The economic limits to modern politics

Murphy Institute Studies in Political Economy
General Editor: Richard F. Teichgraeber III

The books in this series are occasional volumes sponsored by the Murphy Institute of Political Economy at Tulane University and Cambridge University Press, comprising original essays by leading scholars in the United States and other countries. Each volume considers one of the intellectual preoccupations or analytical procedures currently associated with the term "political economy." The goal of the series is to aid scholars and teachers committed to moving beyond the traditional boundaries of their disciplines in a common search for new insights and new ways of studying the political and economic realities of our time. The series is published with the support of the Tulane–Murphy Foundation.

Other books in the series:
Gordon C. Winston and Richard F. Teichgraeber III, eds., *The boundaries of economics*
Nick Baigent and Wulf Gaertner, eds., *The problem of justice in philosophy and economics* (forthcoming)

The economic limits to modern politics

Edited by

JOHN DUNN

King's College, Cambridge

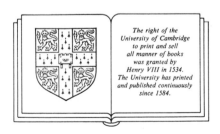

The right of the
University of Cambridge
to print and sell
all manner of books
was granted by
Henry VIII in 1534.
The University has printed
and published continuously
since 1584.

CAMBRIDGE UNIVERSITY PRESS

Cambridge
New York   Port Chester   Melbourne   Sydney

Published by the Press Syndicate of the University of Cambridge
The Pitt Building, Trumpington Street, Cambridge CB2 1RP
40 West 20th Street, New York, NY 10011, USA
10 Stamford Road, Oakleigh, Melbourne 3166, Australia

First published 1990

Printed in Canada

Library of Congress Cataloging-in-Publication Data
The Economic limits to modern politics / edited by John Dunn.
   p. cm. – (Murphy Institute studies in political economy)
  ISBN 0-521-35283-5
  1. Political science – Economic aspects. I. Dunn, John, 1940–   .
II. Series.
JA77.E2 1990
306.2 – dc20   89-38041
                                          CIP

British Library Cataloguing in Publication Data
The Economic limits to modern politics. – (Murphy Institute
  studies in political economy).
  1. Economics. Theories
  I. Dunn, John
  330.1

Contents

v

Contents

Preface

What is "political economy"? The term was coined early in the seventeenth century by Antoine de Montchrétien (a now largely forgotten dramatist) to explain to the French king how the management of a family household could serve as a good model for the management of the polity. His once influential *Traicté de l'oeconomie politique* (1615) inaugurated a tradition of urging rulers and legislators to become "economists," to base policy on the assumption that among the first aims of government were the proper understanding and management of a market economy just in the process of emerging. (Adam Smith's *Wealth of Nations* [1776] was, among other things, the masterwork in that tradition.) Today the study of political economy is sometimes defined – more clearly, if less ambitiously – as an attempt to link the subject matter of political science with the methods and theories of neoclassical economics. But that definition is misleadingly narrow. Indeed, the concept of political economy that the contributors to this volume address describes a broad field of inquiry in which historians and philosophers, as well as economists and political scientists, now make contributions of shared and equal interest. It is arguable, too, that their interdisciplinary research and theorizing represent a recovery and replenishment of political economy as it first emerged in early modern Western thought – namely, an inquiry distinctively concerned with the conduct, institutions, and values of market societies, but always ready to borrow from history, jurisprudence, moral philosophy, and political theory.

Five of the papers published here were delivered as lectures in a series with the general title "The Economic Limits to Modern Politics" at Tulane University in 1986. The series was sponsored by Tulane's Murphy Institute of Political Economy. Professor Dunn's paper, "Capitalism, Socialism, and Democracy" (Chapter 6), was prepared for another occasion but is also published for the first time in this volume. Each contributor offers a distinct perspective on the economic limitations to modern politics, and there is no overarching practical message. What provides unity to the volume is a determination to question dogma and to develop a range of new perspectives for thinking about how economic activities and institutions interact with political forces in the modern world.

Richard F. Teichgraeber III

New Orleans

Contributors

JOHN DUNN, the Murphy Institute Distinguished Visiting Professor, 1985–6, is Fellow of King's College, Cambridge, and Professor of Political Theory, University of Cambridge. He is author of *The Political Thought of John Locke; Modern Revolutions: An Introduction to the Analysis of a Political Phenomenon; Dependence and Opportunity: Political Change in Ahafo* (with A. F. Robertson); *Western Political Theory in the Face of the Future; Political Obligation in Its Historical Context;* and *The Politics of Socialism: An Essay in Political Theory.*

ISTVAN HONT is Professor of Political Science at Columbia University and the former Director of the Political Economy and Society project of the King's College Research Centre of Cambridge University. He is coeditor of and contributor to *Wealth and Virtue: The Shaping of Political Economy in the Scottish Enlightenment* (1984).

J. G. A. POCOCK is Professor of History at Johns Hopkins University. Formerly, he was Professor of History and Political Science at Washington University in St. Louis and Professor of Political Science at the University of Canterbury in New Zealand. He is author of *The Ancient Constitution and the Feudal Law* (1957); *Politics, Language, and Time* (1971); *The Machiavellian Moment* (1975); *The Political Works of James Harrington* (1977); and *Virtue, Commerce and History* (1985). He is also a Director of the Center for the History of British Political Thought at the Folger Shakespeare Library in Washington.

ix

FRANK H. HAHN is Professor of Economics at the University of Cambridge and Fellow of Churchill College. His publications include *The Share of Wages in National Income; Money and Inflation;* and *General Competitive Analysis* (with Kenneth J. Arrow). Among Professor Hahn's many awards are honorary degrees from the University of Birmingham, Strasbourg University, the University of London, and the University of East Anglia.

ROBERT O. KEOHANE is Professor of Government at Harvard University. He is editor of *Neorealism and Its Critics* and *Transnational Relations and World Politics* (with Joseph S. Nye). Professor Keohane is also author of *After Hegemony: Cooperation and Discord in the World Political Economy* and *Power and Interdependence: World Politics in Transition.*

The economic limits to modern politics

Introduction

John Dunn

There is no commanding reason to suppose that a clear and accurate understanding of modern politics really is available to human beings at all. But those who earn a living by purporting to teach others how to understand it must at least try, as best they can, to understand it first for themselves. More pressingly and less parochially, those who choose to take political action need at least some conception of what they are attempting to do, and it is hard to see how they can hope to sustain such conceptions without some sense of what politics today is in fact about or what its human significance now really is.

This collection of essays focuses upon a single key issue in the somewhat groggy history of modern political thinking: the limits set to what is now politically possible by economic structures, processes, and activities. These limits have been a pressing preoccupation, for those in quest of practical just as much as theoretical understanding, for at least two centuries. They have prompted the most ambitious and confident of modern attempts to explain political processes and political development. In the eighteenth and nineteenth centuries, in the heyday first of liberal and then of socialist political ideologies, they underpinned the boldest expectations of moral and material progress and inspired great social and political movements devoted to bringing such progress about. Only in the twentieth century, it sometimes seems, with the impact of the two world wars, the invention and massive deployment of nuclear armaments, and growing fears about the vulnerability of human habitats and the blind dynamic of population growth, has the idea of economic limits acquired more sinister overtones: mocking the futility of even the greatest collective efforts,

1

the perversity of their outcomes, and the pitiful self-deceptions which go into making them possible.

But in fact, any semblance of novelty in this dismay is principally a product of selective inattention. Throughout serious modern reflection on the dynamics of market exchange and international trade and on their implications for the flourishing of human populations, there have always been starkly pessimistic notes also. From the late-seventeenth-century English fears that the prosperity of wage earners must inevitably destroy the price-competitivity of domestic products,[1] through the grim morals of Parson Malthus, to the more detached and sophisticated concerns of Ricardo and John Stuart Mill, there have always been thinkers for whom the idea of economic limits was no occasion for callow optimism.

In the present collection we consider the idea of economic limits to modern politics from a variety of angles. John Pocock, a historian of political ideas, discusses the sharp shift in political priorities marked by the modern concentration on popular prosperity in a highly commercialized economy, stressing particularly the weakening of concern with the capacity of citizens to defend their own political freedoms with their own weapons against enemies at home and abroad. A second historian of ideas, Istvan Hont, describes the realization by thinkers in late-seventeenth-century Britain that military requirements themselves now forced every modern territorial state into international commercial competition, analyzing their exploration of the requirements and options, economic, political, and cultural, for sustaining the prosperity of such a state through domestic manufacturers. Robert Keohane, a theorist of international relations, considers the range of constraints on the freedom of action of national governments imposed by the presence of other states and other economies and assesses the strengths and weaknesses of attempts by modern social scientists to explain why these interact as they do. Frank Hahn, an economist, underlines the indispensability in economic organization of clear reasons for particular agents to act in a fashion which will have benign consequences and the corresponding need for them to ascertain which acts are in fact likely to have such consequences. This focus on problems of information and coordination, echoing argu-

---

[1] See Istvan Hont, Chap. 2 below.

ments of Friedrich Hayek which have been widely broadcast over the last decade, yields an acute skepticism over the prospects of combining the consumption standards of an advanced capitalist society with avoidance of an explicit or tacit regime of private property, determining production and allocating consumption largely through market exchange.

Each of these essays is worth reading closely in its own right – and perhaps especially so in each case by those who do not belong to the captive disciplinary audiences of the author in question. But it is reasonable to hope that they may be particularly instructive if read together and positioned within a somewhat broader framework.

The terrain of modern history may not in the end prove mainly to be (as it has already massively failed to be in all too many instances) one of what Benjamin Constant called "modern liberty"[2] – that special conception of what makes a human being free, so deeply at home in commercial societies, that specifies this in terms of doing what one happens to enjoy and acting just as one pleases: the liberty of preference or, indeed, of whim. But whether this terrain eventually proves on balance more one of modern servitude than of modern liberty, and even if it proves in the end to be one of modern self-immolation, what is clear is that a very large portion of it will continue to be defined, either positively or negatively, and for as long as it lasts, in relation to the logic of the market. It is the Law of the Market and the imperatives laid down by participation in international trade which principally fix the range of possibility for modern societies. To think seriously about modern politics can never be solely to think about production, distribution, and exchange. But it can never be to neglect these considerations for any length of time, and its assessments of even apparently rather distant issues will always be framed, openly or covertly, by an understanding of the constraints imposed by, and the options afforded by, economic organization.

To think of politics in terms of limits can involve either of two strongly contrasted perspectives. It can be to consider politics from the viewpoint of agency, in terms of judgment and choice: to assess

---

[2] Benjamin Constant, *De la liberté des anciens comparée à celle des modernes*, in Constant, *Cours de politique constitutionelle*, Bechet, Paris and Rouen, 1820, 4, Pt. 8, 238–74. English translation in Biancamaria Fontana (ed.), *The Political Writings of Benjamin Constant*, Cambridge University Press, 1988.

the constraints upon and the options open to political action. But it can also be to consider politics in a less involved manner – in terms of determinants and outcomes, necessity and explanation, even of detached and dispassionate prediction. This is not a difference of subject matter but one of orientation. Each perspective, in its turn, is itself infinitely differentiated in time and space, in cultural presumption, and in ultimate imaginative motivation. Each is apt, from occasion to occasion, to exchange places with the other: not least because any real explanatory achievement will have urgent implications for the prospects of success and failure in political action, while skillful and imaginative exploration of the options for political action will not merely alter routine expectations of what can be politically accomplished but, in doing so, will also transform what can in fact be politically accomplished in the future.[3]

To look at the political history of mankind as a whole and hope to identify just what compelled it to follow the course that it has adopted is an ambitious project. Indeed, there is good reason to believe that even Karl Marx himself regarded it as excessively, perhaps even absurdly,[4] ambitious. But in their comfortably parochial style the modern social sciences, where they have made attempts of any vigor to explain the outcomes of political processes or the workings of political structures, have also drawn their confidence largely from models

[3] See John Dunn, "Understanding Revolutions," in Dunn, *Rethinking Modern Political Theory,* Cambridge University Press, 1985, Chap. 4; and Dunn, "The Success and Failure of Modern Revolutions," in Dunn, *Political Obligation in Its Historical Context,* Cambridge University Press, 1980, Chap. 9.

[4] Compare Marx's comment on Mikhailovsky's criticisms: "[T]hat is too little for my critic. He feels he absolutely must metamorphize my historical sketch of the genesis of capitalism in Western Europe into an historico-philosophic theory of the general path every people is fated to tread, whatever the historical circumstances in which it finds itself, in order that it may ultimately arrive at the form of economy which ensures, together with the greatest expansion of the productive powers of social labour, the most complete development of man. But I beg his pardon. (He is both honouring and shaming me too much.)" (November 1877 letter to Editors of *Notes on the Fatherland,* Karl Marx and Frederick Engels, *Selected Correspondence,* Foreign Languages Publishing House, Moscow 1956, 379). For the historical background see A. Walicki, *The Controversy over Capitalism,* Clarendon Press, Oxford 1969. For assessments of the character of Marx's theory see G. A. Cohen, *Karl Marx's Theory of History: A Defence,* Clarendon Press, Oxford 1978; Terrell Carver, *Marx's Social Theory,* Oxford University Press, Oxford 1982; Richard W. Miller, "Producing Change: work, technology, and power in Karl Marx's Theory of History," in Terence Ball and James Farr (eds.), *After Marx,* Cambridge University Press, 1984, 59–87; and, more reconstructively, Jon Elster, *Making Sense of Marx,* Cambridge University Press, 1985.

first developed to explain economic processes.[5] No doubt there are a wide variety of reasons for this propensity – from the sheer ideological resonance of market exchange at one extreme to the far greater intellectual elegance of economics as an academic subject and its markedly greater success at combining cognitive discipline with conceptual intricacy at the other. The epistemic status of theory in economics itself is eminently questionable, less because of the dubious descriptive realism of most of its assumptions or the severely practical difficulties of judging how precisely to apply it to the historical world to minimize disagreeable future surprises,[6] than because of the fundamental unclarity of the idea of necessitarian laws of human action expressed through the category of rationality.[7] Whatever makes a natural science a true science of nature, the idea of imputing causal necessity to well-considered (let alone to perfectly considered) choices by human agents seems a genuinely heroic assumption. At present there remains every reason to doubt whether application of the model of the laws of nature to human agency and human history has been more than an extremely protracted (and expensive) blind alley.

Within human history considered as the consecutive outcomes of a sequence of necessitarian determinations, limits (economic or otherwise) need play no special theoretical or practical role. One can inquire about them, as one can about any other feature of the unitary causal process, but it is not apparent that one, in any sense, *must* do so. In the perspective of agency, however, limits clearly occupy a far more important and privileged position. For an agent to fail to consider limits, except for extremely strong and specific reasons, is necessarily perverse, irresponsible, or inept. The limits on possible out-

---

[5] This is not true simply of Marxist writers (amongst whom see especially Adam Przeworski, *Capitalism and Social Democracy,* Cambridge University Press, 1985). See, for example, Joseph Schumpeter, *Capitalism, Socialism and Democracy,* Allen & Unwin, London 1959; Anthony Downs, *An Economic Theory of Democracy,* Harper & Row, New York 1957; Mancur Olson, *The Logic of Collective Action,* Harvard University Press, Cambridge, Mass., 1965; James M. Buchanan, *Liberty, Market and State: Political Economy in the 1980s,* New York University Press, New York, 1986.

[6] The last fifteen years should have demonstrated the appalling importance of these practical difficulties to any minimally informed person.

[7] These issues are sketched helpfully in the Introduction to Frank Hahn and Martin Hollis (eds.), *Philosophy and Economic Theory,* Oxford University Press, 1979, and explored, to varying effect, in the ensuing contributions to that collection.

comes define the space of possibilities for human actors or agencies, establish what these can or cannot bring about, inform them of what there really is for them to fear or hope for, and focus, as nothing else could, the question of what they do in fact have reason to do. Nowhere is this more evident or more important than it is in the case of politics.

There are certainly other important limits to political agency in the modern world than those established by economics. But in the routine politics of any but the most grotesque travesty of a modern state the issue of what is economically possible and feasible is not merely the most prominent, but also the most consequential, matter at issue.[8] Because this is so, virtually all political choices, from the narrowest puzzles of individual rationality, through the most intimidating dilemmas of national and international strategy, to the most abstract questions about criteria for a legitimate political order or the content of social good or justice, have a crucial economic dimension. Since the late seventeenth century there has been a steadily increasing number of human beings struggling to grasp the implications of this confinement. Political theorists, in particular, have done their best to show either why, in some particular form or other, it should not be truly regarded as confinement at all, or how it could in due course be decisively eluded. But each of these entirely natural goals has militated against the very attempt to identify the implications of this confinement or render these more transparently intelligible than everyday life has already made them for workers or managers, consumers or bureaucrats, politicians or policemen. For this purpose, the classic preoccupations of political theory with the good constitution or polity (more recently, the good party) or with the theory of social justice have proved singularly unilluminating. The former, under most political circumstances, features in the practical appraisal of political hazard and opportunity as little more than a reassuring myth

---

[8] See Frank Hahn, Chap. 4 below; John Dunn, *The Politics of Socialism*, Cambridge University Press, 1984; Charles E. Lindblom, *Politics and Markets*, Basic, New York 1977, esp. p. 138: "Down the ladder moves information and persuasion on what is possible or most feasible, as well as what leaders propose. A good deal of misinformation moves up and down too. Volitions are endlessly reconsidered in the light of what is thought possible or most feasible. What is possible and feasible is constantly reconsidered – and the possibilities themselves reconstructed – in the light of citizen and leader volitions."

or a denunciatory slogan, whereas the latter, despite its evident charms for the philosopher, offers little but calming or inflammatory fancies.

The best criterion for enhanced understanding of modern politics' economic limits would have to be a practical improvement in political judgment. Modern political theory is endlessly evasive on the question of whose practical judgment really does require improvement – let alone on the question of how such improvement is to be concretely provided or developed. Its concern with the question of political judgment is seldom more than whimsical, and where it does commit itself heavily on the question, as most importantly in the Leninist tradition, its treatment of the political division of labor is massively disingenuous. One helpful imaginative preliminary for enhancing political judgment is simply to acknowledge what a bewildering heterogeneity of agencies does make the political history of the modern world and how starkly unreasonable it would be to suppose their judgment in general sound – let alone impeccable.

What are the implications of the economic limits to modern politics for harassed and understandably parochial private individuals, female and male, young and old, in Tashkent and Ouagadougou, Stoke on Trent and Brixton, Ciudad Bolívar, Madurai and New Orleans? What are its implications for conscientious and committed citizens of countries which permit a wide range of political expression? What are its implications for equally conscientious individuals, deeply imaginatively at odds with their own state but fulsomely cosmopolitan in their social affections and concerns? What are its implications for classes, domestic or transnational (capital, labor)? For states, international agencies, or transnational actors like the managements of multinational corporations? For the United Nations – the set of all states now more or less recognizing each other as such? For the human species as a whole, today and for its as yet indefinite future?

The economic limits to political agency for all but the wealthiest of private persons are always, at least in their private capacity, very narrow indeed – if no doubt in some respects less narrow than they contrive to imagine and in others narrower than they fondly hope. For those deeply and reasonably disinclined to concern themselves with politics, the political history of the world is a domain of pure fate. In the wrong place at the wrong time (Germany in the 1920s or 1930s, the

Wehrmacht in occupied Yugoslavia, Israel in the 1980s, almost always somewhere in the world) this attitude may prove in retrospect a massive practical misjudgment. But it is certainly unreasonable to hope for the politically indifferent to remedy it for themselves. And, of course, even for the most dizzily positioned and effective of political actors, for better or worse (Lenin, Roosevelt, Gorbachev, Hitler) the political history of the world is only very mildly adulterated fate. To assess how this history could go better on any scale requires some imaginative detachment from when and where a person happens to find himself. It calls on strategic judgment, bold counter-factual exploration, adventurous reconstruction of routine expectations, and practices.[9] But to try to make this history go better in practice, by the same token, always requires us to begin from where and when and what we now are.[10] Miracles can happen. But the only sound recipe for acting for the better demands a crisply realistic sense of the human world as it now is and of the resources that lie to hand.

Except for the briefest of periods, in conditions of dire crisis or brief and dramatic opportunity, the fulcrum of political realism for any modern society is always an understanding of the conditions for its economic flourishing. The practical implications of this intractable prominence concern virtually everyone now alive on earth, though on the shrinking outer fringes of human habitation there still remains a modest scattering of those on whom its effect is still comparatively marginal. It is politically important that these implications are extremely difficult to understand – that they are as extravagantly complicated as they are cognitively elusive. (Consider the tart judgment passed by an Aberdeen pamphleteer in 1777 on Adam Smith's case for freeing the grain trade: "[I]t is hardly to be supposed that any wise nation will place such confidence in a system, however ingenious the arguments may be by which it is maintained, as to risk its prosperity

---

[9] For a striking statement see Roberto Mangabeira Unger, *Politics*, 3 vols., Cambridge University Press, 1987.

[10] Dunn, *Political Obligation*, Chap. 10; and see Dunn, "Unger's *Politics* and the Appraisal of Political Possibility," *Northwestern University Law Review*, Summer 1987, and more locally, Dunn, "Defining a Defensible Socialism for Britain Today," in Peter Nolan and Suzanne Paine (eds.), *Rethinking Socialist Economics*, Polity Press, Cambridge, 1986, 35–52, and Dunn, "The Politics of Representation and Good Government in Postcolonial Africa," in Patrick Chabal (ed.), *Political Domination in Africa*, Cambridge University Press, 1986, 158–74.

on the trial."[11] Today every state has to rest fundamental aspects of its policies on some "system" or other. The vagaries of economic theory are ineliminable elements in the strategies of any modern government.) Yet it is also just as important that the human significance of the preconditions for economic flourishing is often deeply discomfiting. Few modern interpreters of politics acknowledge either of these features at all adequately. But almost none can bring himself to acknowledge both with any great frankness. And if this is true of the theoretical interpreters of modern politics, how much more so of the latter's hapless practitioners.

To see how we have come to this pass requires above all else historical imagination. John Pocock's essay, recapitulating more than two decades of tenacious inquiry,[12] brings out the brusque inversion of priorities which this transformation has entailed and the disconcerting conflicts between different social, political, and economic goods that have followed from it. Still more clearly, Istvan Hont's record of half a century of British deliberation on the dilemmas of national trading policy shows some of the most fundamental problems of modern politics taking shape before the reader's eyes. The issues of governability and the reproduction of a strongly commercialized prosperity that Charles Davenant confronted in the 1690s are still today discernibly key issues in the politics of South Korea and Brazil, Greece and Hungary, even the Soviet Union, the United Kingdom, and Japan. Modern politics does at times have other and more hectic rhythms, as it did in Germany in the 1930s or in the appalling carnage between Iran and Iraq. But the steady working through of Davanent's central problems goes on everywhere where modern politics has penetrated – by now far the greater part of the globe – and it goes on virtually without interruption. As they first come clearly into focus, these problems are, as Hont strikingly indicates, very much problems of raison d'état, of the effective exercise of state power in the quest for military security or

---

[11] *Considerations on our Corn-Laws*, Aberdeen 1777, 17. (Quoted by Richard F. Teichgraeber III, " 'Less Abused than I had Reason to Expect': The Reception of *The Wealth of Nations* in Britain 1776–90," *The Historical Journal*, 30, 2, June 1987, 337–66, at p. 353).

[12] See especially his classic 1964 article, "Machiavelli, Harrington and English Political Ideologies in the Eighteenth Century," in J. G. A. Pocock, *Politics, Language and Time*, Methuen & Co., London 1972, Chap. 4; and, more expansively, idem, *The Machiavellian Moment*, Princeton University Press, Princeton 1975, and idem, *Virtue, Commerce and History*, Cambridge University Press, 1985.

territorial expansion. But as Hont has also shown here and else-where,[13] they have never been merely problems of raison d'état. The Christian view that the world was given to human beings for them to enjoy served to denounce violations of human rights in the property orders and labor regimes of seventeenth-century Europe.[14] But it also served to vindicate the requirements of commercial efficiency through time as preconditions for the populations of civilized societies – prosperous, commercial, urbane[15] – to realize their entitlement to enjoy. By the end of Hont's story here, Henry Martyn, unabashed apologist for England's East India Company, had worked through a comprehensive vision of efficiency in production as the sole guarantee of an ample popular consumption and had drawn just those morals that serve today as the ideological cement of prospering capitalist societies. For Martyn the protection of employment for employment's sake was already a futile goal: "If the Riches of the Kingdom are not greater, they are not less for being procur'd by fewer Hands."[16] Rigidity in nominal wage rates could directly menace real standards of consump-tion. And the tension between the high and rigid wage rates of prosper-ous manufacturing nations and the pressures of international price competition could be resolved only by the endless *fuite en avant* of technical innovation – the austere disciplines of the product cycle.[17] The threats posed by the resulting instabilities in employment to the coherence of individual lives and communities and to the sense of social solidarity have changed little in the intervening centuries.[18]

[13] Istvan Hont and Michael Ignatieff, "Needs and Justice in the *Wealth of Nations:* an Introductory Essay," in Hont and Ignatieff (eds.), *Wealth and Virtue,* Cambridge University Press, 1983, 1–44; and Hont, "The Language of Sociability and Com-merce: Samuel Pufendorf and the Theoretical Foundations of the 'Four-Stages' Theory," in Anthony Pagden (ed.), *The Languages of Political Theory in Early-Modern Europe,* Cambridge University Press, 1987, 253–76.

[14] John Dunn, *Locke,* Oxford University Press, Oxford 1984, Chaps. 1 and 2.

[15] Hont, "The Language of Sociability," esp. p. 275.

[16] Cited by Hont, Chap. 2, this volume.

[17] On the significance of the product cycle see, conveniently, Raymond Vernon, *Storm over the Multinationals: The Real Issues,* Macmillan, Press, London, 1977, esp. Chaps. 2 and 3. Compare Hont's analysis of Martyn's views (Chap. 2 below) with the clear and illuminating discussion of the considerations that have led American multinational firms in such numbers to choose to site a wide array of subsidiary plants (*maquilas*) in a narrow band just south of the U.S. border with Mexico in an article on the editorial page of the *Financial Times,* Aug. 31, 1987: David Gardner, "The Rich Pickings of America's Backyard."

[18] Compare John Dunn, "Paying for the Past Without Hope for the Future," *Times Literary Supplement,* Apr. 24, 1937, 442–4. But with sufficient skill and continuity of

The implications of these constraints were disputed as spiritedly in the 1690s as they have been ever since. But in the last ten years the weight of judgment has on the whole swung back strongly towards Henry Martyn – further, almost certainly, than is epistemically at all justifiable – and figures as diverse as Deng Xiao Ping and Neil Kinnock, President Mitterrand and Secretary Gorbachev, have come to endorse Davenant's view that a government's role in relation to trade must be essentially "to take a Providential Care of the Whole, but generally to let Second Causes work their own way."[19] This shift itself, however, had done nothing to alleviate the sense of discomfiture which in so many intervening instances has driven political thinkers and actors, as it has driven great societies across the world, to try to take a stronger and more decisive control over the shapes of their economies and over the ways of life, social values, and structures of personal character which emerge from these over time. As Pocock and Hont both emphasize, a politics of purity and virtue has always required an economics to go with it, and an economy founded on speculation and the restless quest for profit and material advantage has always appeared to many both corrosive of citizenship and corrupting of the labor force on which it depends. On the whole, ideologues, intellectuals, university teachers, and politicians have been just as undependable judges of what benefits or impairs the character of those who labor extensively with their hands in twentieth-century China, Kampuchea, Cuba, or Frankfurt as they were in England or Scotland of the seventeenth century.

But the perception that the central organizing principle of a commercial society, the division of labor, has dynamic and often perturbing cultural consequences has proved sound enough. Twentieth-century experience may not wholly endorse the verdict that the main threat it poses has been one to the military prowess or capacity to

purpose, something can certainly be done to meet these: See "Sweden's Economy," *The Economist,* Mar. 7, 1987, 19–24; and for the political and economic background to this achievement see (for Scandinavia) Gosta Esping-Andersen, *Politics Against Markets: The Social Democratic Road to Power,* Princeton University Press, 1985, and (for the now less convincing instance of Austria) Peter J. Katzenstein, *Corporatism and Change: Austria, Switzerland and the Politics of Industry,* Cornell University Press, Ithaca N.Y., 1984.

[19] Cited by Hont in Chap. 2, this volume. For the underlying rationale of the shift see Hahn, Chap. 4, this volume; Alec Nove, *The Economics of Feasible Socialism,* Allen & Unwin, London, 1983; Dunn, *Politics of Socialism.*

protect their own political independence of modern populations. But it has done nothing whatever to confirm that entrusting the shaping of human personality and motivation, with ever diminishing resistance, to the logic of commercial competition is a humanly well-considered option in itself. It is quite impossible in good faith to see any modern polity as well designed to combine prudent regard for the economic limits to modern politics with delicate and effective concern for the sorts of human beings whom its economic momentum fashions.

Even in the less dizzy sphere of political activity, it is hard to believe that the political implications of the division of labor, a central theme in modern political understanding since the democratizing tumult of the French Revolution,[20] are yet at all clearly understood. The main impulse behind the present volume is the simple political judgment that modern political theory and practice have still made only the most superficial progress in working out just how responsibility for assessing the implications of its economic confines could be effectively democratized in a modern population.[21] Modern political theory, accordingly, fissures disreputably into a miscellany of evasive or blatantly offensive elitist projects and a series of just as blatantly offensive or still more fatuously confused egalitarian slogans. To reconstruct it in a more benign form would require, above all else, an unblinking focus on the political component of the division of labor and an unyielding inquiry into just what forms, in each particular setting, this might defensibly take. There is every reason to believe that we urgently need today more acute and powerful elite versions of political economy – conceptions of economic causality and the possibilities this furnishes in the real world which equip us better to face the gloomy final years of the century. But in modern politics it is above all not elite but popular versions of political economy about

[20] See, especially, Pasquale Pasquino, "Emmanuel Sieyes, Benjamin Constant et le 'Gouvernment des Modernes': Contribution à l'histoire du concept de représentation politique," *Revue Française de Science Politique,* 37, 2, April 1987, 214–28, and more broadly, Dunn, *Western Political Theory in the Face of the Future,* Cambridge University Press, 1979, Chap. 1.

[21] I do not mean to suggest, of course, that they have made no attempt to do so. Contrast, for example, Max Weber's Freiburg inaugural lecture of May 1895, "The National State and Economic Policy (Freiburg address)," *Economy and Society,* 9, 4, November 1980, 428–49, and Joseph Schumpeter, *Capitalism, Socialism and Democracy,* Chaps. 21–3, with Charles E. Lindblom, *Politics and Markets,* and Robert A. Dahl, *A Preface to Economic Democracy,* University of California Press, Berkeley and Los Angeles, 1985.

which we remain most helplessly bemused. In the realms of popular political economy, as Mrs. Thatcher has so dismally demonstrated, we have made little, if any, progress since the days of *Hard Times* or Harriet Martineau. The well-founded mutual contempt of demos and professional politicians in the societies of today is not a sound basis for any form of human flourishing through time. No doubt, to reverse a classic sneer, we must do our best to educate our masters. But most pressingly perhaps, the time has surely come to educate ourselves.

CHAPTER 1

The economic limits to modern politics

JOHN DUNN

How is it possible to understand modern politics, say, the modern politics of the United States and Britain, of Japan and North Korea, of the Philippines and Burkina Faso, of the Soviet Union and Brazil?

It is, of course, impossible to understand the politics of anywhere at any time without knowing a great deal about that place at that time. But in addition to such immersion in the particular it is also always helpful to consider techniques of understanding or approaches towards understanding: *how* to understand, not what is the case. In this respect at least, in its comprehension of the scope and limits of its own techniques of understanding and its own approach, the academic discipline of political science has been a fairly unmitigated intellectual disaster. This is no doubt, so far as it goes, an occasion for legitimate merriment. But it reflects a much wider cognitive failure (a failure which runs in some measure through the entire citizenry and governmental circles of nation states across the world today). In this form it seems exceedingly unlikely that the limits on the intelligibility of modern politics are to any degree a good thing: not least, because it is now apparent even to such reluctant learners as the political leaders of the United States and the Soviet Union that only a drastic and imaginative extension of its collaborative political skills can give the human race a reasonable prospect of protracted survival in the world in which we now live.[1] A world in which the tacit inherited savoir

---

[1] A helpful setting from which to begin to get the measure of the hazards is Robert W. Malcolmson, *Nuclear Fallacies,* McGill–Queens University Press, Kingston & Montreal 1985; Paul Bracken, *The Command and Control of Nuclear Forces,* Yale University Press, New Haven, 1983.

faire of the ruling classes could hope politically to suffice died along with the *douçeur de vivre* of the French Ancien Régime. The view that governing can safely be left to the governors belongs to a world that is dead and gone. We may begin, accordingly, with a view from that byegone world; from the death throes of the Ancien Régime.

At some point in the years 1792 or 1793, probably whilst in prison awaiting trial and the guillotine, the Feuillant orator Joseph Barnave set himself to try to explain the vast historical convulsion of the French Revolution. It was a scene in which he had for a time played a role of some prominence; but it was now on the point of engulfing him as it had engulfed so many others. Barnave's *Introduction to the French Revolution* is seen by many modern Marxist scholars as the epitome of the political and social consciousness of the class which they see as the key actor in the Revolution, the revolutionary bourgeoisie.[2]

What matters for our purposes, however, is not Barnave's own political commitments and social sensibility but rather the strength of his conviction that the revolution, like all major transformations in human society and political organization, could be *explained,* shown to result from, structural necessities of social development. In this explanatory insistence, his orientation towards the Revolution was not sharply distinct from that of prominent reactionary thinkers like Barruel, Maistre and Bonald, or indeed from that of the thwarted revolutionaries of 1796, Gracchus Babeuf and Filippo Buonarroti.[3] But whereas all of these figures in their very different ways conceived the Revolution above all as a gratuitous or glorious political adventure or as a sacred or secular drama of social guilt and redemption,

---

[2] J. A. Barnave, *Introduction à la révolution française,* ed. F. Rude, Armand Colin, Paris, 1960. E. Chill (ed.), *Power, Property and History,* Harper & Row, New York 1971. Albert Soboul, *The Parisian Sans-Culottes and the French Revolution 1793–4,* Clarendon Press, Oxford, 1964, 2. Ralph Milibrand, "Barnave: a case of bourgeois class consciousness," in Istvan Meszaros (ed.), *Aspects of History and Class Consciousness,* Routledge & Kegan Paul, London, 1971, 22–48.

[3] Jacques Godechot, *The Counter-Revolution: Doctrine and Action 1789–1804,* tr. S. Attanasio, Routledge & Kegan Paul, London, 1972. *The Works of Joseph de Maistre,* ed. and tr. Jack Lively, Macmillan, New York, 1964. J. M. Roberts, *The Mythology of the Secret Societies,* Secker & Warburg, London, 1972. R. B. Rose, *Gracchus Babeuf: The First Revolutionary Communist,* Edward Arnold, London, 1978. *The Defense of Gracchus Babeuf before the High Court of Vendome,* ed. and tr. J. A. Scott, Schocken Books, New York, 1972. F. M. Buonarroti, *Conspiration pour l'Égalité, dite de Babeuf,* Editions Sociales, 2 vols., Paris, 1957. Elizabeth L. Eisenstein, *The First Professional Revolutionist: Filippo Michele Buonarroti,* Harvard University Press, Cambridge, Mass., 1959.

Barnave, more stolidly, saw it as just a natural outcome of the historical development of French society over the preceding two centuries
or so.[4] What he emphasized at the very beginning of his text was the
structural intelligibility of major social and political change: what, as
he says, prepares the great epochs of history:

Certainly the revolutions of governments, like all of those phenomena of
nature that depend upon the passions and the will of man cannot be subjected
to those fixed and calculable laws that apply to the movements of inanimate
matter. But amongst this multitude of causes whose combined influence produces political events there are some that are so tightly linked to the nature of
things, whose constant and regular action so firmly dominates accidental
causes, that over a period of time they almost necessarily exert their effect. It
is they, almost invariably, that change the face of nations. All the minor
events are engulfed in their general results. It is they that prepare the great
epochs of history, whilst the secondary causes to which these are almost
always attributed only serve to lend them a particular form.[5]

What did make the great epochs of history in Barnave's view was in
essence three things: the organization of armed force, the system of
ownership and economic production, and the weight of opinion.[6]

This is a simple and realistic summary, as far as it goes; and it is a

---

[4] It is still, of course, a profoundly vexed issue in the modern historiography of the
Revolution how far he was *right* to see it in this way: Colin Lucas, "Nobles, Bour-
geois and the Origins of the French Revolution," *Past and Present*, 60, August 1973,
84–126. George V. Taylor, "Non-capitalist Wealth and the Origins of the French
Revolution," *American Historical Review*, 72, 2, January 1967, 469–96; "Revolution-
ary and Non-revolutionary Content in the Cahiers of 1789: An Interim Report,"
French Historical Studies, 7, 4, 1972, 479–502. François Furet, *Interpreting the
French Revolution*, tr. E. Forster, Cambridge University Press, 1981. William Doyle,
Origins of the French Revolution, Oxford University Press, 1980. Patrice Higonnet,
Class, Ideology and the Rights of Nobles during the French Revolution, Clarendon
Press, Oxford, 1981; "The Social and Cultural Antecedents of Revolutionary Discon-
tinuity: Montagnards and Girondins," idem, *English Historical Review*, C, 396, July
1985, 513–44. Keith Michael Baker, "On the Problem of the Ideological Origins of
the French Revolution," in Dominick LaCapra and Steven L. Kaplan (eds.), *Modern
European Intellectual History: Reappraisals and New Perspectives*, Cornell University
Press, Ithaca, N.Y., 1982, 197–219. Guy Chaussinand-Nogaret, *The French Nobility
in the Eighteenth Century: From Feudalism to Enlightenment*, tr. W. Doyle, Cambridge University Press, 1985.
[5] Barnave, "Introduction," 1.
[6] Ibid. 3. "Parmi les différentes bases sur lesquelles le pouvoir peut être étabi, il en est
trois principales dont l'influence domine toutes les autres, et qu'il importe surtout
d'étudier. Ce sont: 1 la force armée, le commandement militaire; 2 la propriété; 3
l'empire de l'opinion. Ce sont ces puissances naturelles qui, quelquefois réunies,
quelquefois opposées, (servent à constituer les gouvernements)." It is apparent from
the remainder of his text that Barnave regarded property as linked indissolubly with
the organization of production.

very nice point whether subsequent thinkers have really contrived to surpass it. But if they have failed to do so, it has certainly not been for want of trying.

Let us consider first of all the principal strategy which modern thinkers have deployed in their efforts to surpass it. Barnave's three factors make up what might be pretentiously described as his theory of history. In his own treatment it is of the essence of history that the three factors can be variously combined: that none permanently and incontestably dominates the others. Modern political and social thinkers who resent such easy plurality have on the whole adopted the strategy of seeking to reduce analytical plurality to analytical unity by rendering one of the three factors 'dominant in the last instance'.[7] This phrase was initially drawn from the English translations of the peculiarly dogmatic and opaque rendition of Marxist theory of history offered by the French philosopher Louis Althusser. But it can serve here for a quite general strategy of analytic reduction which is common to a wide variety of modern social, political and economic thought.

Not all modern social or political thought aspires to anything as ample as a general theory of history, or even a general theory of modern history. Nor is there any very evident reason why it should do so. But insofar as modern social and political thought is a genuine attempt to understand what occurs and what may occur – insofar as it is not simply a form of persiflage – it has no option but to adopt a general strategy of understanding. And since modern social and political experience occurs in a determinate historical setting, under conditions directly encountered, any general strategy of understanding that is to stand the least chance of grasping it validly must be designed to insert itself, and be *capable* of inserting itself, into this determinate setting with some precision. It must, that is to say, be able to take due account of the highly specific historicity of modern social and political life. In this sense it has no option, however prudent and becoming its

[7] Louis Althusser, *Pour Marx,* Francois Maspero, Paris, 1966, 219: "[L]a détermination en dernière instance par l'économie s'exerce justement dans l'histoire réelle, dans les permutations de premier rôle entre l'économie, la politique, et la théorie, etc." On the theoretical vicissitudes of Althusser's thought see, helpfully, Susan James, *The Content of Social Explanation,* Cambridge University Press, 1984. For a crisper reading of Marx's own theory see G. A. Cohen, *Karl Marx's Theory of History: A Defence,* Claredon Press, Oxford, 1978. For a more skeptical assessment of Marxism as a theory see Jon Elster, *Making Sense of Marx,* Cambridge University Press, 1985.

avowals of intellectual modesty, but to be a theory of the intelligibility, the susceptibility to explanation, of at least aspects of modern
history as such. (And this is as true of the intellectual heroes of the
academic discipline of economics – Adam Smith, Quesnay, Maynard
Keynes, Ricardo, Schumpeter, even Kenneth Arrow – as it is, for
example, of James Mill, Karl Marx, Lenin or Robert Dahl.) To put
the point more forensically, it is only because of its capacity to refer
determinately to the world that any modern system of political, social
or economic thinking can be anything more than a complex system of
tautologies. (It can, to be sure, all too readily be decidedly *less* than
this: a tangle of dubiously intended confusions, an unholy mess.)
Even the most abstract and algebraically refined modern system of
economic analysis can only offer instruction on the properties of real
human practices by mastering the specific intellectual problem of its
own applicability to a historically determinate human world. (You
only have to glance through the daily newspaper to see how far we
still at present are from having solved that problem today.)

Because the field of modern experience which we are here seeking
to understand is the field of politics, the problem of applicability[8] is
inevitably a central preoccupation. Within this field I wish to focus on
a quite specific perception about modern history. It is a perception
fundamental to serious thinking about modern politics: that a crucial
range of constraints on modern political possibilities is given by the
workings of a global system of production and exchange. The phrase
"political economy" in recent academic speech refers to a multitude
of respectable intellectual preoccupations and to a variety of not
always very clear or definite analytical procedures. But we may employ it here, shamelessly, to denote any and every attempt to understand just how the workings of a global system of production and
exchange has affected, and does and could affect, the historically
possible organization of collective human life. The advantage of using
it in this way to refer to a field of inquiry rather than a method of
explanation is that it avoids commending a particular method as capable of capturing successfully this field of determination and possibility. (This seems no more than prudent since the attempts since
Barnave's head went under the guillotine to give his analysis a crisper

[8] Analytical complexity and refinement for their own sakes will always make severely
limited contributions to political understanding.

and more conclusive analytical reduction, and explain why all modern history had to go and must in the future go just as it has or will, have all failed. And more drastically, since it seems extremely likely that this accumulated record of failure is not just the product of a lengthy historical sequence of contingent intellectual mishaps but a necessary outcome of the essential validity of Barnave's own judgment. To be essentially right about such questions, naturally, does not require one to be cleverer or in general more profound than those who are not essentially right about them. It merely requires one to display in this respect, if not necessarily in any other, a more sensible intellectual judgment.)

Since the middle of the eighteenth century, political theorists have equivocated with some perseverance over the question of which of Barnave's three factors does in general prevail. Some of their equivocation has been intended to manipulate their readers. Some, no doubt, has resulted from sheer intellectual confusion. But much, it seems clear by now, has been produced by a persisting tension between the explanatory and the normative components of the two principal modern traditions of political understanding and commitment: the liberal and the socialist.[9] A true science of politics, in the postwar positivist understanding of the 1950s, promised understanding *without* commitment. Its fruits would at most be practical advice for the pursuit of externally given ends: instrumental or technical advice. There is a realist tradition of political understanding, stretching back at least as far as Machiavelli and Guicciardini,[10] and most persistently and prominently exemplified in the analysis of the conduct of state policy towards other states, which does at times approximate this technical or Weberian model of political understanding. But even here, a purely technical understanding of the tradition neglects what is often its most vivid and animating preoccupation – that bitter assault, as evident in We-

---

[9] Compare John Dunn, *Rethinking Modern Political Theory*, Cambridge University Press, Cambridge, 1985, esp. Introduction.

[10] Felix Gilbert, *Machiavelli and Guicciardini: Politics and History in Sixteenth-Century Florence*, Princeton University Press, 1965. For aspects of its history see in particular Friedrich Meinecke, *Machiavellism*, tr. D. Scott, Routledge & Kegan Paul, London, 1957. Nannerl O. Keohane, *Philosophy and the State in France*, Princeton University Press, 1980. William F. Church, *Richelieu and Reason of State*, Princeton University Press, 1972.

ber's essay on *Politics as a Vocation* as it is in Machiavelli's *Prince,* on the excessive cultural weight lent by the Christianization of Europe to the standing of benign intentions in the practice of politics. This was, of course, not the *only* possible lesson to be drawn from Christianity for how politics is to be conceived. But there is no doubt that Machiavelli and Weber were addressing themselves to a prominent cultural phenomenon. This realist tradition of political understanding is certainly of great intellectual and practical importance. It also includes some of the most decisive and alarming of modern contributions to political understanding: Carl von Clausewitz's dazzling dissection of the logic of modern war, Marx's studies of politics and class conflict in mid-nineteenth-century France, Lenin's restless and subversive exploration of the political vulnerability of twentieth-century capitalist regimes, Michel Foucault's harsh and anxious vision of the shades of the prison house of modernity closing round the denizens of the world in which we live. At a somewhat more abstract level – and at least equally ambiguously – it dominates the modern practice of nuclear strategy, with its terrifying fusion of primitive emotion, social and political stereotyping, bureaucratic conflict, economic competition, and highly refined and intellectually intricate game-theoretic calculation: the presence that broods over all our lives, and of which we may be as sure as we may be of anything now on earth that no human being has yet fully understood it, perhaps even that none ever *will* fully understand it.

It is, of course, principally the realist tradition that has attempted to do justice to the historical role of armed force in shaping modern politics. (Armed force, one should note, comes first in Barnave's list.) In the aftermath of the two great world wars of the twentieth century, and beneath the looming shadow of the nuclear bomb, it is impossible to doubt the cogency of this emphasis. I shall not discuss it further here, not for any doubt about its vast and dreadful importance, but simply because we have as yet so little convincing analysis of the interactions between economic interest and capability on the one side and military interest and capability on the other.

All Western statesmen of any finesse since at least the seventeenth century have been well aware of the crucial dependence of coercive power upon the ready availability of economic resources.[11] But if it is a modern truism that wealth furnishes the sinews of war, there is no clear analytic rendering in any idiom of modern political understanding of the structure of mutual dependence, or the trade-off matrix, between social wealth and military force. Only an imbecile would doubt that there are (and always have been) economic limits to the availability of military force, and that these limits are of great political importance. Nor can there be much doubt that the cost of servicing repressive capacity continues to constrain other economic allocations. We live in a period in which the provision of military *matériel* is unlikely in itself to furnish handsome opportunities for international depredation. The Soviet Union, for example, is scarcely showing a commercial profit on its ventures in Afghanistan; and it seems improbable that the costs of American military 'assistance' in El Salvador are at present covered by the profits earned by American enterprises within that territory. What might be true, perhaps, is that the funding and intermittent application of modern levels of military and police power have been, and remain, a necessary condition for preserving whatever level of international depredation *is* intrinsic to the current workings of the trading systems of the capitalist world economy and of the *soi-disant* socialist states. And what one can say at present with confidence is that the precise degree of dependence of military power upon the efficacy of the domestic economy, and of compatibility between domestic economic welfare and military expenditure, are obsessive concerns of the administrations of President Bush and Mr. Gorbachev.[12] That the two greatest powers on earth should also happen to represent the two most evocative (and in some respects, mutually inimical) of modern political doctrines may yet prove to be the terminal misfortune of the human species. But, given the poor performance of the Soviet economy in recent years and the growing world market exposure and international competitive weakness of many sectors of the United States economy, it is hard to imagine this complex of military and economic concerns becoming

[11] J. H. Elliott, *Richelieu and Olivares,* Cambridge University Press, 1984, esp. 141, 160. William H. McNeill, *The Pursuit of Power,* Basil Blackwell, Oxford, 1983.

[12] Cf. Michael Mandelbaum and Strobe Talbott, *Reagan and Gorbachev,* Random House, New York, 1987.

less salient in the near future. Contemporary Japan is an interesting case to think about in this context.[13]

The world of politics as I am here discussing it thus leaves something massive and decisive out. What it leaves out is not, of course, all bad in its consequences. It helps to guarantee[14] (is maybe even a necessary condition for) the levels of domestic and international peace that at present prevail throughout the world and earn the appreciation of those who have become accustomed to them largely only as and where they break down.[15] But the organizations and instruments that provide these guarantees are at the same time capable of inflicting the most appalling harm. Indeed, in the streets of Beirut, the marshlands of southern Iraq, the hillsides of El Salvador and the police barracks of Chile, it is all too likely that they are doing just that at this very moment.

But let us for the moment set aside these grim and hectic thoughts, and turn back to consider the two principal modern traditions of political understanding and commitment – the liberal and the socialist. What sharply distinguishes both of these from earlier traditions of political understanding is the weight which each of them gives to the *economic* sphere in the shaping of political society. This is not true in the case of every liberal or socialist thinker. It is only true in a complicated and tangential way, for example, in the case of an early liberal thinker like John Locke.[16] In some of the more recent versions of liberalism the economy plays no explicit role in the specification of the political good itself.[17] And one may well question how far this centrality of the economy remains extant even in a socialist thinker like Herbert Marcuse for whom an alternative property regimen becomes more an aesthetic necessity than a causally responsible politi-

---

[13] Compare also the somewhat oversanguine argument of Richard Rosecrance, *The Rise of the Trading State,* Basic, New York, 1986.

[14] One should remember that at present the only circumstances in which it might fail to provide such a guarantee are ones in which it may well instead render extremely probable the extermination of mankind.

[15] It would not now be good to be a citizen of the Lebanon (not so long ago one of the prize exemplars of "modernization").

[16] John Dunn, *Locke,* Oxford University Press, 1984.

[17] It is rational consent and the requirements of autonomy that define political justice both for Rawls and for Dworkin. Economic welfare (and even the broader concept of utility) enjoys a purely instrumental and derived status within their theories. Compare Dunn, *Rethinking Modern Political Theory,* Chap. 9.

cal recommendation.[18] But the great majority of serious political thinkers in the liberal and socialist tradition, however virulently they may and do disagree over other matters, agree closely on one particular judgment. They agree that it is the requirements and possibilities of economic organization that lie at the very center of modern politics. It is these requirements that set the acceptable limits to modern politics and prescribe the key problems which any modern political community must solve for itself. Of course all political communities throughout recorded history have had to attach *some* significance to economic necessities. There can be no rule without subjects to rule over and no means of guaranteeing the physical sustenance of a human population of any scale except by the careful management and modulation of a natural habitat. But throughout most of human history the benign contribution of coercive power and its organization to guaranteeing the physical subsistence of human populations has been more or less exhausted in excluding the coercive power of others from the opportunity to appropriate the preconditions for physical subsistence. Protection was a strong claim to allegiance not merely because it was a claim difficult and imprudent to contest in practice, but more decisively because protection was often an urgent collective need. (It is a very nice point in many areas of the world just how far this genuinely remains the case today. And there is of course never any guarantee that places where no urgent need is at present apparent will find this happy state of affairs at all enduring.) In some parts of the world for lengthy periods of time – in imperial China for example – governmental power did play an important role in large-scale hydraulic engineering, flood control, and the management of irrigation. But for the most part the provision of reasonably cheap physical protection was not only a real service; it was also the only real service which the best intentioned of governments had the capacity to supply. As late as the seventeenth century in western Europe, good government for the majority of the population was virtually exhausted by the combination of defensive military effectiveness

---

[18] Herbert Marcuse, *One-Dimensional Man,* Routledge & Kegan Paul, London, 1964. It is not clear how far such a regimen survives as a causally responsible recommendation for any contemporary socialist thinkers. See Alec Nove, *The Economics of Feasible Socialism,* Allen & Unwin, London 1983; John Dunn, *The Politics of Socialism,* Cambridge University Press, 1984.

and fiscal restraint. And even in this modest guise it was in distinctly short supply.[19]

The conviction that the modern governments of territorial states can and should play a central and decisive role in fostering the welfare of their subjects first began to take clear shape in seventeenth-century England, following the upheavals of the Civil War, though it had of course a vast range of more nebulous historical precedents. It was not a conviction that at first achieved any great impact on the ideological and geopolitical struggles of the day, in contrast with the intermittent surges of religious bigotry and the more persistent impulse towards dynastic aggrandizement.[20] In its initial forms, as for example in the political theory of Locke,[21] it fused comfortably enough with the immemorial aversion of more prosperous property holders towards arbitrary fiscal exactions, and with the strategies of representative obstruction which these social groups had contrived to develop. No doubt it is right to see the pace and incidence of its subsequent political impact as partly a working through of the obstructive powers of these wealthy and privileged social groups. But it is also right – and modern political theorists are all too obsessively aware of this – to see it from a very different angle.

The immense enhancement in the scope of governmental capacities both for benefiting and for harming subject populations certainly accentuated the charms to these subjects of rendering their government in some measure responsible to them. But more importantly, this enhancement in the governmental capacity to affect human welfare lent quite new ideological resonance and scope to the exercise of political power itself. More intriguingly, it also brought into a tense and delicate relation the degree of ideological resonance and the scale of power available for exercise. A government which, in its own eyes, held enough power to benefit its subjects handsomely could (and did) make

---

[19] This claim may perhaps do less than justice to the aspirations of many rulers. (Compare Marc Raeff, *The Well-ordered Police State,* Yale University Press, New Haven, 1983.) But it is a fair appraisal of the consequences of their actions.

[20] A reasonable sense of the severely limited purchase of such preoccupations in Europe in the period before 1660 can be obtained from Perez Zagorin's two-volume study, *Rebels and Rulers 1500–1660,* Cambridge University Press, 1982.

[21] Dunn, *Locke,* Chaps. 1 and 2. Richard Ashcraft, "The *Two Treatises* and the Exclusion Crisis: The Problem of Lockean Political Theory as Bourgeois Ideology," in J. G. A. Pocock and Richard Ashcraft, *John Locke,* William Andrews Clark Memorial Library, Los Angeles 1980, 25–116.

new appeals to the loyalty, energy and cooperation of its subjects.[22] Indeed it could hope on occasion to combine the very evident externality of modern rule over subjects with the more intimate and involving rewards of ancient citizenship. This combination certainly worked most successfully in wartime, when the indispensability of authority and unity of will was especially evident, and the struggle to provide the more antique and palpable benefit of protection was part of the shared venture. But there can be no doubt that it also featured, albeit erratically, in peacetime political endeavors: Sansculotte *journées,* Stalin's push to industrialize the Soviet Union, the New Deal, the establishment of the British welfare state, even, for some, in the ugly chaos of the Cultural Revolution. Less spectacularly, but on the whole more benignly, it has also featured in that continuous seething turmoil of voluntary associational activity which Tocqueville first identified as the glory of American democracy and which American political scientists have since dissected with such pertinacity. When eighteenth-century political thinkers – Montesquieu, Madison – thought about power, it was natural for them to consider it predominantly in terms of the capacity of human wills to obstruct one another or impose themselves upon one another. But that is emphatically not the way that Stalin or Roosevelt or Robespierre or Mao thought about power – and it is not even the way that paler successors like President Bush or Mrs. Thatcher or Mr. Gorbachev think about it. Modern rulers, virtually without exception in any state of importance, see themselves as engineers of public beneficence; and all of them, with of course very variable success, do their utmost to solicit the cooperation of the fortunate recipients in furnishing the benefits. It is a mistake to see this shift in the self-consciousness of rulers as a consequence of the greater sanctimoniousness or skill in self-deception of the modern exemplars. True, the frank egocentricity and self-indulgence of building handsome palaces has gone a trifle out of fashion, at least outside Africa and a handful of residual monarchies (Saudi Arabia, Brunei). And certainly it is easier to believe that this disappearance has been caused by a lessening in frankness than it has by a rise in altruism or libidinal self-

---

[22] Such appeals were new, to be sure, in relation to the subjects of territorial states. They were familiar enough in the cases of the city republics of ancient Greece and Renaissance Italy. Compare M. I. Finley, *Politics in the Ancient World,* Cambridge University Press, 1983.

restraint. But what is important is not the motivations or ideological styles adopted by modern rulers. It is the drastic change in the nature and significance of the activity in which they are engaged that is marked by these shifts in public affection.

There are two analytically separable, though causally interrelated, aspects to this change. The first of these is not in in itself strictly economic at all, though like all other socially extended human powers it too depends on the human organization of scarce resources through time. This first element is the vast technical increase in the human capacity to control and coordinate on a large scale and at a long distance.[23] The key to this capacity is the handling of information. In the last six or seven millennia it has moved through writing, record-keeping, printing and wireless telegraphy to the most sophisticated forms of modern electronic information processing and transmission. It represents a prodigious extension of human power. But it is not on the whole this extension, awesome though it is, that has marked modern political experience and its understanding off from its earlier antecedents. Information itself certainly greatly extends the opportunity for some wills to coerce others; and it certainly can accentuate, and has phenomenally accentuated, the ancient modalities of governmental power. Modern tyrants dispose of resources of which ancient tyrants could only dream. (Consider the famous description of Josef Stalin as Genghiz Khan with a telephone.) Information plainly also extends more humane human opportunities: the capacities for transparent mutual communication so indefatigably explored by Jurgen Habermas.[24] But it is not, *pace* Habermas, our elaborately structured saturation with information which distinguishes the modern political condition from its miscellaneous predecessors. Rather, it is our common dependence for our daily welfare upon a global system of production and exchange. This dependence is not evenly distributed across the world. Until recently, for example, it was a good deal less intense in the United States than in Great Britain; and it is certainly even now less intense in the upper reaches of the Amazon than it is in Rio de

[23] The impact of this upon military power is well described in McNeill, *The Pursuit of Power.*
[24] Compare also Condorcet's optimistic assessment of the political capacity of enlightened communication to enforce and protect itself. *Esquisse d'un tableau historique des progrès de l'esprit humain,* ed. O. H. Prior, Boivin & Cie, Paris, 1933.

Janeiro. But in contrast with the human world of two thousand years ago it marks a staggering and bemusing transformation.

It is this transformation which lies at the center of the two great pivotal works of modern liberalism and modern socialism: Adam Smith's *Wealth of Nations* and Marx's and Engels's *German Ideology.* What holds modern political theory together and makes it something more than a deluge of fantasies or an interminable and ill-tempered squabble is the twin projects of (1) identifying and explaining the scope of this transformation and (2) judging its implications for how human beings now have good reason to act. The realist tradition of political understanding is definitely capable of contributing to the explanation. As William McNeill has shown in his dramatic study *The Pursuit of Power,* the fusion between organizational control and the deployment of coercive force lies at the very center of the history of the modern state. It would be difficult to exaggerate the effect of military competition on both the extension of political control and the scale of economic organization in the world today. Where the realist tradition falters – and falters as much by sheer inattention as by lack of relevant analytical resources – is in its understanding of the politics of distribution and ideological commitment. By contrast, this is the terrain on which both liberal and socialist theories feel most at home. Both, for example, like Barnave himself, see arms – military force, coercive power – as naturally and relatively readily subordinate in a modern society and economy shaped by the imperatives of effective production. Both also endorse in their conceptions of the future, that contrast which Saint-Simon classically drew between an industrial and essentially pacific society and an agrarian and essentially bellicose society.[25] As matters have turned out this particular expectation has proved to show rather little insight. But it has been remarkably difficult to replace it with more plausible expectations without simply obliterating modern political theory. Stalinism, for example, is from one point of view merely a socialist apotheosis of the realist tradition; and it is not difficult to identify comparable deformations of the liberal sense of political value in the understanding of the needs and

---

[25] Compare also Benjamin Constant, *De l'esprit de conquête* (*Oeuvres,* ed. A. Roulin, Gallimard, Paris, 1957) 949–91; *De la liberté des anciens comparée à celle des modernes* (*Cours de politique constitutionelle,* Bechet, Paris & Rouen, 1820, Vol. 4, 238–74). John Dunn, "Liberty as a Substantive Political Value " (unpublished paper, UN University, August 1984).

destiny of the postwar American state elaborated by intellectuals like Brzezinski or Huntington or Kissinger. Raison d'état, of course, has always been an alarming political doctrine and one which its most determined exponents in practice have preferred to keep as discreet as possible. The necessities of state were as difficult to reconcile with public sanctimoniousness in the days of Richelieu as they have proved in the days of Richard Nixon, or Ronald Reagan, or François Mitterrand. But only the most sanguine of political moralists can doubt that civilization or community may sometimes stand in real peril and imperatively require defense. (There are very few British advocates of the view that it would not particularly have mattered if Hitler had won the Battle of Britain, and probably no Jewish or Korean advocates of the view that it would not especially have mattered if the United States had chosen to make an abject peace with both Germany and Japan in 1942.) But if defense is sometimes urgently needed, there certainly is today – and not only for dogmatic pacifists – some real doubt as to whether the standard modern techniques for defending advanced civilizations are actually *compatible* with civilization itself.[26] Except perhaps in private hands, arms in the United States do not do the sort of domestic damage that they have recently perpetrated in Uganda or Beirut. But it would be a bold analyst of any major modern state who was altogether convinced that its military capabilities were nothing more than the deft and passive instruments of its collective social interests. (Bolder still, perhaps, one that was confident that they were bound indefinitely to remain such. Think of the hapless population of Chile. Think of the successive bloodbaths of Kampuchea. Almost *any* army can, if it really chooses, take over almost *any* modern state. How can anyone rationally be certain that the army of their own state will always choose not to? Think of Argentina. Think of France. Think of Japan. Think of Spain. And then go *on* thinking . . .)

Modern political theorists do not so much resolve these difficulties as determinedly avert their eyes from them. The theoretical space to which modern political theory condescends to address itself – and which at times it does address with real energy – is defined by the

---

[26] Compare Malcolmson, *Nuclear Fallacies;* Bracken, *Command and Control;* and more agitatedly, Anthony Kenny, *The Logic of Deterrence,* Firethorn Press, London, 1985.

remaining pair of Barnave's triad: property (control over the production and distribution of economic goods) and opinion (the causal beliefs and conceptions of social and political value held by citizens). It is helpful to redivide these two factors further into, first, elements that serve to specify what is in itself socially or politically desirable (the normative component of the theories) and, second, elements that serve to specify the causal preconditions for realizing or frustrating such intrinsic values (the explanatory component of the theories). These last items, the causal elements, are plainly envisaged as objective: independent of human taste on the part of the analyst. But the former, the intrinsic values, are seen as in the last instance subjective: not just dependent upon but constituted by human taste. (This is at least one reason why John Locke, however negligently one interprets him, was emphatically not either a modern liberal or a modern socialist.)

Perhaps the most important single fact about modern political theory is the fact that the division between wealth and opinion does not correspond at all precisely to the division between objective and subjective elements. The solid presence of the objective (in itself a precondition for elementary political sanity) furnishes a basis for effective modern doctrines of political authority. But the somewhat more nebulous opening towards subjectivity establishes a measure of countervailing strain. It is this opening towards subjectivity which lends the idiom of democracy its powerful critical edge within modern politics.[27] Even if the organizational reality of any modern state is radically incompatible with its being a system of popular rule,[28] the mere fact that a modern government is keenly disliked by its own demos remains intensely degrading: a lethal ideological blemish. Islamic states can still justify themselves without contradiction just by endeavouring to make possible the living of a truly Islamic life, and if the *Umma* proves disinclined for such a life, then it is the *Umma* and not the government that is discredited by the aversion. But a socialist

---

[27] Compare John Dunn, *Western Political Theory in the Face of the Future,* Cambridge University Press, 1979, Chaps. 1 and 2; idem, "Country Risk: Social and Cultural Aspects," in Richard J. Herring (ed.), idem, *Managing International Risk,* Cambridge University Press, 1983, 138–67; idem, *Rethinking Modern Political Theory,* Chap. 7.

[28] *Works of Joseph de Maistre,* (*Sovereignty,* bk. 1, Chap. 1), "[T]he people which *command* are not the people which *obey.*"

populace that loathes its socialist masters, or a liberal economy that can be preserved only by the torture chambers of the secret police, demolish the pretensions of those who rule over them, however sincere, intelligent and even well-intentioned the latter may be. In the modern world once the most enlightened of despotisms becomes popularly misliked, it denounces itself. How can effective doctrines of political authority consort with such limitless facilities for self-righteous insubordination? (This, I take it, is roughly what has preoccupied anxious recent interpreters of the ungovernability of modern societies, a concern which is in fact roughly coeval with the existence of governmental power.)

Much of modern political theory – and perhaps most modern governmental practice – is taken up with the effort to devise a more comfortable accommodation between the two. Populist political theory (which comes in liberal as well as socialist versions, and which is most authentically represented by libertarian anarchism) fatuously denies the existence of any need for governmental power, though it seldom today goes so far as to suggest any imminent prospect of divesting ourselves of the latter. The more intellectually penetrating versions of modern political theory, by contrast, fasten on the coexistence within popular (and presumably governmental) opinion of causal beliefs and direct evaluations. The direct evaluations of the demos are privileged and beyond criticism; but their causal beliefs are eminently fallible – and since they are in fact often rather frivolously derived and casually entertained, they clearly lack the dignity of the painstakingly formulated and lovingly nurtured nostrums elaborated by the Treasury, MITI, the Ministry of Finance or the Bureau of the Budget. Wealth may be defined in the last instance by the subjective (contingent individual preferences) within capitalist economics, but once it has been so defined, the analytic apparatus which explains how it can be created and sustained is – at least in intention – awesomely objective. If all a modern demos needed was a ready flow of belief and preference, it could safely be left to its own devices. But since, on the most optimistic analysis, every modern demos also requires a dependable tide of goods and services on which to deploy its preferences, it plainly also needs some trustworthy guarantee that this tide will indeed continue to run.

Modern liberal and socialist political thinking has been a serried struggle to show how such a guarantee can be provided. On the whole it cannot be said to have been impressively successful in showing anything of the kind. No one today really knows for sure just why its success has been so limited. (To know for sure would be either to have succeeded already oneself – or to see how to prove that an ampler measure of success is in principle impossible.) I suspect that the principal reason for its relative failure lies in the intrinsic difficulty of combining a respect for subjective evaluative whim (the tastes of the demos) with a respect for objective causal judgment (the assessment of objective constraints by whoever is epistemically best placed to assess them). To reconcile these two orientations does not require unusual theoretical penetration. (There is no obvious and intractable contradiction between the two.) What it does require is a high measure of practical agility and flexibility, a degree of real political prowess. And it requires this agility not just of professional rulers and economists but also of the individual members of the demos in their capacities as consumers, producers and political agents.[29] (There are none so ungovernable as those without the least inclination to be governed.)

But there are, of course, plenty of other impediments to modern political flourishing besides the habitual muscular or imaginative rigidity of human populations and their would-be leaders. For one thing, even the more optimistic versions of modern political theory claim to identify merely how good social and political orders are now possible. Only the most credulous version of Marxism, for example, genuinely insists that the requirements for the dynamic development of the forces of production must necessarily succeed in imposing themselves upon the contingent disarray of the relations of production. The alternative version of Marxism which emphasizes the centrality and causal efficacy of class struggle[30] has little difficulty in accommodating itself (at least at an explanatory level) to the discouraging lessons of politi-

[29] Compare Joseph Schumpeter, *Capitalism, Socialism and Democracy* 4th ed., Allen & Unwin, London, 1954, 261: The "core of the trouble is the fact that the sense of reality is so completely lost. Normally the great political questions take their place in the psychic economy of the typical citizen with those leisure-hour interests that have not attained the rank of hobbies, and with the subjects of irresponsible conversation. These things seem to be so far off. . . . one feels oneself to be moving in a fictitious world . . . the private citizen . . . expends less disciplined effort on mastering a political problem than he spends on a game of bridge."

[30] See Elster, *Making Sense of Marx.*

cal experience. Another factor that impedes the political articulation of the populace's subjective will is the distinctly limited conviction of rulers or would-be rulers that contingent popular tastes really do deserve any such deference. The most morally imposing of existing versions of both liberalism and socialism set an overwhelming value upon human autonomy, the right and capacity of each human being to *choose* as much of their life as, at the historically prevailing level of social and economic efficacy, they can be given the opportunity to choose. This is as decisively the case with the more clear-headed of modern socialist moralists (Cohen, Elster, Przeworski) as it is with the devoutly Kantian exponents of recent American political philosophy (John Rawls, Ronald Dworkin, even, after his fashion, Robert Nozick).[31] It is at the least a defensible interpretation of the more coherent views of Marx himself,[32] and it is a natural and unforced reading of the central figures of the liberal tradition from Smith and Constant to John Stuart Mill, Tocqueville and Isaiah Berlin. But even in this determinedly autonomy-centered interpretation there is an opening for important intrusions of moral paternalism in the potential tensions between the right to autonomy at a particular time and the capacity of the same or other agents for autonomy at some other later time. It is this loophole that has made possible the dismal synthesis of socialism with tryanny with which we are all so familiar. It has also served to rationalize (if not to justify) the extended practice of tutelary dictatorship in many areas of the world on behalf of the long-term prospects for capitalist enterprise.

At least as weightily – and on socialist just as much as on capitalist terrain – the finality of individual subjective choice and will has been set aside in favor of an alternative moral theory, utilitarianism, which

---

[31] Ibid.; G. A. Cohen, *Karl Marx's Theory;* Adam Przeworski, *Capitalism and Social Democracy,* Cambridge University Press, 1985; John Rawls, *A Theory of Justice,* Oxford University Press, Oxford, 1972; idem, "Kantian Constructivism in Moral Theory," *Journal of Philosophy* 77, 1980, 515–72; Ronald Dworkin, *Taking Rights Seriously,* Duckworth, London 1977; idem, "Liberalism," in Stuart Hampshire (ed.), *Public and Private Morality,* Cambridge University Press, 1978, 113–43; "What is Equality? Pt. 1: Equality of Welfare," *Philosophy and Public Affairs,* 10, 3, 1981, 185–246; "What is Equality? Pt. 2: Equality of Resources," ibid., 10, 4, 1981, 283–345; Robert Nozick, *Anarchy, State and Utopia,* Basil Blackwell, Oxford, 1974.

[32] Steven Lukes, *Marxism and Morality,* Clarendon Press, Oxford, 1985; Elster, *Making Sense of Marx.*

has a far more natural and intimate affinity with political authority.[33] If autonomy is truly the criterion of human value, then all of us (at least after a certain age) must just be left to value for ourselves. But once value is abstracted from the separateness of persons and lumped together in the medium of welfare, then it morally requires aggregation and strategic calculation even to determine its own prescriptions. Still more importantly, it also licenses (perhaps even demands) its own application on the amplest and least obstructed scale possible. Utilitarians, if they are honest, must certainly be alert to the potential disutilities of concentrating power. But once all the utility calculations are in, it is an imperative of their own theory that they should will its implementation on the widest possible canvas. No true utilitarian can be wholly happy with anything less than a dependably utilitarian global political authority: a world government indefatigably devoted to the maximization of utility.

At a less ambitious and clear-headed level, there are still in every real ruling apparatus in the modern world ample residues of more or less bigoted moral (and not so moral) paternalism. Most modern rulers are some way from being value skeptics, and the practice of rule does little to inspire them with genuine respect for the refractory values of others. It is easy enough to explain why even those governments most intent on expressing their liberal or socialist political commitments should in practice diverge rather markedly from taking the contingent wills of their subjects as a final authority. There is no reason to believe that they are necessarily either confused or morally in error in so doing, just because it is not clear that a genuine respect for contentless preference or choice in others is either psychologically possible or morally appropriate. And it is all too clear that the absolutization of individual autonomy as a *standard* of value is not in itself imaginatively a very helpful basis on which to set about the attempt to understand politics. Perhaps, indeed, it is not even a very helpful basis on which to attempt to understand the value of autonomy.[34] Just because it deliberately begins so far away from explanation, it offers little external aid in determining at all coherently or

---

[33] Compare Amartya Sen and Bernard Williams (eds.), *Utilitarianism and Beyond,* Cambridge University Press, 1982, Introduction.
[34] Joseph Raz, "Right-based Moralities," in Jeremy Waldron (ed.), *Theories of Rights,* Oxford University Press, Oxford, 1984, 182–200.

delicately what it is and what it is not in fact a good idea for political agents to do.

So even if the central moral precepts of liberal and socialist theories of politics are altogether valid (which may well be doubted), they are certainly in themselves insufficient to constitute a sound theory of politics. To provide the latter it is necessary to work more directly from the historically given materials of current political circumstance: the way politics now actually is.[35] As a gloss on the realities of modern politics, liberalism and socialism may be taken principally to claim that there exist definite ways of organizing economies, societies and governmental institutions which dependably combine free popular choice with the successful reproduction and further embellishment of the material preconditions for such choice. Liberals differ from socialists (and each of course differ extravagantly amongst each other) on just *how* these combinations must be organized to be possible at all: on the minimal conditions for modern civilized life. They differ further, characteristically, on how these could in principle be best arranged. They do however agree, as we have noted, that the zone which is decisively important in ensuring this combination is the organization of the economy. And in this conviction at least they can draw on a large measure of popular support. Modern populations may rather seldom accept a governmental view that economic prosperity is a sufficient condition for civilized life; but they are increasingly inclined to regard it as a necessary condition. Both for private citizens and for rulers, accordingly, the choice of effective economic policies is, under normal conditions, the most important and permanent of modern political needs. It is also a need which has proved over the decades remarkably difficult to satisfy.

Both liberalism and socialism in their earlier renderings offered a reasonably clear and confident account of how this need could in the future be expected to satisfy itself. For classical liberals this was the unimpeded working of domestic and international markets; for socialists it was the planned rational subordination of human productive powers to the conscious will and collective choice of the species which had developed them. Neither of these convictions has proved to be a pure and unmitigated fantasy. But each, sadly, has also

[35] Dunn, *Rethinking Modern Political Theory,* Introduction and Chaps. 4–10.

proved to be, at least in the form in which it first imposed itself upon human credulity, devastatingly overoptimistic. Both market exchange and economic planning have enormously extended human productive powers and the facilities for material enjoyment. And within the world economy and over the last century it has become extravagantly difficult to disentangle their respective impacts and to see precisely across space and time just where the one starts and the other stops.[36]

Both markets and plans, to be sure, still have their devotees. But each now finds increasing difficulty in extending such devotion politically to a large enough proportion of the politically relevant nation to realize either at all uninhibitedly in the real world. Still more embarrassingly, it is that these difficulties increase in direct ratio to the percentage of the populations concerned that is in fact politically relevant. The full dominion of either market or plan today requires a narrow and socially insulated dictatorship.[37] This is partly a consequence of the structure of modern states. It is, for example, quite generally true that the greater the real democratization of political life the less the opportunity for coherent economic policy, and the less the real democratization the greater the real opportunity for economic coherence. (The shadow of utilitarianism here falls again.) But the gross political unviability of pure market or pure planning approaches to economic management also stems from analytic deficiencies of the political economies of market and plan that have emerged in the two centuries since Adam Smith and which were certainly at first some way from being self-evident features of either mode of economic coordination. The reason these deficiencies are so important in modern politics is that they are individually necessary and jointly sufficient to preclude the depoliticization of modern economic management, either on a capitalist or on a socialist basis. It was only because he was so confident that the rational collective direction of production would preserve and enhance the productive dynamism of capitalism that Marx could be so casual in his attitude towards the

---

[36] It is obviously not analytically defensible to treat large-scale economic actors, like multinational corporations, as though their market interventions were not a product of the attempt to plan rationally.

[37] For a particularly vivid protest at the implications of this assessment in the case of planning see Nove, *Economics of Feasible Socialism*.

political institutionalization of the socialist or communist future.[38] It was because the free working of the market, domestically and internationally, was in their view such an evident public good that Tom Paine, and the Abbé Sieyes, and James Mill were so confident that a fully nationally representative political order would not be fatally riven by structural conflicts of interests.[39] Unfortunately, however, a modern government combines an extensive capacity to modify the workings of markets and a rich variety of motives for so doing with an extremely unimpressive capacity to replace their workings in their entirety by its own directing rational will.

Both liberals and socialists aspire today, with some variations in assurance, to specify forms of political organization that can sensibly be expected to combine through time free political choice with effective economic production. (They differ rather more, between themselves and from each other, over how far they desire or expect that the economic goods produced will be distributed in a manner which is plausibly just. But neither, naturally, is radically indifferent to this issue, since it is hard to combine free political choice indefinitely with excessively palpable social injustice, at least towards a stable majority of the population. That is why free political choice is not as yet on offer to the majority of the South African population.)[40] The charms of free political choice for the choosers are evident enough, and they become even more evident in settings where for any length of time they are absent or decisively withdrawn. But it is important to realize firmly that, even if free political choice may be compatible with effec-

---

[38] This is not, of course, to suggest that he was wise to be casual about this matter. Compare Dunn, *The Politics of Socialism* and *Rethinking Modern Political Theory* with John M. Maguire, *Marx's Theory of Politics,* Cambridge University Press, 1978; Alan Gilbert, *Marx's Politics: Communists and Citizens,* Martin Robertson, Oxford, 1981; R. N. Hunt, *The Political Ideas of Marx and Engels,* 2 vols., Macmillan, London, 1975 and 1984.

[39] Thomas Paine, *The Rights of Man,* J. M. Dent & Son, London 1915; Emmanuel Joseph Sieyes, *What Is the Third Estate?* tr. M. Blondel, Pall Mall Press, London 1963; James Mill, *Essay on Government,* in Jack Lively and John Rees (eds.), *Utilitarian Logic and Politics,* Clarendon Press, Oxford, 1978, 53–95); Pasquale Pasquino, "Introduction to Lorenz von Stein," *Economy and Society,* 10, 1, February 1981, 1–6; "E. J. Sieyes e la Rapprasentanza Politica: Progetto per una Ricerca," *Quaderni Piacentini,* 12, 1984, esp. 75–81.

[40] See Heribert Adam and Kogila Moodley, *South Africa Without Apartheid,* University of California Press, Berkeley and Los Angeles, 1986, for a level-headed study of the prospects for rendering social, economic, and political injustice less blatant in this setting.

tive production in a wide variety of social and political orders, it necessarily and permanently also carries the power to disrupt this. Even within a single generation (and quite apart from the moral risks of generational egoism) a society can (and sometimes will) freely choose to consume fecklessly. Even perfectly rational and perfectly informed human agents could choose to impair the economic prospects of their less immediate human successors; and perfectly informed (and on some readings perhaps even perfectly rational)[41] human agents might well choose to diminish even their own future prospects of consumption. (Waiving the perfection of rationality and information, just these choices have in fact been made in Great Britain over at least the last ten years, as they have in Nigeria over at least the last twenty and in Ghana over at least the last thirty.) Political freedom in fact *entails* the opportunity to impair the future real wealth of a community.

But it is not principally the folly or vice of the wastrel that menaces the coherence of modern political values. Rather, it is the extreme difficulty both in designing and in realizing in practice systems of political and economic choice which work effectively together for the better and do not select too drastically or arbitrarily the values of which they take account.

There are three intractable barriers to such design. (There are also, of course, a considerable number of further obstructions, some of them possibly insurmountable in principle,[42] to realizing the best of designs in practice. And behind these barriers in turn there lie two main pressures: the conflicts between human interests and the difficulties which human beings face in understanding clearly just what they are doing.) The first of these barriers is the absence of a reasonably transparent and efficiency-preserving standard of justice in economic distribution. The second is the formidable array of puzzles of collective rationality inherent in any system of public choice and dramatically multiplied by the prior existence of elaborate and morally arbitrary divisions of interest: divisions which exist in every real historical society at almost every point in time. (It is in the analysis of this array

[41] See Derek Parfit, "Later Selves and Moral Principles," in Alan Montefiore (ed.), *Philosophy and Personal Relations,* Routledge & Kegan Paul, London, 1973, 137–69. But compare the implications of the far fuller treatment in idem, *Reasons and Persons,* Clarendon Press, Oxford, 1984.

[42] Dunn, *Politics of Socialism;* idem, *Rethinking Modern Political Theory,* Chaps. 4–6.

of puzzles, following particularly the work of Kenneth Arrow, Mancur Olson and the architects of the modern theory of games, that recent political theorists have most decisively deepened nineteenth-century liberal or socialist understandings of the dilemmas of modern politics.)[43] The third barrier, in itself well beyond the analytic resources of political theorists but nonetheless salient today amidst their concerns, is the overwhelming opacity of the workings of the world economy.[44] Each of these barriers has received ample academic attention in the last few decades. But none show much sign of succumbing to these attentions. In contrast with the evident (if perhaps largely illusory) equity of the modern standard of justice in political distribution (formal political equality)[45] the standards of economic justice now on offer combine dismaying levels of complexity with almost equally dismaying levels of intellectual implausibility. Sustained analysis of the problems of collective rationality, precisely by its rather steady intellectual progress, has demonstrated to all but the willfully obtuse that there simply cannot be systems of public choice for real modern societies that combine simplicity of design, apparent fairness, and the avoidance of perverse outcomes in a wide variety of politically relevant instances. Even with the working of the world economy, a particularly unstable and murky zone in modern understanding, what little has come to be clearly understood serves principally to underline the forlornness of any hope of rendering the formulation of national economic policies transparently acceptable even to the denizens of a domestic economy and predictably effective in sustaining this in the wider ecology within which it has to subsist. (Let alone any hope of devising a model for the relations between domestic economies which meets the same standards.)

On an optimistic view, therefore, we still have good reason to see

---

[43] Mancur Olson, *The Logic of Collective Action,* Harvard University Press, Cambridge, Mass., 1965; idem, *The Rise and Decline of Nations,* Yale University Press, New Haven, 1982; Russell Hardin, *Collective Action,* Johns Hopkins University Press, Baltimore, 1982.

[44] A cognitive field that plainly fuses politics with economics: Robert O. Keohane, *After Hegemony: Cooperation and Discord in the World Political Economy,* Princeton University Press, 1984; John H. Goldthorpe (ed.), *Order and Conflict in Contemporary Capitalism,* Clarendon Press, Oxford, 1984.

[45] Compare Dunn, *Western Political Theory,* Chap. 1. But see Gregory Vlastos's splendid assertion of the rationale for the standard, "Justice and Equality," in Waldron (ed.), *Theories of Rights,* esp. 53–4, 58.

the analysis of the economic limits to modern political possibility as the key to the understanding of modern politics (at least on that domestic stage, which is still the widest arena in which even the most optimistic observers have contrived to see modern populations as choosing collectively for themselves). What in the last few decades political theorists have been struggling patiently to grasp is how little idea they genuinely possess of how to cut this key so that it will turn the lock. To understand modern politics well today is most emphatically to realize how *very* little of it there is of which we yet have the least real comprehension. But it is also to see, and to see with ever more nightmarish clarity, just how urgently we *need* to understand it as soberly and clearly as we can. In that mixture of habit, hope and self-deception that makes up the modern academic world, we all need in this context to learn to be a lot lighter on our feet, to see how to turn the clever range of intellectual tricks accumulated over the last two centuries into effective tools for making this a better world, or just for stopping it from becoming an even worse one, or perhaps in the very last instance just for stopping it from coming to a hideous and deserved end.

CHAPTER 2

Free trade and the economic limits to national politics: neo-Machiavellian political economy reconsidered*

ISTVAN HONT

Trade is now becoming the golden ball, for which all nations of the world are contending, and the occasion of so great partialities, that not only every nation is endeavouring to posess the trade of the whole world, but every city to draw all to itself.

Andrew Fletcher of Saltoun

There are many kinds of economic limits to politics, by no means all of them distinctively a product of the "modern age." Here we shall consider only the specific limit to politics set by the imperative need of modern nations to succeed in international trade, arguing that this particular limitation in substantial territorial states came into existence only when a number of European countries were transformed into what eighteenth-century political economists called "commercial societies."

In the 1660s the former English ambassador William Temple, in his influential analysis of its politics and commerce, observed that Holland was then facing an entirely novel adverse situation in international markets, one which he predicted would soon put an end to the coun-

*The first version of this chapter, presented at the Murphy Institute for Political Economy, was entitled "The Wealth of One Nation and the Dynamics of International Competition." John Dunn, Albert Hirschmann, Michael Landesmann, Aladár Madarász, Nicholas Phillipson, J. G. A. Pocock, John Robertson, Keith Tribe, and Jonathan Zeitlin helped me considerably during the rethinking and rewriting of the original paper. The Institute for Advanced Study in Princeton and the Max Planck Institute for History in Göttingen provided me with excellent working conditions during this period. I acknowledge the generous support for this project by the John M. Olin Foundation and the Council for Research in the Humanities and Social Sciences of Columbia University in New York City. I am grateful to John Dunn for his help with editing the manuscript.

41

try's miraculous development.[1] He did not advance the familiar moralistic analysis in terms of the impact of luxury and the decline this must inevitably promote. He predicted the decline of Holland not because all good things must at some point come to an end or because of the supposedly corrupting impact of increasing opulence. Rather, he insisted upon the reality of a transformation in the world trading regime which was wholly independent of the practical merits or demerits of Dutch trading policy. Holland was a commercial republic, a specialized maritime trade carrier serving the large territorial–military states of Europe by servicing those of their external economic needs that could be supplied by peaceful foreign trade. It now faced fresh competition, not from a new maritime republic seeking to undercut its trade by offering similar services more cheaply or reliably, but from a quite new type of "commercial," or trading, state: the territorial monarchies of Europe themselves.

In the course of the seventeenth century, as Temple shrewdly noted, the structure of international trading relations had altered sharply. In place of a close and complementary relation between territorial states and small but specialized commercial polities (most of them republics or city-states) a new regime had come into existence in which the territorial states had become international commercial agents in their own right. It was not that these monarchies had wholly changed their nature, but rather that their habitual political ambitions now spilled over onto the terrain of international commerce. In David Hume's famous words, in the seventeenth century commerce, for the first time, became a "reason of state".[2] The needs

---

[1] Sir William Temple, *Observations Upon the United Provinces of the Netherlands,* ed. George Clark (Oxford, 1972), chap. 6, "Of Their Trade," pp. 108–26. The book was first published in 1673. Temple entered the diplomatic service of the king in 1665 and served as ambassador at The Hague from 1668 to 1670. For three years afterwards he withdrew from public service and in temporary retirement devoted his time to writing. There were six English editions of the *Observations,* besides Dutch and French translations, in his lifetime, the second with a few additions and corrections. His memoirs, correspondence, and essays were published after his death by Jonathan Swift, his protégé and private secretary in the 1690s. His collected works were published seven times in the eighteenth century. Temple was very highly regarded in his time and was offered high office several times, which he refused. For his life (1628–99) see "The Life and Character of Sir William Temple" by his sister Lady Giffard, written when Temple was still alive (1690), in *The Early Essays and Romances of Sir William Temple Bt.,* ed. G. C. Moore Smith (Oxford, 1930), pp. 3–25.

[2] David Hume, "Of Civil Liberty" [1741] in *Essays Moral, Political and Literary,* ed. E. F. Miller (Indianapolis, 1985), pp. 88–9.

of modern warfare created an ever increasing demand for finance on a scale that simply could not be met by the expedients of the past. It compelled even the most reluctant of territorial monarchies to concern themselves with trade both as a reliable source of income and as an ultimate resource for their own defense and military efficacy.[3] The international marketplace came to be crowded by warring monarchies pursuing their rivalries as commercial competitors and vying for every apparently lucrative market. Instead of seeming a clear antithesis to warfare between nations and a peaceful bond connecting every type of state, republic and monarchy alike, commerce, under this new impetus, menaced rivalries as intense as – and perhaps even more uncertain in their outcome than – any earlier forms of conflict.

But the rules of this new game were in some respects novel. The market, it was now recognized, had its own laws, and laws which differed sharply from those of politics. It was, for one thing, in a number of ways beyond political control. Markets were constituted by the meeting of sellers with buyers, and competition was measured in prices. Whoever could sell cheaper secured the market. This was an obvious fact of economic life, well known and frequently repeated by merchants and directors of trading companies. But for the nation, the state, to submit itself to this kind of arbitration, to ground its military strength, national glory, and political stability upon commercial success in foreign markets created a wholly new situation. It required a redefinition, or at the least a significant modification, of the very notion of strength, for if one asked, as many contemporaries did, what was the key to cheap and competitive prices, the answer they returned was surprisingly uniform. In competitive trade, trade not based simply on supplying goods and raw materials otherwise unavailable at the point of sale, prices were determined mainly by the costs of transport and the wages required to produce the goods in question. A successful commercial nation was a nation of cheap prices and consequently a nation of low wages. Wealth, glory, and military power could achieve a great deal, but on open and free markets, that is, on *true* markets,[4] they

---

[3] See the recent accounts of William H. McNeill, *The Pursuit of Power* (Chicago, 1982), particularly pp. 102–16; and Paul Kennedy, *The Rise and Fall of the Great Powers: Economic Change and Military Conflict from 1500 to 2000* (New York, 1987), esp. pp. 70–115.

[4] For an extremely clear statement of what true markets entailed for a late-seventeenth-century political theorist, see John Locke's 1695 manuscript essay "Venditio," first

might well constitute a disadvantage, since they did not imply – and seldom in fact coincided with – a regime of low wages. From now on there was a new precondition for political success. Survival for a state now required not only wealth and power, but also the ability to sell cheap, and hence ultimately the ability to keep wage costs firmly under control. The requirements for effective political action had encountered a whole new range of constraints.

These were in fact limits to politics in a profound sense. Not only did competitiveness require successful commercial nations to maintain cheap prices and hence low wages, but the determinants of an appropriate price level also lay firmly beyond the competence of the domestic politics of any individual competitor nation. Politics, by strict definition, had long been understood to be concerned with the ordered and peaceful life of the *polis,* the *civitas,* a "distinct society." Seventeenth-century theories of politics or of the conditions for legitimate political authority (contract theories, for example) always focused on the politics of a single and distinct sovereign community and assessed the best structure of common life for those who chose, or found themselves compelled, to live together in a given *civitas,* whether a monarchy or a republic. The legitimate political order of such a polity was conceived as qualitatively different from prepolitical life, the state of nature. It was also the opposite of the structure of international society, the real remaining "state of nature."[5] International society was conceived as a realm of freedom, albeit a freedom full of hazard. International "politics," accordingly, if the term was appropriate at all, was seen as a matter of self-defense and of the variety of preemptive activities aimed at minimizing armed conflict and averting the threat of loss of sovereignty. The politics of each

published in John Dunn, "Justice and the Interpretation of Locke's Political Theory," *Political Studies,* 16 (1968), 84–7.

[5] In seventeenth-century jurisprudence the state of nature, "as it was really," the condition of "natural liberty," was not some imaginary condition of beginning (that was only methodological fiction), but a product of history; it had developed as mankind separated into communities, tribes, and eventually nations. The state of nature, announced Samuel Pufendorf in the most successful natural law textbook of all times, "at this Time is the Case of many Kingdoms and Communities, and of the Subjects of the same, with respect to the Subjects of the other; and the same was anciently the State of the Patriarchs, when they liv'd independently." See his *De officio hominis et civis juxta legem naturalem libri duo,* 2.1.6, as translated into English by Andrew Tooke under the title *The Whole Duty of Man According to the Law of Nature; The Fourth Edition with the Notes of Mr Barbeyrac, and many other Additions and Amendments* (London, 1716).

distinct society in this international state of nature was effectively constrained by the need of each state to possess adequate national defense. But the rise of commerce as a reason of state added a whole new dimension to the constraints which the anarchical relations between sovereign states imposed on national politics. To launch the *civitas* into international trade was to commit the nation not only to an international politics of military self-protection, but also to a hazardous and active participation in a domain which was subject to no effective overall authority at all.

A particularly acute sense of the dangers of commerce was developed in the middle of the eighteenth century by the French *économistes,* who firmly preferred a large territorial monarchy to anchor its wealth and power in a strong agricultural base. The severely analytical language which Quesnay and his fellow members of the sect deployed in their economic theory should not blind us to the fact that as political theorists the *économistes* justified their preference for the stability of an agricultural state in terms closely similar to those of the English and Scottish theorists of commercial society. Like that of their counterparts in Britain, their political vocabulary associated trade and liberty, presenting their own defense of modern civilized monarchies in terms of a sophisticated analysis of the relative advantages and disadvantages of republican and monarchical government. Ronald Meek has already noticed, in his quest for the elusive roots of the notorious "four stages theory of history," that Mirabeau, in his *Philosophie rurale,* had developed a theory of commercial society remarkably similar to, though quite different in its conclusions from, that of the Scottish philosophical political economists.[6] As Meek remarked, the source of this differ-

---

[6] See The Marquis de Mirabeau and François Quesnay, "An Extract from *Rural Philosophy*" in R. L. Meek (ed.), *Precursors of Adam Smith* (London, 1973), pp. 104–13. The fragment translated by Meek is a modern English rendering of pp. 9–26 of vol. 2, chap. 8, "Rapports des dépenses avec la population" of the *Philosophie rurale ou économie générale et politique de l'agriculture, pour servir de suite à l'ami des hommes.* Par M. de Mirabeau, (3 vols., Amsterdam, 1766). Mirabeau and Quesnay worked together on the book, but it was probably only chap. 7 which can be attributed entirely to Quesnay. It was their first attempt to provide a comprehensive positive system of the school of *économistes.* On its appearance it was regarded as a fundamental work, and it played a significant role in establishing the reputation of the Physiocratic "sect." On the genesis and reception of the book, see Georges Weulersse, *Le mouvement physiocratique en France (de 1756 à 1770)* (2 vols., Paris, 1910), vol. 1, pp. 78–86. Mirabeau's contribution to the shaping of the theoretical history foundations of political economy are sadly neglected. For a general discussion of his political economy, see Lucien Brocard, *Les doctrines économiques et sociales*

ence lay in the *économistes'* reluctance to accept commercial society as a fourth stage into which modern territorial agrarian societies must inevitably develop. Instead of labeling this, with Meek, a failure in achieving modernity, it is more helpful to inquire why they insisted so strongly on the need for a stable agrarian base for modern monarchies. Mirabeau and Quesnay were drawing a deliberate contrast between the way of life and the politics of commercial states and those of territorial monarchies. Rather than showing the latter how to adopt the posture of the former, they aimed to alert their readers to the perils for large territorial monarchies like France in any attempt to transform themselves into commercial societies.

In the *Philosophie rurale* Mirabeau and Quesnay stressed systematically how the satisfaction of man's basic needs and desires furnished a foundation for social life and politics. They insisted uncompromisingly that man had first to eat before he could engage in other activities and argued that the politics of a society was structured by its mode of subsistence. Drawing on well-established analyses of the legitimization of property rights and the history of property forms, they listed three fundamental modes of subsistence which had been open to mankind from its initial occupation of the world: hunting, fishing, and gathering; the herding of flocks; and the cultivation of land. These were the primary activities which had ensured the survival and growth of human populations. They insisted that man's attempt to satisfy his basic needs had definite mental consequences, establishing a dynamic of desires which, once established, had become central to the politics and political economy of modern societies.

Commerce, they argued, was an inevitable consequence of the establishment of private property among agricultural peoples, peo-

du Marquis de Mirabeau dans l'ami des hommes, (Paris, 1902) and the essays in Part 1 of *Les Mirabeaus et leur temps. Actes du Colloque d'Aix-en-Provence, 17 et 18 decembre 1966* (Paris, 1968), particularly Paul Chénier's piece, "Le dilemme de Mirabeau: Cantillon ou Quesnay," pp. 23–36. For a broader overview of the development of eighteenth-century French political economy see Jean-Claude Perrot, "Economie politique" in R. Reichardt, E. Schmitt, G. van den Heuvel, and A. Hofer, *Handbuch politisch-sozialer Grundbegriffe in Frankreich 1680–1820*, vol. 8 (Munich, 1988), pp. 51–104. The rise of the group around Gournay transplanting English ideas of trade and commercial polity is discussed in Antoin E. Murphy, *Richard Cantillon, Entrepreneur and Economist* (Oxford, 1986), chap. 15. Adam Smith quoted Mirabeau, remarking that he was a "very diligent and respectable author" (*Wealth of Nations*, IV.ix.39). Together with Mercier de la Rivière's *L'ordre naturel et essentiel des sociétés politiques* (1767), the *Philosophie rurale* most probably served as the general basis of Smith's account of the system of the *économistes*.

ples who had developed a wide variety of desires. Settled nations and settled individuals, because of their new situation, inevitably faced shortages in some products and surpluses in others. It was precisely the exchange of their surpluses that became the primary factor binding together societies of private property owners and separate nations settled within their own sovereign boundaries. This exchange of surpluses, once regularized, became part and parcel of social life, and the very activity of facilitating it could become a source of subsistence for some. In this way a fourth mode of subsistence could emerge, the commercial mode, a way of living which was, by its very nature, secondary and additional to the primary modes of ensuring man's survival. "Thus alongside the agricultural societies" – Quesnay and Mirabeau explained – "there could be, and were bound to be, set up commercial societies, just as granaries are set up alongside crops."[7] A whole society organized to fulfill this function was for Quesnay and Mirabeau, therefore, virtually an enormous clearinghouse or *comptoir:* an integrally commercial society or trading polity.

Though commerce, the trading of surpluses, had been part of the life of all modern agricultural monarchies, the *Philosophie Rurale* argued that it was in the best interest of mankind and more specifically of the agrarian territorial states that only specialized trading polities should elect to make trade a raison d'état. Territorial states which must feed and defend large populations, even if they had once enjoyed free constitutions, were likely to find themselves transformed into monarchies. It was natural that monarchical governments should set their sights on matching the wealth of the most successful commercial societies. But any route to such wealth was fraught with grave difficulties. Conquest had become well nigh impossible, since no sooner was it accomplished than the very purpose of undertaking it promptly became unattainable. To intrude power politics into the free realm of international trade must undermine the very foundations of commerce. In reality, they argued, the foundations of commercial societies lay "in their industry, their knowledge of routes and the surpluses and needs of different areas, and the reputation which they acquired because people grew accustomed to finding

---

[7] De Mirabeau and Quesnay, *Rural Philosophy,* p. 111. Meek's translation is imprecise in a crucial respect. Mirabeau, instead of commercial societies, simply talks about trading or merchant societies, "les sociétés marchandes."

them always successful and always scrupulous in fulfilling their obligations." If the trading polity was conquered, its commerce could disappear and its eminently mobile wealth would escape capture. The wealth of merchants, echoing Montesquieu's well-known argument, was by nature unsuited to the territorial control of monarchical politics. For similar reasons the hope of "the governments of those agricultural nations which take such pains to school themselves to become merchants,"[8] that they might continue to "plunder" domestic mercantile wealth through taxation, was equally futile.

Trade, the institution of a *comptoir*, Quesnay and Mirabeau insisted, was free by its very nature. The seeds of freedom in the activity of market exchange itself demanded a republican form of government. Trading societies required a properly constituted system of sovereign power in order to settle their internal disputes and to protect their citizens from one another, to "make for themselves laws relating to association, warehousing, and security." What they did not need was the institution of a single leader or a reorganization of the state to serve military purposes. The best defense of such a commercial state lay in its ability to fulfill its specialized function well: "Helpful to its neighbours and engaged in serving them," the trading polity could civilize them "in making them wealthy, or rather in conferring the attribute of wealth on their goods." But it was not only because tampering with the mechanisms which generated their wealth would simply destroy the latter that the flexible political structure and freedom of trading polities had become indispensable. The logic of trade itself required mobility and flexibility in political organization. In the eyes of Mirabeau, "the basis of sovereignty is stability," but he saw little prospect for stability in a society which earned its wealth through trade. Trade was fickle and ever changing; it was a profoundly "uncertain means of subsistence." In commercial societies, accordingly, life was based on "continual activity." The maintenance of internal order required that their most fundamental laws be fixed, but they also required a "large number of regulations relating to the

---

[8] A. V. Judges argues that this account had a great influence on Adam Smith's famous critique of the mercantile system. When Mirabeau ridiculed "the approximation of the commercial policy of great empires to the standards of a counting house" the marginal running title said, "absurd inconsistency of the mercantile system" (*système mercantile*); see "The Idea of a Mercantile State," reprinted in D. C. Coleman (ed.), *Revisions in Mercantilism* (London, 1969), pp. 37–8.

internal economy and civil administration" which constantly adjusted to "changing circumstances." Such deliberate adjustment could be secured only if those who were winning the profits were regularly consulted. A commercial society had to find a subtle balance between flexibility and a most "orderly and methodical way" of dealing with the multiplicity of new challenges thrown up by "changes in the operations from which profit is made." Though commerce could be extremely profitable, it also made social life changeable and uncertain, rendering the survival of a trading state far more dependent on the continued health of its constitution and on the effective curbing of the turbulent ambitions and seething corruption created by its very commercial success.

From the different interrelationships and drawing together of the different societies there is born a new kind of secondary and artificial society, less secure so far as its basis and duration are concerned, less capable of extension, and unable to form a great empire, but nevertheless free, wealthy, and powerful within its narrow boundaries. Such societies, however, are transitory and subject to change, owing to their excesses, to their carelessness, or to the enterprise of their neighbours, since the way in which they are constituted renders them too much exposed to competition. These are commercial societies.[9]

In a series of powerful analyses John Pocock has argued that the understanding of commerce and commercial society in late-seventeenth-century England was most advanced by just those political thinkers who saw the political health of the English nation as jeopardized by the pervasive corruption that resulted from the intrusion of the demands of the war economy into the sphere of domestic politics.[10] Pocock emphasized the centrality of debates on the organization of national defense to the redefinition of an acceptable framework for English power politics. He also emphasized, convincingly, the crucial importance both of the debate between partisans of the standing army and the militia and of the growing awareness of the distortions which the new kind of war finance, the running of a huge public debt, might cause to the balance of the English constitution. Not only did a political and military regime financed by public debt

---

[9] De Mirabeau and Quesnay, *Rural Philosophy*, p. 111.
[10] J. G. A. Pocock, *The Machiavellian Moment: Political Thought and the Atlantic Republican Tradition* (Princeton, 1975), chap. 13., p. 423.

imply a danger of the rising influence of a financier class, which could exercise power without enjoying a proper and legitimate place in the politics of the country; it also meant that the fate of the nation now rested on a most delicate and uncertain foundation. In the eyes of these critics of the English financial revolution, credit – and more particularly paper credit – was among the least stable and dependable institutional expedients ever invented. In comparison with it, even trade, the exchange of real goods, satisfying the mutual needs of agents in a market, appeared altogether more benign and less disquieting.

This contrast was certainly widely perceived, and many of the opponents of standing armies or paper credit undoubtedly approved of England's increasing involvement in international trade. But it is necessary to be cautious in assessing the implications of these reactions for English politics and judging their impact on those who sought to assess the constraints which England's new position as a trading nation imposed on the character and legitimacy of its domestic polity. It would be odd, to say the least, if the dangers involved in living off international trade in this way had escaped their attention.

The clear continuities between William Temple's analysis of the Dutch trading republic and the changing structure of international trade in Europe in the 1660s and Mirabeau's understanding of the nature and dangers of commercial societies a century later require a careful reinvestigation of the role of foreign trade in the political thought of late seventeenth-century England. Temple's influential argument must be set beside the understanding by thinkers like Charles Davenant (whose importance in the shaping of English political thought has long been underlined by Pocock) of the consequences of England's transformation into a nation dependent on trade. Davenant fully recognized that its status as a commercial society now limited England's options and required it to adapt drastically to its new role as an active agent operating on open international markets. A close consideration of his arguments casts a new light on English debates over the effect of commerce on politics. These issues first came to a head in England when the Glorious Revolution government of William III faced a sudden request from Ireland to trade freely with its mother country along with all foreign nations. Since England held full political control of Ireland, this was an instance in which market opportunities were potentially under direct political control. The dubious faith of free-trade ideology in English politics, in both its republican and its natural law forms, was blatantly exposed. Davenant's agonized justification for denying a right of free trade to Ireland and his careful exploration of England's painful options for gaining control of its markets make it possible to study his understanding of the relationship between trade and politics and to contrast it with the understandings of a number of his contemporaries.

I

Temple's analysis of Holland's trade centered on the fragility and the artificial nature of commercial polities. Holland, he thought, constituted a particularly interesting example because the Dutch had created a trading polity whose wealth and sophistication surpassed all previous examples. Nonetheless, Holland's wealth in his view was not of a wholly unprecedented character. Its greatness was a natural product of the same causes that had produced all the great trading centers throughout history. Holland's greatness was entirely manmade; it was in no sense due to the natural resources of the country, either the excellence of harbors or the fertility of lands. Holland had "grown rich . . . by force of Industry." To grasp the causes of its "industry" he proposed a historical inquiry into "what it is that makes people industrious in one Countrey, and idle in another."[11] For Temple to ask this was itself to inquire into "the true original and ground of Trade."

Like Mirabeau, Temple here turned to the conjectural histories of the rise of private property.[12] Like him he laid particular emphasis

[11] Temple, *Observations*, pp. 108–9.

[12] Temple's model, however, was derived not from natural law but the skeptical humanist tradition. Temple was critical of the idiom of natural sociability and he denied that government arose from a contract in a natural state of war. See his "Essay upon the Original and Nature of Government" written in 1671, the year before he composed the *Observations*, in *The Works of Sir William Temple* (4 vols., London, 1814), vol. 1, pp. 9–14. His theory of the paternal origins of political authority was built on these sceptical foundations, although sometimes confused with the quite different idiom of Filmer. For Temple's erudition and understanding of political and moral theory see his rambling but remarkable "Essays by Sir W. T. Written in his Youth at Br* in 1652 when he was about *" in *Early Essays and Romances*, pp. 137–77. There is no satisfactory account of Temple's political thought, although the skeptical theme is brought out by Clara Marburg, *Sir William Temple: A Seventeenth-Century "Libertin"* (New Haven, 1932). The most recent account is R. C. Steensma, *Sir William Temple* (New York, 1970). See also C. B. Macpherson, "Sir William Tem-

upon the differences between territorial and commercial states. Trade as a way of living became a necessity for an entire society when a

> . . . great multitude of people crowded into small compass of Land, whereby all things necessary to life become dear, and all men who have possessions, are induced to Parsimony; but those who have none, are forced to industry and labour, or else to want.[13]

These constraints demanded a remedy, to "supply the defect by some sort of Inventions or Ingenuity." The cause of the commercialization of an entire political society might be necessity, but the engine of its development was emulation or "imitation" until these attitudes became the manners or "habit" of the country. For a small but densely populated country it was then natural to open sea trade, partly to obtain foreign goods for consumption, partly to break out from the constraints of diminishing returns in the struggle to improve the limited amount of land available. This thesis Temple illustrated, notoriously, by adducing the counterexample of Ireland, which, he claimed, had the best deep-water harbors and the best "native commodities" in Europe. That it was necessity which generated industry, he argued,

> . . . cannot be better illustrated, than by its contrary, which appears no where more than in Ireland; Where by the largeness and plenty of the Soil, and scarcity of People, all things necessary to life are so cheap, that an industrious man, by two days labour, may gain enough to feed him the rest of the week; Which I take to be a very plain ground of the laziness attributed to the people: For men naturally prefer Ease before Labour, and will not take pains if they can live idle; Though, when by necessity they have been inured to it, they cannot leave it, being grown a custom necessary to their health, and to their very entertainment.[14]

ple, Political Scientist," *Canadian Journal of Economics and Political Science* 9(1943), 39–54. The famous nineteenth-century controversy between Courtenay and Macaulay over Temple's character and politics is still very illuminating; see T. P. Courtenay, *Memoirs of the Life, Works, and Correspondence of Sir William Temple, Bart.* (2 vols., London, 1836), and Macaulay's review essay in the *Edinburgh Review* in October 1838, reprinted in the numerous editions of his works.

[13] Temple, *Observations*, p. 109.

[14] Ibid. pp. 109–10. This statement rose to fame in the late seventeenth and in the eighteenth century. David Hume cited it prominently in his essay "Of Taxes" (1752). It was also immediately noticed by contemporaries. In the summer of 1673, soon after the publication of the *Observations*, Temple was asked by the Earl of Essex, Lord Lieutenant of Ireland, to provide advice for the improvement of Ireland's economy. For the result see "An Essay upon the Advancement of Trade in Ireland" in *Works*, vol. 3, pp. 1–28, first published in Temple's *Miscellanea* in 1680. In this

This derivation of trade and industry from the ratio between land and population seemed to Temple far more important than the political constitution of the city or territory in question. Eight of the outstanding examples of a trading community – Tyre, Carthage, Athens, Syracuse, Agrigentum, Rhodes, Venice, and Holland – had been republics, an index that there is "something in that form of Government proper and natural to Trade in a more peculiar manner."[15] It was also true that the first six had declined precisely at the point when they succumbed to "Arbitrary Dominions." But two recent examples, Bruges and Antwerp, were not republics. Hence the dividing line must lie not between republics and monarchies, but between free states and legal monarchies ruled by good princes on one hand and "Arbitrary and Tyrannical Power" on the other. Without security for private property, trust among private men, and a confidence in the government, trade could not survive. Whether the regime was based on the "Constitutions and Orders of a State" or on the "personal Virtues and Qualities of the Prince" was less important than whether it enjoyed a stable legal and political order.[16]

In these conditions, the natural growth of the population and immigration from abroad were guaranteed. Liberty of religion, sound private mores, the absence of restraints on economic initiatives were the way to success. The Dutch were also very careful to model their trading institutions to facilitate security and order. Their banks, their compulsory legal registration of property in land, their severe judiciary all ensured a feeling of general security. Rates of interest, as well as customs duties on imported goods, were kept low, and quality was closely regulated. The culture of the Dutch, at first shaped by necessity, spontaneously developed into the true manners of a trading

piece Temple repeated his judgment that Ireland had no hope for development while it remained a "cheap" country, thus the population to resources ratio had to be increased first as a prerequisite of improvement.

[15] Temple, *Observations,* p. 110.

[16] Temple was highly critical of Aristotle (preferring both Plato and Confucius) (see *Early Essays,* p. 144) and regarded the "form of government" analysis as trivial. He preferred monarchies, but in general his view was that "though old distinctions run otherwise, there seem to be but two general kinds of government in the world; the one exercised according to the arbitrary commands and will of some single person; and the other according to certain orders or laws introduced by agreement or custom, and not to be changed without the consent of many," "Essay on Government," *Works,* vol. 1, p. 2.

nation.[17] Merit and honor were not attained through ostentatious consumption, and parsimony and frugality could coexist with great efforts to make profits. The less that was consumed at home, the more that could be exported. Since exports were independent of the domestic way of life, prices could be adjusted to export markets. Because of the low prices at which they could sell, Dutch traders were not easily constrained by lack of demand, "there being no Commodity, but at one price or other will find a Market, which They will be Masters of, who can afford it cheapest: Such are always the most industrious and parsimonious people, who can thrive by Prices upon which the Lazy and Expensive cannot live.[18]

Foreign trade had to be determined by the quest for the most profitable markets for each good, but at home the Dutch continued to consume what was cheapest, whether or not this had to be imported. "They sell the finest of their own Cloth to France," explained Temple, "and buy coarse out of England for their own wear."[19] "They furnish infinite Luxury, which they never practice," in sharp contrast with the English presumption that home production could best be stimulated by first generating a domestic demand for its own luxury products. National gains, Temple explained, could be produced only by a favorable trade balance, not by insisting either that home consumption be entirely supplied by English products or that imports should be brought in only by means of barter. The key lay rather in the kind of demand that existed on the home market. To stimulate luxury at home was dangerous, because "the custom or humour of Luxury and Expence, cannot stop at certain bounds: What begins in Native, will proceed in Forreign Commodities; and though the Example arise among idle persons, yet the Imitation will run into all Degrees, even by those men by whose Industry the Nation subsists."[20]

Temple addressed his advice to the contemporary English expecta-

---

[17] The term "manners" is rarely used by Temple, but he frequently uses the terms "general habits," "dispositions," "affections," "customs," "veins," "use," "opinions," "educations," and "humours" of people. But see his dictum that those forms of government "are the best, which have been longest received and authorized in a nation by custom and use; and into which the humours and manners of the people run with the most general and strongest current," "Essay on Government," *Works,* vol. 1, p. 22.

[18] Temple, *Observations,* p. 119.

[19] Ibid.

[20] Ibid., p. 120.

tion that Dutch competition would fall away once the Dutch too fell prey to the fate which had brought all earlier trading republics to an end, the destruction of their free state by a foreign military power. In Temple's opinion the Dutch might well continue to retain their internal freedom by joining the federally organized Holy German Empire. But in any case, the English hopes for Holland's fall were simply futile. It was vain to hope that the commerce of the Dutch would fall into English laps unless the English could develop domestic morals on the Dutch model which were appropriate for sustaining their commercial and industrial strategy. This was more particularly the case, since, in his view, competitive pressures were intensifying throughout Europe. The English had now to survive in an environment in which even the Dutch were beginning to face a crisis. England itself was, of course, among the new trading nations, but as Temple noted, the French, the Danes, and the Swedes were also turning toward trade.[21] The peace of the 1650s and 1660s favored this. Even if these countries, with their rich endowment of natural resources, were less assiduous than the Dutch, they were enjoying a measure of success. The hope of retaining as large a share of the trade as the Dutch had earlier enjoyed as the sole trading center for a largely uncommercial Europe (along with correspondingly high profits) was an illusion:

> . . . there seem to be grown too many Traders for Trade in the World. So as they can hardly live one by another. As in a great populous Village, the first Grocer or Mercer that sets up among them, grows presently rich, having all the Custom; till another, encouraged by his success, comes to set up by him, and share in his gains; At length so many fall to the Trade, that nothing is got by it; and some must give over, or all must break.[22]

---

[21] Temple, as a practicing diplomat, was well aware of the European situation. See his "A Survey of the Constitution and Interests of the Empire, Sweden, Denmark, Spain, Holland, France, and Flanders with their Relation to England in the Year 1671," which Temple submitted as his final report when leaving his post as English ambassador to The Hague, *Works,* vol. 2, pp. 209–33.

[22] Temple, *Observations,* p. 123. Temple's interpretation was "reinvented" in modern economic history and now is the dominant view. In opposition to the "moral" view of Dutch decline, i.e., that luxury ruined their manners, "more recent observers [i.e., twentieth-century ones] have suggested that the change in the condition of the Dutch economy was merely the necessary consequence of structural changes in the economic life of Europe. It is suggested that the efflorescence of the seventeenth century was possible for this small nation, poor in natural resources, only because *external* conditions were particularly favorable – in practical terms, because other states were preoccupied with wars or internal practical troubles. If this be accepted, then the course of events in the eighteenth century was merely a natural adjustment

In Temple's view the simultaneous expansion of commercial activity in several European countries coincided with the collapse of a number of export markets. In these peaceful years the corn production of Poland and Prussia grew rapidly by taking more and more land into cultivation. This depressed corn prices, restricting the capacity of the countries concerned to act as export markets for others. The profits of the Dutch East India trade were similarly falling because of oversupply. The monopolizers of trade were thus obliged to "give over" their business to the masters of new industries, new trade routes, new markets. This was just what had befallen the Italian city-states, the Hansa towns, and Portugal in the recent past.

Temple could also see a cyclical pattern reasserting itself in the structure of European states. Both the great nations of Europe, which had been preoccupied since the Middle Ages with empire building and with wars, and the small trading centers were subject to a common frustration:

The Kingdoms and Principalities were in the World like the Noblemen and Gentlemen in a Countrey; the Free-States and Cities, like the Merchants and Traders: . . . Some of these came to grow Rich and Powerful by Industry and Parsimony; and some of the others Poor, by War and by Luxury: Which made the Traders begin to take upon them, and carry it like Gentlemen; and the Gentlemen begin to take a fancy of falling to Trade.[23]

to normality when Holland resumed a position in the European hierarchy appropriate to her population, resources and power," Charles Wilson, "The Decline of the Netherlands" in his *Economic History and the Historian: Collected Essays* (London, 1969), p. 40. Compare this with Roger North's early-eighteenth-century comment: "It was a shrewd mistake of a politician, Sir William Temple, who, writing memoirs of the United Provinces, showed the reasons of their rising, and concluded with showing the reasons of their fall *before they were down,*" *Examen* (London, 1740), p. 471.

[23] Temple, *Observations,* p. 124. Immanuel Wallerstein describes this process as the emergence of the world system and asserts that Holland was the hegemon of its first period; see his *The Modern World System, Volume 2. Mercantilism and the Consolidation of the European World Economy, 1600–1750* (New York, 1980), pp. 36–71, and his essay "The Three Instances of Hegemony in the History of the Capitalist World-Economy" in *The Politics of the World-Economy: The States, the Movements and the Civilisations. Essays by Immanuel Wallerstein* (Cambridge, 1984), pp. 37–46. This view of the Dutch golden century was questioned by several authors. Temple's own interpretation clearly shows that he did not regard the flourishing of the Dutch as a typical part of the newly emerging European structure. Rather it seems that the last of the old type of commercial republics flourished precisely during the gestation period of the new world system, before a proper hegemon could arise, and indeed, as the English saw it, delaying their own rise to domination which had its beginnings in the latter part of the sixteenth century. For an explanation of what hegemony

In this way the Dutch were compelled to face new competitors, with a consequent decline not only in their share of world trade but also in its overall profitability. The new canals of Amsterdam with their luxurious houses had also shown the natural effects of riches and the corrupting consequences of luxury. Hence, despite his praise for the principles which had contributed to Dutch greatness, Temple closed his chapter on the trade of the Netherlands with a more general historical lesson. For the English the message was both optimistic and sobering: "So as it seems to be with Trade, as with the Sea (its Element), that has a certain pitch, above which it never rises in the highest Tides; And begins to ebb as soon as ever it ceases to flow; And ever loses ground in one place, proportionably to what it gains in another."[24]

II

Charles Davenant[25] was probably the most influential English analyst of trade and its implications in the closing years of the seventeenth

means in the terms of this debate see Robert O. Keohane, *After Hegemony: Co-operation and Discord in the World Political Economy* (Princeton, 1984).

[24] Temple, *Observations*, p. 126.

[25] For Davenant's life see D. Waddell, "The Career and Writings of Charles Davenant" (unpublished D. Phil. thesis, Oxford University, 1954), and idem, "Charles Davenant (1656–1714) – A Biographical Sketch," *Economic History Review*, 2nd ser., 11(1959), 279–88; with the complementary bibliography in Waddell, "The Writings of Charles Davenant (1656–1714)," *The Library*, 5th ser. 5(1956), 206–12. The works considered here were published in a nine-year period between 1695 and 1704, Davenant producing one printed work per year. They were all reprinted in the eighteenth century by a successor of Davenant in the office of Inspector General of Exports and Imports, Sir Charles Whitworth, as *The Political Works of that Celebrated Writer Charles D'Avenant, LL.D.,* (4 vols., London, 1771). Davenant had two careers in office. As a young man, under the reign of James II, he was a commissioner of excise (1678–88) and M.P. from 1685. After the Glorious Revolution he was out of government employment until 1703, when the new Tory government of Queen Anne appointed him to the post mentioned above. In the intervening fourteen years he was assiduously trying to obtain a stable income and regularly offered his services to both the government and the East India Company. In the modern literature this gave rise to a profound suspicion concerning his character, issuing in the resigned and harsh judgment of his biographer, Waddell, that "he lacked the force of personality and obvious integrity necessary for the role which he appears to have tried to play – that of a partisan pamphleteer who was yet a man of independent judgment and not a mere hack. . . . He was neither an original thinker, nor practical man of affairs, but merely a competent journalist" (p. 288). For Davenant's role in the rise of the English political journalism regime in the post–Glorious Revolution decades, see J. A. Downie, *Robert Harley and the Press. Propaganda and Public Opinion in the*

century. He is particulary interesting because of his unique attempt to sustain and articulate the "Old Whig" theory of government, while at the same time developing a coherent set of commercial policies compatible with, or even sustaining, whatever was still genuinely viable in "revolution principles." In this way he struggled to adapt the Whig theory of politics as it had been before 1688 to the novel circumstances that succeeded the Revolution, in which the theory had to be realized in a country which, after an unprecedented commercial boom under the Restoration, had plunged immediately into fresh European wars after the Revolution, with severe strains upon, and further transformations in, both its finances and its economy. Davenant's attempt to combine ideological politics with commercial *Realpolitik* required fundamental rethinking.

The resulting idiom was so influential precisely because it continued to transpose the imagery of a powerful vision of politics into Davenant's discussion of trade. Pocock characterized the new commercial theory founded on "revolution principles" as "a neo-Machiavellian, as well as neo-Harringtonian, style in the theory of political economy,"[26] since it drew its moral energy from the English republican theory of the 1650s and 1660s, seen at its weightiest in the works of Harrington himself. However, though he did occasionally refer to Harrington, Davenant preferred to present his own moral theory of government in an almost purely Machiavellian form. In a number of his influential commercial writings he devoted considerable space to "a short view of practical Ethicks,"[27] which he defended by explicit reference to Machiavelli's *Discourses:*

And if it should be asked, Why the care of liberty and preserving our civil rights should be so much recommended in a paper relating to Trade? we

---

Age of Swift and Defoe (Cambridge, 1979). No attempt was ever made to set his valuation as a hired pen for the country party and then for the Tory ministry against a thorough reading of the ideas contained in his literary output. The only monographic attempt to deal with his ideas is the dated account of Willy Casper, *Charles Davenant. Ein Beitrag zur Kenntnis des englischen Merkantilismus* (Jena, 1930).

[26] J. G. A. Pocock, *The Machiavellian Moment: Political Thought and the Atlantic Republican Tradition* (Princeton, 1975), p. 423.

[27] "On the Plantation Trade," *Discourses on the Public Revenues, and on the Trade of England which more immediately Treat of the Foreign Traffick of this Kingdom, Part. II,* Discourse 4 [1698] in *The Political and Commercial Works of that Celebrated Writer Charles D'Avenant, LL.D,* ed. by Sir Charles Whitworth (5 vols., London, 1771), vol. 2, p. 76

answer, that herein we follow Machiavel, who says, "That when a free state degenerates into a tyranny, the least mischief that it can expect, is to make no farther advancement in its empire; and no farther encrease either in riches or power, but for the most part it goes backward and declines.[28]

Davenant faithfully reconstructed what he believed to be the main elements of a Machiavellian science of politics. Its central motif was the assertion of a close link between freedom and wealth. "Machiavel has asserted, 'That no cities have augmented their revenues or enlarged their territories, but whilst they were free and at liberty.' "[29] The liberty envisaged here was a double one. It meant the independence of a country: "They who either are slaves, or who believe their freedom precarious, can neither succeed in trade or meliorate the country."[30] But beyond this it meant primarily the security of property and protection from legalized plunder carried out in the name of taxation. Davenant emphasized that for the "Old Whigs," whose theory he was propounding, "*Meum* and *Tuum* was sacred."[31] Adding an element of a theory of rights to his Machiavellian foundation he distinguished firmly between "good and bad reigns, frugal and careless management":

. . . under the first they [the common people] find themselves rich and easy, under the second poor and oppressed by taxes. Besides, they are apt to think such conduct in a court an invasion of their properties. For in a free nation, or in a government of laws, and not of men, as Princes have a right to such revenues as may support the royal dignity, and enable them to protect the publick, as well in its honour as its safety; so the body of the people collectively considered, have likewise a natural right to such a proportion of their country's wealth and product, as is sufficient not only for the necessary but comfortable subsistence of life.[32]

In a government of laws, not men, everything depended upon the quality of the system of laws. The Machiavellian science of politics suggested that these were determined at its initial foundation, which was best executed on the advice of a single legislator operating with the

---

[28] *An Essay upon the Probable Methods of making a People Gainers in the Balance of Trade* [1699] in *Works*, vol. 2, p. 336. Davenant's reference was to *Discourses on Livy*, Lib.ii.c.2.
[29] *Balance of Trade, Works*, vol. 2, p. 337.
[30] "Plantation Trade," *Works*, vol. 2, p. 35.
[31] *Balance of Trade, Works*, vol. 2, p. 332.
[32] *Essays upon Peace at Home and War Abroad. In Two Parts. Part I* [1709] in *Works*, vol. 4, pp. 427–8.

utmost parsimony in the design of legislative regulation. The fewer laws, the better. But following Machiavelli's analysis, Davenant suggested that the question was less one of designing a coherent and well-considered set of regulations than one of devising acceptable systems which could be expected to endure. The seeds of future ruin could always be traced back to the system adopted at the "first founding" of any state. There were famous constitutions, still admired, like that of Solon, which proved to be notoriously fragile. And, of course, a tyrant or an absolute monarch could also devise the most impressive of regulations, – the economic policies of Colbert's administration in France provided a relevant example for Davenant[33] – even if any such reform was certain to be reversed by the eventually inevitable change in the person of the monarch himself. The design of governments "for any duration" was a key project of Machiavelli's *Discourses,* and Davenant rendered the problem faithfully within his own analysis of politics.

In theory, models of government might well be eternal, but in historical fact they were plainly nothing of the kind. "Great empires, in the beginning well constituted" could be "immortal" if only people managed to refrain from "civil dissentions"[34] and faction and if only they could tame their "insatiable appetite"[35] for power, glory, and riches. States had an inevitable tendency to expand in order to build an empire. At first this was a natural and desirable process. For a Machiavellian like Davenant it was a wholly natural axiom that "where things are well administered 'that country will always encrease in wealth and power' "[36] At what point this healthy growth transformed itself into a corruption of the very principles on which the empire had been founded could be ascertained only as and when it actually happened, from the prominence of indices of an internal malady: "When any empire is destined to be undone, or to lose its freedom, the seeds of this ruin are to be first seen in the corruption of

[33] The ambiguity concerning the policies of the great monarchies of Europe cut deep. Davenant was deeply impressed by the efficient administration and virtue not only of Richelieu and Colbert but also of the Spanish statesmen and their system of councils.
[34] *Peace at Home, Works,* vol. 4, p. 281.
[35] "An Essay upon Universal Monarchy," *Essays upon I. The Ballance of Power, II. The Right of Making War, Peace and Alliances, III. Universal Monarchy* [1701] in *Works,* vol. 4, p. 4.
[36] *Balance of Trade, Works,* vol. 2, p. 379.

its manners."[37] Corruption usually manifested itself in the overextension of empire. The original polity, being now the center of the empire, acted as a magnet not only to all who wished for political power, but also to the entire trade of the extended dominion:

As we see in a particular kingdoms, where there is one great city, it draws to it all the trade; so in a large dominion, composed of several provinces, be it a commonwealth, or a principality, whatever country is the head of affairs, there will all the traffic center.[38]

The empire, built initially on military virtue, was now undergoing a process of relentless corruption through the constant flow of wealth toward its center. Davenant saw this process as a sequence of clearly defined stages – from luxury to vice and effeminacy, and the consequent collapse of the state's ability to defend itself:

The natural steps to ruin in politic institutions, that have a mixture in them of popular government, seem to be in this manner: 1st, Extended dominion, power atchieved by arms, or riches flowing in by trade, beget effeminacy, pride, ambition and luxuries of all kind; these vices, as they obtain strength and growth, produce quickly private property, and then public want; private property puts ill men upon wicked arts to get wealth, and public want but too often makes those ill men necessary in a corrupted state.[39]

Corruption of manners had external as well as internal implications. Internally effeminacy arrested the domestic production of wealth. When "industry decays, the people become effeminate and unfit for labour. To maintain luxury, the great ones must oppress the meaner sort; and to avoid this oppression, the meaner sort are often compelled to seditious tumults, or open rebellion."[40] Externally an effeminate rich nation was doomed to become a prey to foreign military invasion.

But as each empire fell, Davenant thought, another was bound to take its place. When the "mighty fabric" of a seemingly universal empire falls, "out of its ruins another building rises, which in time may grow to equal what went before, in strength, extent, symmetry, and height."[41] In this historical vision Rome was the obvious arche-

---

[37] "Plantation Trade," *Works,* vol. 2, p. 50.
[38] "Universal Monarchy," *Works,* vol. 4, pp. 33–4.
[39] "Plantation Trade," *Works,* vol. 2, p. 55.
[40] Ibid., p. 42.
[41] "Universal Monarchy," *Works,* vol. 4, pp. 22–3.

type for any attempt to establish universal monarchy. But Davenant was not concerned with ancient history. Since the dynamics which produce universal monarchy constantly re-create themselves, he saw the re-creation of a modern universal monarchy as a genuine danger in his own lifetime. Spain had been the most recent contender for such universal domination. The next contender in the making, as he saw it, was France.

Universal monarchy could be averted only by the maintenance of a multicentered world of smaller states, sustained by a balance of power. But Davenant's principal preoccupation was with the Machiavellian struggle against corruption within the home country itself. The chances for success in this struggle depended crucially on the strength of the corrupted state's initial constitution. In this sense the English regime of 1688 did have some chance of recovery. In contrast to absolute monarchies, which "corrupted in their morals and discipline, impaired in their wealth, sunk in credit, and weakened by inbred disorders, do very rarely retrieve their condition," in mixed governments the cycle of decline was in principle reversible:

Men, when they are worn out with diseases, aged, crazy, and when besides they have the *mala stamina vitae,* may be patched up for a while, but they cannot hold out for long; for life, though it is shortened by irregularities, is not to be extended by any care beyond such period. But it is not so with the body politic, by wisdom and conduct that is to be made long-lived, if not immortal; its distempers are to be cured, nay its very youth is to be renewed, and a mixed government grows young and healthy again, whenever it returns to the principles upon which it was first founded.[42]

On this point Davenant's principal authority was exceedingly firm. "Machiavel says, That to render a commonwealth long-lived, it is necessary to correct it often, and reduce it towards its first principles, which is to be done by punishments and examples." But if it was in fact possible to reverse the process of corruption, who exactly could hope to carry through the reversal and what resources could they draw on in their enterprise? The main damage inflicted by luxury and corruption was the desertion of public affairs for the sating of private desires. Regeneration, accordingly, depended on the energies of the public spirited. "Wherever private men can be brought to make all their actions and counsels, thoughts and designments, to centre in the

---

[42] *Balance of Trade, Works,* vol. 2, p. 294.

common good, that nation will soon gather such strength as shall resist any home-bred mischief or outward accident."[43] A healthy polity required more than the protection of *meum* and *tuum,* of property rights. Echoing Justinian's classic definition of justice, Davenant insisted that the public virtue needed to preserve a state was essentially "a constant and perpetual will to do our country good."[44] This was very much *virtù* as Machiavelli understood it, and Davenant made clear the contrast with more conventionally Christian conceptions of virtue:

By virtue I do not mean that which is commonly opposed to vice, but by virtue I here understand piety to our country, zeal for its interest or glory, patience under adverse fortune, temper in prosperity, obedience to discipline and the laws, foresight in business, secrecy and firmness in councils, vigour in action, courage, military skill, thirst of honour, magnanimity; and these are the virtues upon which dominion is founded.[45]

This linguistic shift from a moralism of virtue and vice to a dynamics of raison d'état was applied by Davenant to the economic as well as to the political domain. Frugality was always a helpful virtue in commerce. But in the struggle against corruption within a commercial state what was crucial was not private, but public, frugality, "frugality in the state." Again, he took pains to make his language clear:

The frugality treated of here, is not a narrow hoarding up of wealth to keep it in the exchequer, or to save where saving is either timid or dishonourable, but a general good oeconomy in the minister; when he takes care that the publick treasure be never wasted, and yet is really at hand to supply any great occasion, when the Prince's honour and the country's safety requires it.[46]

---

[43] "Plantation Trade," *Works,* vol. 2, p. 72.

[44] *Balance of Trade, Works,* vol. 2, p. 338. According to the famous definition of Justinian's *Digest,* justice was "a constant and perpetual will [*constans et perpetua voluntas*] to render unto everyone his right." Davenant's attempt to assimilate the general definition of virtue to the definition of justice cannot be accidental. He was formally trained in civil law in Cambridge and in another context he called attention to his qualifications as a trained civil lawyer. The definition of virtue quoted above appeared in a prominent place on the first page of Davenant's manuscript "An Essay on Publick Virtue, to his Grace the Duke of Shrewsbury; and the Right Honourable Sidney Lord Godolphin. Part I" (late 1696 or early 1697; it appears that no Part II had ever been written), preserved in the Harleian Manuscripts in the British Library, BM Harleian MSS 1223 (another copy exists in the Goldsmiths' Library, University of London, MS 60), from which it was lifted into the text of the *Balance of Trade.*

[45] "Universal Monarchy," *Works,* vol. 4, p. 23.

[46] *Peace at Home, Works,* vol. 4, p. 431.

This contrast is important for understanding Davenant's views on commerce, trade, and the public debt. In his eyes, any failure in public virtue and frugality was fatal because it rendered decline inevitable. But this did not make him an opponent of trade at all.

Corruption was engendered by luxury, and it also manifested itself in luxury. Luxury might set any nation on the slippery path to decline if it were not counteracted by public virtue. But a condition of opulence and luxury in a state was not the final outcome of a process of social corruption. In itself it was merely a stage of transition. When decline reached a stage at which recovery was no longer possible, the fate faced by a community was not one of conspicuous wealth and luxury, but one of abject poverty. In its ultimate ruin a state would be reduced to economic nullity. Just as freedom and growing wealth could be combined benignly, so could (and would) a final condition of utter corruption and dire poverty. The constitution of the political body was in greater danger from the threat of impoverishment than from the hazards of luxury:

. . . such as propose to thrive by disorder and misgovernment, have a strong interest to beggar the people. The confusion which public wants and private necessities introduce, suits best with their designs: a wealthy nation may be jealous of its rights, and watch any invasions upon its freedom, and a rich gentry may be unmanageable; and such bad men may think that the best course to keep us humble is to make us poor.[47]

Unlike poverty among its citizenry, wealth was a condition with which an appropriately organized state could well live, since, as Davenant argued,

. . . it is not impossible to make wealth and virtue coexist together: it has been seen in particular instances: several private men have been both rich and virtuous: a wise man brings this about by suppressing his appetites and passions: if it is to be done by a single person, why, by general wisdom in those who govern, is not the same to be compassed in a whole commonwealth, which is but a great body, composed of many individuals?[48]

Riches thus played a dual role in Davenant's thinking. Wealth was opposed to poverty on the one hand, but it was also opposed to simplicity on the other. In ideological sympathy and esthetic prefer-

[47] *Balance of Trade, Works,* vol. 2, pp. 309–10.
[48] *Peace at Home, Works,* vol. 4, p. 17.

ence, Davenant stood firmly with those, like Cato, who privileged simplicity. Trade, in this sense, was at odds with the best life:

Trade, without doubt, is in its nature a pernicious thing; it brings in that wealth which introduces luxury; it gives a rise to fraud and avarice, and extinguishes virtue and simplicity of manners; it depraves a people, and makes way for that corruption which never fails to end in slavery, foreign and domestic. Lycurgus, in the most perfect model of government that was ever framed, did banish it from his commonwealth. But, the posture and condition of other countries considered, it is become with us a necessary evil. . . . However, if trade cannot be made subservient to the nation's safety, it ought to be no more encouraged here than it was in Sparta.[49]

The resulting ambivalence cut deep, and it was far from being an idiosyncrasy of a stray Machiavellian Whig. Sparta was not the only image which placed the present in a damaging perspective. Writers in the school of natural jurisprudence, drawing on Aristotle in their treatments of the origins of trade, also saw the latter as at best questionable in its provenance, seeing it as intimately connected with the rise of a regime of private property. Davenant's own account is strongly reminiscent of the ambivalence of John Locke's famous analysis:

Mankind subsisted by their labour, and from what the earth produced, till their corruptions had brought in fraud, avarice, and force, but when the strong began to invade the weaker, and when strength was to be maintained by policy, they built cities, disciplined men, and erected dominions; and when great numbers were thus confined to a narrower space, their necessities could not be all answered by what was near them, and at hand; so that they were compelled to seek for remoter helps, and this gave rise to what we call Trade, which at first was only permutation of commodities.[50]

But this dual opposition to the insatiability of desire with its twin outcomes in private property and social corruption could not readily yield a coherent approach to modern politics. Here Davenant naturally distinguished sharply between ancient and modern prudence. In modern Europe the direct call of ancient virtue for simplicity could no longer be followed. Questions of wealth could no longer be properly judged without the closest attention to time and place.

In general, Davenant argued, it might well be beneficial for En-

---

[49] *Balance of Trade, Works,* vol. 2, p. 275.
[50] "That Foreign Trade is beneficial to England," *Discourses on the Public Revenues, Part II,* Discourse I, *Works,* vol. 1, pp. 348–9.

gland to discontinue its East India trade, "for Europe draws from thence nothing of solid use," but rather "materials to supply luxury, and only perishable commodities."[51] Sumptuary laws were not promising as a solution. Every European country had a mass of sumptuary regulations, but in practice they achieved remarkably little. The people of England, "who have been long accustom'd to Mild Laws, and a loose Administration,"[52] would in any case be wholly unprepared to endure the severity of ancient legislation. Sumptuary laws, Davenant observed, "were somewhat regarded in the Infancy of the Roman Common-wealth, before Riches and Pomp, had banish'd Vertue, and obedience: But their chiefest Strength was always deriv'd from the Sanctity, and Veneration, in which was held the Office of Censor. . . . In England, they would be immediately condemn'd, and derided."[53]

But even if these obstacles had not existed, the attempt to impose strict sumptuary laws upon the East India trade could not succeed if it was implemented in England alone. To achieve simplicity, and to avoid simply damaging England to the advantage of her neighbors, it was necessary that "all Europe by common Consent would agree to have no further dealings to those Parts". However, in light of the fact that the "Western Nations," as Davenant called them, had been wholly content for the last hundred years "to be deceiv'd" by the gains in luxury derived from trade with Asia, the idea that "all Europe will come to an Agrement of Dealing no more to those Parts" was "an absurd and wild Notion."[54] Indeed, in Davenant's view any such attempt to reform the "Collective Body of Europe" might easily provide a danger far graver than the corruption engendered by an influx of luxury products from the East Indies: universal monarchy which he so feared but in which uniformity of laws across countries might, of course, be readily achieved.

The question was not whether modern manners and the modern taste for luxury were desirable in themselves. They were not. But real prudence meant the ability to "live with necessity, for the Laws of all Countries must be suited to the Bent and Inclinations of the People." And in this instance necessity required that "they should be a little

[51] *An Essay on the East India Trade* [1696], in *Works,* vol. 1, p. 90.
[52] Ibid., p. 114.
[53] Ibid., pp. 114–5.
[54] Ibid., p. 92.

accommodated to their deprav'd Manners and Corruption."[55] What was practicable was of fundamental importance in politics. Davenant pressed this point with special vehemence on English legislators because he believed that England required public wealth to retain its liberty and virtue and that any anachronistic interference with trade was likely to damage England's greatness and to prove wholly ineffective into the bargain. It was essential to control passions and appetites and to contain their corrupting consequences without interrupting the growth of the country's riches.

This need was rendered particularly urgent by changes in the character of modern warfare. The strains of modern war placed the most brutal burden on a nation's finances. Even if all other considerations were set aside, this alone would be enough to compel the abandonment of political nostalgia:

We shall hardly be permitted to live in the way our ancestors did, though inclined to. The power of our neighbours, both by land and sea, is grown so formidable, that perhaps we must be for some time upon our guard, with fleets too big to be maintained merely by the natural produce and income of our country. We must therefore have recourse to those artificial helps which industry and a well governed trade may minister.[56]

This "all devouring monster," war and the ever pressing need to prepare for it, demanded constant expenditure. Since military power depended on the resources of a country, those who failed to win sufficient riches were in real danger of destruction or foreign subjugation. So how were the resources for national defense to be secured? In Davenant's view it was impossible for any state to create them by domestic means alone: "The Soil of no Country is Rich enough to attain a great Mass of Wealth, meerly by the Exchange and Exportation of its Own Natural Product."[57] The workings of an internal market could not in themselves generate resources to be deployed abroad, and warfare required many things which conventional trade was in any case incapable of supplying. Modern prudence, accordingly, required a sharp inversion of the priorities suggested by the moralizing ideology of simplicity. "In a Trading Nation the Bent of all

[55] Ibid., p. 114.
[56] "Foreign Trade is beneficial," *Works,* vol. 1, p. 348.
[57] *East India Trade, Works,* vol. 1, p. 86.

the Laws should tend to the Encouragement of Commerce."[58] Commercial society, in other words, set clear limits to ideological politics. What war required was not self-contained simplicity, but rather the fostering of a surplus economy. To reinforce this conclusion Davenant transformed his rhetorical address. Instead of praising the English woolen trade, as proud Englishmen were accustomed to do, he insisted tartly on its severe limitations from the viewpoint of raison d'état:

As Bread is call'd the Staff of Life, so the Woollen Manufacture is truly the Principal Nourishment of Our Body Politick. And as a Man might possibly live onely upon Bread, yet his Life would be ill sustain'd, Feeble and Unpleasant; So though England could probably subsist barely upon the Exportation of its own Product, yet to enjoy a more florid Health, to be Rich, Powerful and Strong, we must have a more extended Traffick than Our Native Commodities can afford us.[59]

Along with this novel emphasis on the importance of commerce, Davenant insisted on the need to incorporate a firm recognition of its significance into the education of those who held responsibility for public affairs. Trade, from now on, must be treated as a "Matter of State," not regarded simply as a "Conveniency or Accidental Ornament" to glory and greatness. The struggle against corruption and potential decline henceforth required that a knowledge of the general laws of commerce become part of a schooling in public virtue. The old practice of listening to "Particular Merchants, and other Interested Persons" must cease. Those who believed in the sufficiency of a simple understanding of ancient public virtue were dangerously in error: " 'Twill be found at last, when all Things come to be Rightly Consider'd, that no Plenty at Home, Victory Abroad, Affection of the People, nor no Conduct, or Wisdom, in other things, can give the Public effectual help, till we can mend the Condition and Posture of Trade."[60]

To incorporate an understanding of trade into the definition of civic virtue was not necessary merely to prevent undue influence of private interest on the government or to stop the special pleading of merchants from overruling public considerations. Two further factors

[58] Ibid., p. 89.
[59] Ibid., p. 88.
[60] Ibid., p. 89.

made it altogether imperative. In the first place, trade was now the way to glory and dominion. Those who possessed the most profitable trade had acquired the best defense against any assault upon their freedoms. Davenant firmly believed that England's trade with the East Indies, even if it must to some degree be shared with the Dutch, could give England real dominion even without formal empire.

Davenant here followed the spirit of Harrington's dictum that "the sea gives law to the growth of Venice, but the growth of Oceana gives law to the sea."[61] The East India trade was the maritime trade best calculated to achieve this, and Davenant now proclaimed firmly that "whatever Country can be in the full and undisputed Possession of it, will give Law to all the Commercial World."[62]

But an empire based on seaborne trade differed crucially from the wealthy empires of the past. These could attract the surplus of much of the world to their home territory and capital city, and Davenant hoped England would also be able to do so, by first exerting their military power. "War and its discipline, was the chief object of their thoughts, as knowing that riches always follow power, and that iron brings to it the gold and silver of other places."[63] But in the conditions of late-seventeenth-century Europe this chain of reasoning had now to be inverted. It was now military, and especially naval, power which depended upon the development of trade. If the English were indeed convinced of the merits of abstemiousness and the need to bring to an end the corrupting trade of the East Indies, the "derelict" trade would be immediately seized by the Dutch and "if to their Naval Strength in Europe, such a Foreign Strength and Wealth be added, England must hereafter be contented to Trade by their Protection, and under their Banners."[64]

It was essential for statesmen to understand trade because it had its rules, just as much as war did. Just as the stronger was the victor in war, in trade whoever sold cheapest secured the market. Since foreign markets were located in sovereign territories, they could not simply be forced to take one's merchandise. To force them to do so,

---

[61] *The Commonwealth of Oceana* [1656], ed. J. G. A. Pocock (Cambridge, 1977), p. 160.
[62] *East India Trade, Works,* vol. 1, p. 94; and repeated in almost identical terms on p. 123.
[63] "Foreign Trade is beneficial," *Works,* vol. 1, p. 349.
[64] *East India Trade, Works,* vol. 1, p. 94.

to capture markets by force, would have been a direct continuation of empire by the sword. Some might think that the only solid recipe for lasting glory, at least in theory, must be the acquisition of universal empire. But Davenant was adamantly opposed to any such undertaking. The old Spanish theorist of universal empire, Pedro Mexia, might argue that trade had been at its most flourishing under the beneficial empire of the Antonines.[65] This ambition however, was now a characteristically French conception. The English, if they desired empire, must found their dominion on trade. Both the maintenance and growth of English glory entailed the acceptance of a single imperative, the rule of the international market.

Davenant's revived Machiavellianism was therefore centrally concerned with the novel question of how a trading nation might best be organized for protracted (and perhaps indefinite) prosperity. Some of the military dangers which threatened its survival would inevitably remain just the same. While conditions in Europe itself were changing rapidly, wealthy, luxurious, and effeminate nations might still fall prey to hardy and impoverished barbarians. But the latter could hardly pose a commercial threat. Davenant was quick to deflate the appeals of such primitive austerity. Sparsely populated and simple countries might be the breeding ground of military valor, but when it came to work and the cultivation of the soil, their citizens were proud, lazy, and inactive. Not only could they not compete in trade, but they were also desperately poor and utterly deprived of all the conveniences of life.

Yet if their territory was potentially rich, this condition could change very rapidly. Just as their poverty might be turned to their advantage in war, it too, once they had chosen the high road from simplicity to riches, might swiftly be transformed into an irresistible

[65] Pedro Mexia, (1499–1551), as Davenant himself noted, "wrote in the time of the Emperor Charles the Vth, and whose historiographer he was." Davenant's reference was to Mexia's *Los Cesares* (Seville, 1545), which was translated into English as *The historie of all the Romane emperors, beginning with Caius Iulius Caesar, and successively ending with Rodulph the Second now reigning . . . First collected in Spain by Pedro Mexia, since enlarged in Italian by Lodovico Dulce and Girolamo Bardi, and now Englished by W. T.* (London, 1604); later republished with a slightly different title and continuation. Mexia's work was particularly influential in France and Italy. On the context of Mexia's promotion of the ambitions of Charles V see J. A. Fernandez-Santamaria, *The State, War and Peace: Spanish Political Thought of the Renaissance* (Cambridge, 1977), p. 14, and H. L. Seaver, *The Great Revolt in Castile* (Boston, 1928), p. 168.

weapon of trade. Advantage in trade could come from only two fundamental sources. As Davenant reflected on the central theme of the natural jurists, that "mankind subsisted by their labour, and from what the earth produced," he came to realize that it was possible to sell cheaply either where the fruits of the earth themselves were available at a low cost or where labor was available cheaply. The cost of raw materials and the cost of labor formed the two principal components of prices. Furthermore, wages themselves depended chiefly on the relative cheapness of subsistence goods.

Poverty or simplicity, the lack of riches, gold, and silver so much coveted and desired by rich nations, also exerted a beneficial effect on prices. Gold and silver, as Davenant well understood, were not the "original spring" of trade; their function was simply to serve as a measure. If it was to move beyond barter, exchange required such a medium of measurement or common denominator. To explain its function Davenant used the metaphor of the (recently discovered) circulation of blood in the human body. A trading country needed money just as a healthy heart needed the circulating blood. But since money measured prices, prices in a monetized economy could not be in any sense natural. The less money that was in circulation in a given economy, the lower must its prices be. Here, too, conditions of poverty appeared to enjoy an advantage over those of wealth. As Davenant observed: ". . . gold and silver being the measure of trade, all things are dear or cheap as that sort of wealth is wanted or abounding. And in all countries of the world where money is rare and scarce, the product of the earth is cheap; as for instance, in Scotland, Ireland, the Northern Kingdoms, Germany, and most parts of Asia and America."[66]

There was thus a prima facie case for believing that poor countries should be able to sell cheaper than rich ones. Rich countries with their higher living standards must be at a disadvantage in price competition. What is more, their corruption in this context emerged once again as a real danger in its own right. Luxury, when it filtered down to the laborers, did not only raise their wages. In addition, in a corrupt country, it undermined the military valor and freedom of the populace and rendered its effeminate inhabitants "unfit for labour." The more frugal and virtuous, or wise, neighbors of such a country –

---

[66] "Means and Methods of restoring Credit," *Works*, vol. 1, p. 160.

and still more its poorer rivals – could then appropriate its markets with apparent ease.

The key to Davenant's novel conception of the politics of commercial society was his view of how permanent national prosperity might be grounded on international commerce. Why did he believe that the possession of the East India trade could endow England with the "dominion of the sea" and enable it to lay down the law to the world of commerce? The answer was simplicity itself. India was the cheapest producer of manufactured textiles in the world. At the same time the Indians presented no military threat to Europe and were unable to trade directly with Europe in the absence of a long-distance merchant navy of their own. Their wages were so low and their skills so elaborate that their products remained cheaper than European ones even when the costs of transport and the profits of the English merchants had been added to their initial price. The East India trade was the best trade of all to dominate since it allowed buying cheap and then selling dear. Much maligned though it was, its beauty lay particularly in the fact that it was based on purely commercial principles and that it followed the basic rule of the market, that the cheapest producer or vendor sells best. No degree of frugality among England's European competitors could enable them to avoid this rule.

As a good Machiavellian Davenant assumed that the fewer laws there were in a state, the better its system of government was constructed. He was equally sure "that few Laws relating to Trade, are the Mark of a Nation that thrives by Traffick."[67] As a *permutatio* of goods exchanged at the market, trade was in fact a system of mutualities. The requirements of mutuality on free markets were barely compatible with interference. The mere attempt to regulate trade constituted corruption in the constitution of a trading country. Davenant's advocacy of laissez faire did not mince words:

Trade is in its Nature Free, finds its own Channel, and best directeth its own Course: and all Laws to give it Rules, and Directions, and to Limit, and Circumscribe it, may serve the Particular Ends of Private Men, but are seldom Advantageous to the Publick. Governments in Relation to it, are to take a Providential Care of the Whole, but generally to let Second Causes work their own way. . . . Laws to Compel the Consumption of some Commodities, and prohibit the use of others, may well do enough, where Trade is forc'd,

---

[67] *East India Trade, Works,* vol. 1, p. 99.

and only Artificial, as in France; But in Countries inclin'd by Genius, and adapted to it by Situation, such Laws are needless, unnatural, and can have no Effect conducive to the Publick Good.[68]

Guided by his two Machiavellian principles of politics – to have as few laws as possible and never to allow sectional interest to dominate the pursuit of the public good – Davenant wished to hand over the fate of a trading and seafaring nation to the laws of the international market. The political rhetoric which he deployed for the purpose should not go unnoticed. When Davenant noted that the French ministers drove their subjects to produce particular types of manufactures, he made no claim that they did so through insufficient concern for the public good. Nor did he deny that the French ban on the imports of East Indian textiles was wise, since it was after all not the French who would have reaped its profits. He did, however, see the artificial support for certain domestic strategies of development and its attendant prohibitions as a natural, if baleful, practice for absolute monarchies, those enemies of freedom and potential champions of universal empire. The notion of political liberty gained a fresh connotation. It now included the firmest abstention from interference with the market. What *virtù* required was not to bend the market, but to ride it.

The force of Davenant's position became particularly clear in the face of England's attempt to ride to empire on the back of the cheapest manufacturing industry in the world, the East Indian. But must the same principles apply to the British economy as a whole? The real test of the principles of "modern prudence" must come when they were applied to goods manufactured not in distant India, but in Britain itself. However, it was not only in the East India trade that Britain had the opportunity to avoid the full force of the free market. Its second major source of trading surplus, as Davenant emphasized, lay in its plantation trade with the West Indies, conducted on entirely different principles from those of the East Indian and based firmly on the empire of the sword and the exploitation of the plantations. It consisted in an exchange of a "great quantity of our Inferiour Manufactures" for a great quantity of natural produce – "Tobacco, Cotton, Ginger, Sugars, Indico, etc." These imports were used partly at

[68] Ibid., pp. 98–9.

home, but their great volume allowed a substantial proportion to be reexported in order to generate surplus for the war economy. In addition, as Davenant saw it, the West India trade kept in employment all the producers of low-quality goods destined for its market. But the key issue of trading strategy for Davenant's contemporaries was the prospective fate of those whose employment depended on trading, not on the captive markets of the plantations, but on markets which were genuinely free.

Some of the charges against the East India trade were easy for Davenant to dismiss. Many clearly reflected sectional interests, and others, like Pollexfen's insistence on the harmfulness of exporting ready cash and bullion in exchange for consumer goods, rested on a misunderstanding of the nature of trade. But allowing the international market price free sway over the home market did pose a very real threat to the viability of English industry. For Davenant this was as much a political, as a purely commercial, issue, since in his view a laborer had a natural right to the necessities and even to the comforts of life, a right which he could scarcely hope to exercise if others could destroy his employment merely by producing similar goods more cheaply. This dilemma forced him to reconsider the fundamental rationale of trade itself.

In trades where one could not rely on the labor of others, as with the East India trade, or on the produce "of other countries subject to our dominion, the West Indies,"[69] commercial possibilities in international markets were determined strictly by the natural endowments of each country. As the natural lawyers had long insisted, it was fundamental to the character of trade that God had created the different regions of the earth with very different endowments so that communities should exchange their natural produce with one another, a point which Bishop Burnet had pressed on Davenant himself. He "did urge a thing which the philosophy seemed very sound and right, and upon which we have since reflected often; he said, that nature had adapted different countries for different manufactures."[70]

For Davenant this was not merely a matter of the inherent mutuality of trading or the logic of bartering qualitatively different products from different climes to the advantage of all concerned. It involved a

---

[69] *Balance of Trade, Works,* vol. 2, p. 228.
[70] Ibid., pp. 235–6. Davenant was referring to a personal conversation with Burnet.

profound reconsideration of the implications of the competitive logic of market pricing in terms of his central images of social and political health and debility. In this ampler context the message of Burnet's theory was that it was only in trades grounded in the natural advantages of one's own territory that it was possible to compete with any real prospect of long-term success. The economic boom of the Restoration period had resulted in a particularly dangerous kind of corruption. Desirable though it might be on other grounds, the fact that by the end of the century Britain had in Davenant's view the highest wage level in Europe placed severe restrictions on its economic options. First and foremost, it constrained the possibilities of retaining employment by diversifying into new industries, like textiles, in which foreign producers were already well established.

Burnet himself had singled out the woolen trade as especially well suited to the temperate and humid climate of Britain and argued accordingly against diversification into the production of silk. For England to complement its woolen trade with silk and linen would be an instance of just the sort of forced and unnatural policy which Davenant believed to be doomed to failure in a wealthy country like England. It was in direct conflict with the laws of the market and clashed with the ruling manners of the country. Not only were silk and linen imported materials, but establishing a silk and linen industry would imply competing against domestic producers utilizing cheap local wool and against other European countries which already possessed established silk or linen industries of their own. Both the linen and silk industries, in Davenant's view, could thrive only in countries "where Parsimony renders Craft and Workmanship not dear." France, Italy, and Holland were in fact already undercutting the silk prices envisaged by British "Projectors."[71] Furthermore, India could undercut even the most frugal and virtuous of European producers by at least 25 percent. For a corrupted country, competing effectively in the prices of silks was a hopeless undertaking. The appropriate policy for such a country was to market cheap Indian silks in Europe for high profits, undercutting the prices and sapping the moral resources of England's European neighbors.

In the linen trade the situation was rather different. England could

---

[71] *East India Trade, Works,* vol. 1, p. 108.

not manufacture fine linens and had to import these from Holland and France. It could, of course, attempt to set up at home a new industry producing high-quality linens, but recruitment of skilled labor to the new industries would drive up wages throughout the economy, blunting the competitive edge of the strategically important woolen staple.[72] In Davenant's view England did not have sufficient skilled manpower to compete in international markets in such a variety of fields. In cheaper products it could compete with the northeast of Europe, securing employment for its own poor. But since those countries could buy English woolens only by bartering linen goods for them, to set up a British linen industry could only impoverish the country's existing and profitable export markets. A rich and not particularly frugal country, operating under external market pressure, could not afford to behave like a newcomer. It inevitably faced competition from both low-wage countries and established quality producers.

In the woolen trade the position was different. In this trade England was the established producer, and it possessed all the necessary ingredients for successful production: cheap raw materials, skills, and markets. This array of advantages served to highlight the crucial role of the wage level in sustaining the country's freedom through commercial success. It was not enough to be an established producer. Here England's very economic success required an exercise of public virtue. It could ensure durable wealth only by remaining cheapest in the market. Otherwise high wages would wreck the woolen manufacturers, "of which most have more value from the workmanship than the material; and if the price of this workmanship be inhanced, it will in a short course of time put a necessity upon those we deal with of setting up manufactures of their own, such as they can, or of buying goods of the like kind and use from nations that can afford them cheaper."[73]

Davenant outlined a dual strategy for retaining England's woolen trade. The first element was to remain the cheapest producer across the existing range of woolen products. "To make England a true Gainer by the Woollen Manufacture" – he argued – "we should be able to work the Commodity so Cheap, as to under-sell all Comers to the Markets abroad."[74] To achieve this there were three requirements.

---

[72] Ibid., p. 111.
[73] Ibid., p. 200.
[74] Ibid., p. 100.

Since wages "must bear some proportion with the expence," the first requirement was to make vigorous efforts to lower the price of wage goods. A large population supported by a thriving agriculture was the basis for cheap food prices. England could support at least twice its existing population on its own land. Although agricultural development and population growth might be attained in the "natural course of time," Davenant insisted that in this instance "the common progression of things may be hastened by art."[75] One means was to put the unemployed to work on the land. It was absurd to allow productive industries to be damaged while part of the population remained unproductive. The entry of the unemployed onto the labor market, by suddenly raising the supply of labor, might somewhat lower wages, and if their labor was deployed in agriculture, the increased food supply might also bring down food prices. The second requirement was to emulate the Dutch policy of provisioning. Though in the 1690s France and Scotland had suffered terrible famines, Holland by contrast had made great profits by selling back to the producer countries grain which it had bought in earlier and cheaper years. Following the Dutch model could serve to dampen or even eliminate fluctuation in subsistence costs. The third requirement, once again, involved emulating the Dutch. In Holland the workers, in their virtuous parsimony, did not consume the products which they produced for export, proving highly successful in this selective frugality and "Consuming at Home what is Cheap, or comes Cheaply, and carrying abroad what is Rich, and will yield most Money."[76] In a relatively corrupt country like England such frugality could not be a realistic goal for policy. But if the English could be supplied with cheap Indian textiles, their wages might be adjusted downward while the English woolens were sent abroad to the "highest markets." Since the cost of production in India was only one-fourth of the British cost, to substitute products in home consumption in case of such a key wage good could yield real export gains. In addition Davenant counseled firmly against forcing up prices on the home market. He doubted the viability of dual pricing, seeing no way in which high home prices could coexist with cheap export prices, without a compensating bounty payment, and judging that any distortion of market pricing was likely to prove in the end bad policy.

[75] *Balance of Trade, Works*, vol. 2, p. 222.
[76] *East India Trade, Works*, vol. 1, p. 103.

He did not, of course, deny that cheap imports of any kind could hurt home producers who had to compete directly with them, and he acknowledged that "England could subsist and the Poor perhaps would have fuller Employment, if Foreign Trade were quite laid aside."[77] But to take this course was incompatible with England's remaining a strong and thus a free country, a condition which required the surpluses generated by foreign trade. If the worst came to the worst, therefore, Davenant advocated a more radical strategy. The least price-elastic of Britain's export goods were the cheapest and medium range of woolens, which actually composed the greater part of British exports, since in these cases raw material supplies of the necessary quality were equally available to foreign competitors. In view of the obstacles to cutting English wages this was the sector in which the country's export markets faced their most decisive threat. New manufacturing countries possessed the modest levels of skill required to start up their own manufacturing in these cheaper and cruder products. In the last instance, therefore, England might well be wise, Davenant argued, to abandon low-quality woolen production. Its best chance of survival lay in a decision "to divert the Wooll used in these of our Home Manufactures, and the Craft, Labour and Industry employ'd about 'em, to the Making Fine Broad Cloth, Coarse and Narrow Cloths, Stuffs and other Commodities, fit for Sale in Foreign Markets."[78]

Instead of seeking to diversify and develop new skills in new trades, Davenant advocated relying on existing skills and manufactures and on shifting production to products of greater value in the face of competitive pressures. At the costliest end of the product range, price elasticity was larger and exports could be maintained despite higher wage costs, unless a low-wage competitor entered the market with natural endowments for pursuing the woolen trade identical or similar to those which England enjoyed. In this case the richer and more luxurious high-wage country had little hope of continuing to rule the international market and hence little hope of durable domestic prosperity. No English contemporary of Davenant's age needed much reminder that Ireland was a country in just this position.[79]

[77] Ibid., p. 103.
[78] Ibid.
[79] *Balance of Trade, Works*, vol. 2, p. 235.

After the Glorious Revolution and with the domination of the rhetoric of liberty in England itself, it was only natural for the English colonists in Ireland to claim at least some of the corresponding freedoms for themselves. As Sir Richard Cox argued, pleading for reasonable treatment of Ireland in commercial matters, the Anglo-Irish, in trying to improve Ireland, were

> . . . not contending for Power or great Riches; they neither trade to the East-Indies, Turky or Africa; they have neither Hamborough, Hudson-Bay, Greenland or Russia Companies; they have no Fleets or Plantations; they ask only the common benefits of Earth and Air. They desire only to change their native Commodities for those they want, and to manufacture a small part of their own Product, which is a liberty seems to be allowed them by the Law of Nature, and which I don't find hath been denied by the most severe Conquerors.[80]

In citing the freedom of trade and the oceans as an accepted principle of the laws of nature and nations, the Anglo-Irish modestly saw themselves as demanding much less than a new constitutional status, let alone a complete independence. They simply wished to pursue their own interests beneath the political aegis of the English monarchy. Despite occasional English encouragement of Irish wool production, its inhabitants had long concluded that it was merely elementary prudence to avoid provocative competition with England's leading manufacture. Sir William Temple had cautioned the Irish against competing with England in this particular sector,[81] and Sir William Petty was

[80] *Some Thoughts on the Bill Depending before the Right Honourable the House of Lords, for Prohibiting the Exportation of the Woolwen Manufactures of Ireland to Foreign Parts* (London, 1698). Cox (1650–1733), a zealous Protestant under the reign of James II and a strong supporter of William Orange had a distinguished legal career. On the accession of Anne the new government turned to him for advice on the proper government of Ireland. His suggestion that "it was for the interest of England to encourage the woollen manufacturers in Ireland in the coarse branches of it" and his considered critical view that "it was the most impolitic step which was ever taken by England to prohibit the whole exportation of woollen manufactures from Ireland" was not heeded. Nonetheless Cox was appointed, in succession to Methuen, as Lord Chancellor of Ireland. For this information see the article on Cox in the *Dictionary of National Biography*.

[81] See his remark in "An Essay upon the Advancement of Trade in Ireland" stating that "one thing must be taken notice of as peculiar to this country, which is, that, as in the nature of its government, so in the very improvement of its trade and riches, it ought to be considered not only in its own proper interest, but likewise in its relation to England, to which it is subordinate, and upon whose weal in the main that of this kingdom depends; and therefore a regard must be had of those points wherein the trade of Ireland comes to interfere with the main branches of the trade of England; in which cases the encouragement of such trade ought to be either declined or

equally adamant that Ireland should form a union with England and transfer some of its population there rather than attempt to compete commercially.[82] Any friend of Ireland in England could see the obvious dangers in attempting to upset England's woolen trade. When John Locke, a member of the newly formed English Board of Trade, was asked to draft an advisory report for the government on the Irish issue, he was just as adamant about the foolishness of any such attempt. Instead, he recommended freely that "the exportation of all sorts of woollen manufacturers out of Ireland should be restrained and penalized," since the improvement of Irish wool manufacturers could not but end up in "very ill consequences" to England.[83] It was better to encourage flax husbandry and linen manufacture in Ireland itself.[84] Most Englishmen were apt to see this division of labor between wool

moderated, and so give way to the interest of trade in England, upon the health and vigour whereof the strength, riches and glory of his Majesty's crowns seem chiefly to depend" (pp. 12–13).

[82] See Petty's last considerable work, his long memorandum submitted to James II, under the title "A Treatise of Ireland" (1687), first printed in C. H. Hull (ed.), *The Economic Writings of Sir William Petty* (2 vols., Cambridge, 1899), vol. 2, pp. 545–621.

[83] The Board of Trade, established in June 1696, started to discuss the linen trade in July 1696. After a longer discussion in August Locke needed the information for his follow-up report. He turned to his friend William Molyneux for up-to-date information. Molyneux gave his answer on September 26, 1696, providing an exemplary précis of the argument: "England most certainly will never let us thrive by the Woollen trade, This is their Darling Mistris, and they are jealous of any Rival. But I see not, that we interfere with them in the least by the Linnen trade, so that is yet left open to us to grow rich by, if it were well Establishd and managed. . . . There is no Country has better land or Water for Flax and Hemp; and I do veryly beleive the Navy may be provided here with Sayling and Cordage Cheaper by far than in England. Our Land is Cheaper, Victuals for Workmen is Cheaper, and Labour is Cheaper, together with the other Necessarys for Artificers," *The Correspondence of John Locke*, ed. E. S. De Beer (8 vols., Oxford, 1976–1989), vol. 5, p. 704. The correspondence about the topic continued in 1697. Locke's 1697 policy document, "pitched upon" by his fellow members of the Board from several competing proposals on August 24 and transmitted to the Lord Justices on the 31 August, was published from the Board of Trade papers by H. R. Fox Bourne, *The Life of John Locke* (2 vols., London, 1876), vol. 2, pp. 363–72. For a general account of Locke's role in the Board of Trade see Peter Laslett, "John Locke, the Great Recoinage, and the Origins of the Board of Trade: 1695–1698" in John W. Yolton (ed.), *John Locke: Problems and Perspectives* (Cambridge, 1969), pp. 137–64.

[84] This was Locke's official advice, endorsed by the Board of Trade: "Since it generally proves ineffectual, and we conceive it hard to endeavour, to drive men from the trade they are employed in by bare prohibition, without offering them at the same time some other trade which, if they please, may turn to account, we humbly propose that the linen manufacture be set on foot and so encouraged in Ireland as may make it the general trade of that country as effectually as the woollen manufacture is and must be of England," Fox Bourne, *Life of Locke*, vol. 2, p. 365.

and linen production as a fair bargain between the mother country and the colony, and it was acceptable to many in Ireland also. Projects to help the development of the Irish linen industry were set on foot at just the time English country opposition to Ireland's woolen trade began to flare up. The backward condition of the country and the need for legislative assistance prompted plans for the forming of chartered linen companies by a number of Anglo-Irish groups.[85] Although Locke doubted the prospects for establishing an Irish linen manufacture in such corrupt times,[86] he had shown distinct sympathy for the enterprise and for the good intentions of its promoters.

Davenant was well aware of the growing English controversy over Ireland's general economic improvement and her wool trade in particular, but he saw the calls for restraint of Irish trade as "pushed on (without doors) rather for private ends, and to serve some particular turn, than calculated to produce any public benefit."[87] In the growing pamphlet war over Ireland, he was firmly "inclined to the milder side." Ireland was subject to England's empire by the sword, and Davenant had no inhibitions over the propensity of imperial centers to draw to themselves all the riches of their provinces, particularly since, as it was in England's case, such centralization was likely to hold even

. . . more strongly where the seat of dominion is in a great emporium, for such a city will not only be the head of power but of Trade, governing all its branches, and giving the rules and price; so that all parts thereon depending, can deal but subordinately to it, till at last it is found that provinces work but to enrich the superior kingdom.[88]

Ireland, he insisted, must be treated as a "Colony for Empire" rather than a "Colony for Trade."[89] In the former, the restriction of

---

[85] See Conrad Gill, *The Rise of the Irish Linen Industry* (Oxford, 1925).

[86] Locke to William Molyneux, February 22, 1697: "I thank you for the account you gave me of your linen manufacture. Private knavery, I perceive, does there as well as here destroy all public good works, and forbid the hope of any advantages by them, where nature plentyfully offers what industry would improve, were it but rightly directed, and duly cherished. The corruption of the age gives me so ill a prospect of any success in design of this kind, never so well laid, that I am not sorry my ill health gives me so just a reason to desire to be eased of the employment I am in," *Correspondence of Locke*, vol. 6, p. 7.

[87] *Balance of Trade, Works*, vol. 2, p. 239.

[88] Ibid., p. 238.

[89] For this important distinction see Cox, *Some Thoughts*, pp. 8–9.

their own trade made sense, but in the latter, where the aim of the state was to keep a neighboring conquered country in peaceful subjection, it was bad policy. At this stage he had to consider the protection of English trade against Ireland as a primary reason of state.

But as bills were submitted by successive MPs for Exeter and as supporters and opposition lined up in Parliament and in the Lords, the debate acquired a political dynamic of its own.[90] Ireland's "colonial" obedience in matters of trade became an issue of real urgency. As the country party agitation against the Irish woolen trade gathered strength, the whole edifice of rights and liberties on which the Irish position rested came under ever more radical questioning. A number of Ireland's leading intellectual figures realized with growing dismay the menace which this campaign posed not just to Ireland's woolen trade but to their own plans to develop a new linen manufacture. What was now in question was the political status of the English Protestant colonists of Ireland.[91]

The frustration of the Anglo-Irish patriots was set out most prominently in a hastily written but vigorous pamphlet by William Molyneux,[92] scion of an important Protestant Dublin family, cosmopolitan philosopher, Irish MP, and supporter of one of the new linen projects. Molyneux threw down a direct challenge to his friend and correspondent, John Locke, demanding the opinion of "the author of the *The Treatises on Government* " on the central argument of *The Case of Ireland's Being Bound by Acts of Parliament in England Stated.*[93] He was at pains to emphasize that he had no personal

---

[90] The best account of the whole Irish wool export debate is in H. F. Kearney, "The Political Background to English Mercantilism, 1695–1700," *Economic History Review,* 2nd ser., 11(1959), pp. 484–96.

[91] See the excellent analysis of Nicholas Canny, "Identity Formation in Ireland: The Emergence of the Anglo-Irish" in Nicholas Canny and Anthony Pagden (eds.), *Colonial Identity in the Atlantic World, 1500–1800* (Princeton, 1987), pp. 159–212. On the influence of the Irish problem on the American colonialists see Owen Dudley Edward, "The American Image of Ireland: A Study of Its Early Phases," *Perspectives in American History* 4(1970), pp. 199–282.

[92] For a biography of Molyneux (1656–1697) see J. G. Simms, *William Molyneux of Dublin: A Life of the Seventeenth-Century Political Writer and Scientist* (Dublin, 1982). A good background analysis is also provided in his *War and Politics in Ireland, 1649–1730* (London, 1986), pp. 251–61.

[93] Despite being the author of the wool-for-linen compromise between England and Ireland, along a clearly understood line of comparative advantages, and hence being a supporter of the prohibitive moves against the Irish wool trade, Locke's position on the interference with Irish parliamentary legislation concerning the linen companies

"concern in Wool, or the Wool Trade."[94] Instead, he drew extensively on the "Civilians, Grotius, Puffendorf, Locke's Treat. Government, etc.,"[95] and on the ancient constitutional history of the parliamentary and legal traditions of England and Ireland,[96] to deny "the dependence of Ireland upon the Parliament of England, or that they were bound by the laws enacted here further than they thought fit themselves." "If they had submitted to any such laws," he insisted, "as they did to that establishing the new Oaths, it was more by voluntary tacit consent, as finding it suited to their present circumstances, than by any compulsion, or that it was of itself binding."[97]

In his dedication to King William III, Molyneux claimed that the rights and liberties established by the Glorious Revolution ought to apply to the king's Protestant subjects in Ireland as much as to those

was clearly expressed by his blunt refusal to sign the Board of Trade's emendations to the bill prepared by the Irish Parliament. Such a refusal to resign himself to the majority view on an issue which for his colleagues appeared as of apparently secondary importance was a marked deviation from the Board's accepted procedures.

[94] Molyneux, "Preface to the Reader," *The Case of Ireland's Being Bound by Acts of Parliament in England Stated,* London, 1720 ed., p. x.

[95] Molyneux, *The Case of Ireland,* p. 130.

[96] J. G. A. Pocock noted Molyneux's "conjoint" reliance on both traditions, Lockean theory and ancient constitution, in the use of the latter detecting the influence of William Petyt's *The Antient Right of the Commons of England Asserted* (London, 1680). See Pocock, *The Ancient Constitution and the Feudal Law: A Study of English Historical Thought in the Seventeenth Century,* 2nd ed. (Cambridge, 1987), pp. 188, 238. Caroline Robbins maintains that the chief source of Molyneux's ancient constitutionalism was the MS treatise of Sir William Domville, his father-in-law, written for the use of the Duke of Ormonde in 1660; *The Eighteenth-Century Commonwealthman* (Cambridge, Mass. 1959), p. 140. For the curious shape of Molyneux's attempt to prove Ireland's independence with appeal to the English ancient constitution see the commentary of Canny, "Identity Formation in Ireland," pp. 204–5. The resulting Anglo-Irish ancient constitutionalism did not fare well with the English representatives of the genre. Note that Petyt's pupil and friend William Attwood produced a lengthy refutation of Molyneux's book in his *The History, and Reasons, of the Dependency of Ireland upon the Imperial Crown of the Kingdom of England. Rectifying Mr. Molineux's State of the Case of Ireland's Being Bound by Acts of Parliament in England* (London, 1698). For the crucial impact of this debate on the debates concerning the union of England and Scotland in the first years of the eighteenth century see William Ferguson, "Imperial Crowns: A Neglected Facet of the Background to the Treaty of Union of 1707," *Scottish Historical Review* 53(1974), pp. 22–44.

[97] *Calendar of State Papers of the Reign of William III., Domestic Series, 1698,* p. 262, a report of the Chancellor of Ireland, Methuen, to the House of Commons concerning Molyneux's book. Earlier Molyneux had described Methuen as acceptable to "all Moderate and Good Men" in Ireland, in a letter to Locke, February 3, 1697, *Correspondence of Locke,* vol. 5, p. 766. Locke unhesitatingly acted as a host during Molyneux's visit to London precisely at the time when Parliament had hysterically banned *The Case of Ireland.*

who lived in England, seeing the Irish Protestant community not as a colony but as a distinct society in union with England under a common monarch.

In his preface to the reader, Molyneux defied the advice of those who suggested that his daring book would hurt rather than help the Anglo-Irish cause. It was a matter of virtue, serving the good cause of his own country, to stand up for the rights on which the true relationship and common interest of England and the Irish colonists ought to rest.[98] But the effect was entirely predictable. His book was condemned both by the English and by the Irish parliaments and induced a spate of refutations, the first by John Cary, the Bristol merchant and a prominent and respectable theorist of free trade, with Davenant also joining in the fray rather late in the day.

Davenant's undue confidence in the Machiavellian theory of empires did not survive Molyneux's intervention. It was now clear that even those who supported the English military occupation of Ireland and freely acknowledged their loyalty to the king of England could at the same time claim independence not merely by political and constitutional separation, but also on grounds of the right to free trade. Though Davenant had previously regarded Ireland as a special part of the English empire and trusted that the metropolitan center could dictate to the provinces without dispute, he was now compelled to realize that trading empires differed in their political principles from empires based simply on military control of territory. Freedom of trade, accordingly, became a crucial constitutional issue in itself. If Ireland claimed the rights of a distinct society within the empire, the threat of commercial competition had become urgent.

The focus of concern therefore shifted from the problem of security to the behavior of markets. Here Davenant adopted arguments deployed by the English woolen interest. He quoted prominently from the recent pamphlet of Simon Clement, *The Interest of England with relation to the Trade of Ireland*,[99] a work designed specifically to re-

[98] For Molyneux's links to the Anglo-Irish party of republican virtue see Caroline Robbins, *The Eighteenth-Century Commonwealthman*, pp. 138–9.
[99] [Simon Clement], *The Interest of England, as it stands with relation to the trade of Ireland, considered; the Arguments against the Bill, for prohibiting the Exportation of Woollen Manufactures from Ireland to Forreign Parts, fairly discusst, and the reasonableness and necessity of Englands restraining her colonies in all matters of trade, that may be prejudicial to her own commerce, clearly demonstrated. With short remarques*

fute the arguments of Sir Richard Cox and pressing strongly for legislation against Ireland. Clement had warned English politicians that "if any one offers his goods cheaper than the usual price, that will then become the market price; and every one else must sell at the same, or keep his goods."[100] Davenant now noted: "All that have either writ or spoke upon this subject agree, that the whole controversy turns upon this single point, whether they can make the same woollen goods cheaper there than here."[101]

If trade was free, then it was prices which mattered, not the political structures of empire. Convinced that international free markets must fall to the cheapest supplier, Davenant accepted the conclusion that the Irish, once they were allowed to trade freely with England and Europe, would expel the English from all their existing markets. In the face of Molyneux's political attack and the insistence of Clement and others on the imperative of mastering markets, Davenant abandoned his initial advocacy of abstention from political interference with the workings of trade. In sheer self-defense, he argued, England must prohibit Irish woolen exports by law. Molyneux had wholly misconstrued the true meaning of Ireland's colonial status. If the "supereminent dominion and supreme and uncontrolable regiment over themselves"[102] which the Irish demanded could lead to such cutthroat competition, then Ireland must be restrained "at least in a capacity to ruin England."[103] It was "the right of England . . .

---

on a book, entitled, Some thoughts on the bill depending before the right honourable the House of Lords, for prohibiting the exportation of the woollen manufactures of Ireland to forreign parts (London, 1698). Clement, whose aim was to show "the Necessity there is upon us to stop the progress of such Manufacturys in Ireland, which directly interfere with those of England" (p. 2) in an appendix was also attacking vehemently Cox's *Some Thoughts.* The arguments of this debate, with clear, albeit slightly veiled, reference to Davenant's intervention, were summed up in *The Substance of the Arguments for and against the Bill, for Prohibiting the Exportation of Woollen Manufacture from Ireland to Forreign Parts, Deliver'd at the Bar of the House of Lords. Together with Some Remarks on a Printed Paper, Entituled Some Thoughts on the said Bill* (London, 1698). For Clement's later position in the country party propaganda machinery see Downie, *Harley and the Press,* pp. 43, 121–2.

[100] *The Interest of England,* p. 7, cited by Davenant in *Balance of Trade, Works,* vol. 2, p. 253.

[101] *Balance of Trade, Works,* vol. 2, p. 252. This identification of the fulcrum of the debate is accepted in *The Substance of the Arguments* (pp. 4–5), which insisted that the "point on which the Stress of the Controversie depends" was "whether the Irish can send their Manufactures cheaper to Foreign Markets than the English."

[102] Ibid., p. 248.

[103] Ibid., p. 250.

that the legislative authority . . . should, upon all emergencies, make such regulations and restrictions, relating to Trade especially, as shall be thought for the weal-public of both countries."[104] Davenant's *volte face* was a decision in true Machiavellian spirit. The belief that the Irish would strangle England's staple woolen trade was grounds for a "reasonable jealousy of state." *Virtù* counseled the "severe wisdom" in defense of one's patria that it was "not only prudent, but just . . . to interrupt the too sudden growth of any neighbour nation."[105]

The issue was no longer one of whether one should tolerate backward Ireland's rudimentary efforts at improvement. If the Irish claimed the rights of free trade, the threat to England's staple was direct and immediate. England's wealth ensured that its only chance for successful foreign trade in its own products was to channel its efforts to produce what it was best suited to produce: woolens, in which it could expect lasting profits despite its high wage costs. This strategy relied on England's comparative natural advantages in the face of other trading countries. Compared with Ireland, England had no fixed natural advantages, and in a situation of equal advantages low-wage nations presented a deadly threat to rich countries. Ireland was potentially a more dangerous competitor of England than anybody else. Davenant pressed his assessment of the Irish case into an analysis of the prospects of poor countries in free trade that was more thorough than any offered by his English contemporaries.

Opinion on Ireland's competitive prospects was far from uniform, supporters of the view that a poor country was always a dangerous enemy in free trade on account of its cheap wages being matched by forceful opponents who insisted that the genuine advantages of poverty over corruption could not be exploited in practice without great difficulty. Human resources, skill, and capital mattered as much as wages. Since Ireland shared the same climate and resources as England, materials like wool were just as good in Ireland as in England. Davenant and others estimated that since food represented half of the subsistence costs governing wages, "the cheapness of provisions" would enable the Irish "to afford their commodities cheaper than England can do in foreign markets"[106] and might well be able to

[104] Ibid., pp. 250–1.
[105] Ibid., p. 254.
[106] Ibid., p. 252.

produce the same quality of wool as England "a third cheaper." But poverty was not simply a condition of cheap prices. It also meant a lack of skill, and discipline in the work force, and in general a lack of a culture of industry in the backward country. Hence the question of the real price of Irish workmanship was more complicated. Spinning, as a simple rural occupation, could be very cheap in Ireland, but more skilled tasks, like combing and weaving, were costlier than in England, because of the shortage of skilled Irish labor.

Here the issue was not one of cheap wages, but of the excessively high price of skilled labor in poor nations. The key issue was how much time, capital, and import of more skilled labor the Irish economy would need before its initial advantage of cheap resources and cheap but unskilled labor could render it a truly formidable exporter. The advantages of backwardness were inherently transitory. Once the population-to-land ratio, which, as Temple had emphasized, was the crucial index of development, began to rise, the Irish wage advantage could well disappear. What was crucial was the intervening period, when wage goods were still cheaper than elsewhere but skills had become more abundant and hence less expensive. The very high wages of skilled labor, Davenant accepted, would have to drop "as workmen encrease; for handycraft in countries where living is cheap, can be dear no longer than till artists are bread up." To recruit and train a skilled labor force needed time, but it was likely to be implemented much faster than the erosion of the wage advantage. There would therefore be a considerable period of high competitiveness in which skills would develop rapidly and wages remain relatively low since "a great many artists will be instructed before the multitude of inhabitants can render provisions dear in such a place as Ireland."[107] Even if the price advantage of Irish wool were to diminish from one-third to a tenth, Davenant pointed out, this was enough to throw Ireland's high-wage competitors "into more disorders, than the most knowing man in England can readily describe."[108]

It was unclear whether Ireland could attract skilled immigrant labor and import dyes and other chemicals needed for the quality wool production that was necessary for the setting up of a serious textile industry. But Davenant assumed there was considerable international

[107] Ibid.
[108] Ibid., p. 253.

mobility of labor and that the direct recruitment of skilled labor in the short run would present no great problem:

Where there is plenty of material, which, manufactured, yields a good price, hands will be soon invited over to work it up. . . . But this holds more strongly, where not only the material, but all sorts of provisions are cheap; and in countries which have not been yet improved, where every new comer hopes to make a sudden fortune.[109]

The lure of high profitability in upstart countries was also important. If the gains were sufficient to attract labor to the country, the same motives and mobility would certainly be apparent in the case of money capital. Entrepreneurs in corrupt and rich countries were unlikely to prove themselves paragons of public spirit:

. . . to ask where will be the stocks of money to set up so large a manufacture? is but an evasive way of arguing; for where the prospects of gain is certain, money never fails to come. . . . foreigners will carry stocks to an improving place, where they may reasonably expect many more advantages than what shall arise from this manufacture. As for example, to lay out money upon good securities, at 10 per cent interest, to buy land capable of great melioration at 10 years purchase; and to have almost all the necessaries of life half as cheap again as in other parts; are not all these circumstances sufficient to invite thither, not only foreign stocks, but very much of our own money, and a great number of our workmen, where their industry will turn to a better account than it does here.[110]

Public virtue therefore demanded that the legislators of the richer imperial center crush the competitive pressures of their ambitious but dependent neighbor. On this account Davenant wished to deny even the freedom of linen manufacturing to Ireland. It would be of no benefit to encourage the linen interest in Ireland if the result was that Ireland ruined the other European linen producers and these, in turn, ceased to be viable trading partners and markets for English woolens of the cruder sort. He proposed, accordingly, to suppress the entire textile trade of Ireland. As a colony, Ireland must be excluded from the trading system of comparative advantages. The consolation prize which he graciously offered to the Irish was pitiful, but entirely in keeping with his conception of trade. Since there were hazards in forcing the Irish into such poverty that they openly rebelled, they

[109] Ibid., p. 251.
[110] Ibid., pp. 253–4.

should be given back the opportunity to export cattle to England, long prohibited to them, in compensation for the loss of their manufacturing trade. The cattle trade would be wholly in keeping with their backwardness, since "countries thinly peopled, can sooner improve in the bread of cattle than any other way, because it is a work which few hands may manage."[111] At the same time the cheapness of Irish meat would enable the English to reduce wages without encroaching on the corrupt manners of their luxury-loving people. Public-spirited butchers in England, accordingly, must reconcile themselves to the primacy of national interest and accept their individual losses for the benefit of the whole community.[112]

As always, Davenant's reasoning rested ultimately on the necessities imposed by war. Whatever the Irish might think "it must be their interest as well as ours, that the supreme power, and the chief wealth, should be ever preserved to center here in the seat of empire."[113] To withstand the strains of modern war, states must accept the imperatives of trade, even if commerce was plainly inimical to ideals of social austerity. But living on trade had many other pernicious and potentially destructive implications. To live in a trading empire and shrink from imposing the empire of the sword on one's markets was to build castles on sand. Far from guaranteeing stability and the provision of the means for national defense, it committed wealthy nations to permanent price wars and required an endless adaptation of their productive systems. "Duration" and trade were deeply at odds with one another.

Davenant's opposition to the public debt was a natural complement to this viewpoint. He was certain that modern war finance was possible only through access to surpluses in foreign trade. He was well aware, however, that war in fact interrupted foreign trade and that the English government in the face of temporary financial difficulties had turned instead to another instantly available method of war fi-

---

[111] Ibid., p. 251.
[112] Although the act of prohibiting the export of woolen goods from Ireland to foreign parts was enacted in 1699 (10 & 11 Wm.III.c.10), the famous anti-Irish Cattle Acts of the 1660s were first suspended in the 1750s and finally repealed only in 1776. For the vicissitudes of English legal regulation of cattle imports from Ireland see J. O'Donovan, *The Economic History of Livestock in Ireland* (Cork, 1940), and for the general economic background, L. M. Cullen, *An Economic History of Ireland since 1660* (London, 1972).
[113] *Balance of Trade, Works,* vol. 2, p. 250.

nance: the creation of a system of public debt, borrowing money against its future tax revenues. It was an age, above all, in England of myriad projects of banking, paper money, and loans to the state. Davenant fully understood the economic principles behind these developments. His opposition to the English public debt system was in no sense an opposition to paper money as such. If money was first and foremost a measure of trade, there was a clear need for money throughout the country. Davenant thought that there was good reason to believe that paper money could make a real contribution to satisfying this need. He was sure that if

. . . such tallies as shall be proposed to go in payments of the fleet, ordinance, civil list, or for stores, or for repayment of money to be actually lent, should be placed upon such funds as will every year clear off the interest, and a certain proportion of the principal. If such funds can be found out, and set on foot, the tallies struck thereupon will be as so much new stock in the kingdom; and because they carry interest with them, may perhaps in time be more esteemed than money itself.[114]

Paper money circulation could assist the country after the war as well as during it. In wartime it could aid greatly in financing the war effort. Afterward it could help to cushion the slump in foreign demand that followed the restoration of the peacetime trade channels. The sudden drop in demand anticipated with the return to peacetime financing would mean a sudden shortage of money, and since "all things are dear or cheap" in relation to an existing supply of money in the economy, in the postwar slump English prices might well drop

---

[114] "Concerning Credit, and the means and methods by which it may be restored," *Discourses on the Public Revenues, Part I,* Discourse 2, [1698] *Works,* vol. 1, p. 154. The origin of this essay or discourse is in "A Memorial Concerning Credit and the Means and Methods whereby it may be Restored" (1696), which was submitted to the government in support of Davenant's application for a place in the Excise administration. It is now printed in Charles Davenant, *Two Manuscripts,* ed. by A. P. Usher (Baltimore, 1942). Davenant's biographer D. Waddell suggests that "this tract is remarkable for the moderation of its tone and for its apparent acceptance of the necessity of the previously condemned policy of public borrowing at high interest rates. The mood soon passed, perhaps because Davenant did not get the post in the Excise, and he was soon in an uncompromising opposition" (p. 281). Usher also thinks that the 1698 discourse, cited above, differed significantly from the 1696 "Memoriall" whose position was closer to Davenant's 1706 *An Essay upon National Credit.* The praise of paper money, cited above, appeared in the "Memoriall" too: "By this Artificall help, and at least appearing Enlargement of our stock, the Kingdomes business was supported," (pp. 68–9). In its main lines, and in most important detail, the 1696 and 1698 writings represent the same position.

suddenly. A shortage of money in a developed economy might create acute tension. It was "of such pernicious consequence to any nation for the money not to circulate, that the disease cannot be cured at too high a price."[115]

A cure would therefore certainly be welcome, but a quack recipe would only be likely to imperil the health of the patient. In Davenant's considered view the projectors responsible for setting up the Bank of England and devising the new methods of war financing of the 1690s were quacks in just this sense:

> The paper-credit, which, with such encomiums to themselves, they boast to have set up, what effects has it produced, but only to lull the nation asleep, . . . It is an opiate that quiets the patient for a time, but it is no cure for the disease their ill combat has brought upon us: can this imaginary wealth stand the shock of any sudden calamity? Is it not by experience found a rotten building, which the least storm from abroad is ready to throw down?[116]

An economy based on credit posed particular threats to the goal of duration. While repayments were regularly made and confidence in the government lasted, paper bonds would circulate "from hand to hand" with great ease, encouraging the government to issue more and more of them to cover the increasing burdens of war. While the people believed that these bonds were "secured upon solid and substantial funds," their confidence made the paper money as good as specie. But their standing depended abjectly on the maintenance of such confidence:

> Of all beings that have existence only in the minds of men, nothing is more fantastical and nice than Credit, it is never to be forced; it hangs upon opinion; it depends upon our passions of hope and fear; it comes many times unsought for, and often goes away without reason; and when once lost, is hardly to be quite recovered.[117]

In the face of the news of a single lost battle the sudden, and perhaps entirely unreasonable, collapse of credit might well cause the loss of the whole war. Even in peacetime, if the government's intention or ability to continue repayments came to be seriously doubted, the paper money, "in the nature of a quick stock in the nation, where-

---

[115] "Means and Methods of restoring Credit," *Works,* vol. 1, p. 156.
[116] "An Essay upon the Balance of Power," *Essays,* in *Works,* vol. 3, p. 329.
[117] "Credit," *Works,* vol. 1, p. 151.

with the people may transact their bargains,"[118] could lose its value
and bring the entire circulation of money to an abrupt halt. Davenant
saw great danger in this ill-judged means of handling the economic
problems of the nation. By no means all virtuous men agreed that to
build an opinion was necessarily to build on fragile ground:

It is true, some modern politicians have run upon another notion; and several
persons have thought that the more funds are erected, the more people are
engaged to preserve the present government. This policy indeed of theirs
would hold good, if they could make out that the lenders are stronger, and
more in number than such as are concerned in Payments to the Public.[119]

Davenant was haunted by the specter of a sudden loss of confidence in the country's monetary media and a consequent collapse of
all credit. He was especially concerned, accordingly, at the prospect
of extending rather than restricting the credit economy now that the
war was over. No collapse of credit did in fact occur during the period
in which he was writing, and the party of credit naturally went from
strength to strength. But Davenant himself remained convinced that
a continuation of the public debt would ruin both the political fabric
and the economy of the nation. The "huge engine of credit" was itself
an engine of corruption. To take up new credits before the old were
paid back, to assume more credit than could be repaid from existing
resources, was an inevitable road to ever-rising taxation. High taxation made the country expensive and served to price it out of international markets. This must lead to "certain ruin":

It will be found, that in no long course of time we shall languish and decay
every year, by steps easy enough to be perceived by such as consider of these
matters. Our gold and silver will be carried off by degrees, rents will fall, the
purchase of land will decrease, wool will sink in its price, our stock of shipping will be diminished, farm-houses will go to ruin, industry will decay, and
we shall have upon us all the visible marks of a declining people.[120]

To levy high taxes to pay the debts meant robbing the public at large,
taking away the property they had earned by their labor in order to
transfer it into the pockets of state creditors, speculators, and finally
even foreigners. The resources of a rich country might suffice to repay
the arrears. But the debt was likely in practice to prove endless since

[118] Ibid., p. 154.
[119] *Balance of Trade, Works,* vol. 2, p. 297.
[120] Ibid., p. 283.

"in all likelihood it must chiefly arise from exorbitant premiums, unwarrantable interest, and other ways of laying out money, hurtful to the King and destructive to the people."[121] It was a process like the classic cycle of imperial corruption. It would constantly drain the resources of the provinces to the governing center where the public creditors congregated. In its quest for further credits, the government could only fall still further under the baneful influence of its luxurious and bloated capital. The private and party interests of its corrupt head would overwhelm the health of the body politic, deafening the government to the advice of the wise and virtuous.

In such a situation the public debt system might well end by pulling "down all our civil rights." The mechanism of public debt creation was not merely the financial base of a standing army; it was a virtual financial equivalent to one. "Suppose," Davenant argued, "that in some future reign, the ministers should be either weary or afraid of Parliaments, and desire to govern by the sword, and without law."[122] Such political leaders, "an ambitious and desperate set of men, and resolved to make their master absolute," would have a marvelous opportunity to consolidate their private power base by deliberately misrepresenting the country's debt position. They could reduce cash revenues and claim wholly fallacious needs for incurring still further state debt and employ the latter to subvert the constitution, "especially if they should be backed with the support of a standing army."

Davenant sought, as ever, to identify the symptoms of impending danger in order to give virtuous men time for effective countervailing action. In this particular case, he was confident, "the symptoms of their [i.e., 'the wicked ministers'] approaching frenzy will be evident enough." While calling for further loans, they would do their best to see "that the people may be kept in the dark, both as to what they give, and as to what each branch is likely to yield." This possibility reflected an important defect in the English Constitution. There were no legal means for impeaching a government which stopped the repayment of the public debt, and there was no legal obligation on government to provide Parliament with a detailed report of the nation's accounts. Davenant's own political arithmetic, fondly offered as a

[121] Ibid., p. 282.
[122] Ibid., p. 285.

powerful check on the finances of the government, was only as effective as a virtually impotent private citizen could make it. In a modern trading state any system of political checks and balances required some distinctively modern features: "At a time when there is such an immense revenue collected every year, it seems a fault in our constitution that sufficient provision is not made against diverting and misapplying the public treasure, and against breaking into appropriated funds."[123]

Though Davenant chose to formulate these threats, with understandable caution, very much as a long-term possibility, he pressed his contemporaries to see the issue of the public debt as a choice between liberty and slavery. Even for the short term it might do great harm to the country's economy. A debt economy would lead to negligence in the financial administration of the state

. . . and with very little more carelessness, the raising more and more will grow unavoidable for our common defence till at last we shall come to pay constantly between five and six millions per.ann. And when this Kingdom shall be arrived at that period of ill conduct, we may venture to pronounce, that the common people of England will in all circumstances be then as poor and miserable as the common people of France were before the war. And we desire all good patriots to carry this reflection in their minds.[124]

Even in purely economic terms the presence of high-interest-bearing government bonds in the economy meant that there was little incentive to earn profits through investment and labor. "Will men who can safely, and without trouble, reap such gains, bread their children to be merchants? Will they venture great stocks to make discoveries, and employ their industry to enlarge and extend our dealings in distant parts?"[125] Money earned in this way would be spent on imported luxury goods, and these, in their turn, were bound to undermine the country's balance of trade. This emphasis on the constant and relentless distortion of the economy by the mere existence of a permanent government borrowing requirement was crucial for Davenant, for the sole solution which he could see was one which must itself damage the short-term interests of both traders and producers. If further borrowing was stopped and funds were diverted to a

[123] Ibid., p. 286.
[124] Ibid., p. 288.
[125] Ibid., p. 295.

regular schedule for the repayment of existing debts, then a temporary scarcity of money for the ordinary course of trade was unavoidable. But such a squeeze on public borrowing, and hence on what had
come to be regarded as the ordinary money supply of the country, was
a necessity to be endured by all who understood both the public
interest and the private interests of the vast majority. To establish the
economy on a sound monetary footing and foster trade and shipping,
even if it might create a short-term crisis, would at least offer a
durable cure for its ills and permit it to flourish in the future.

III

Davenant's preoccupations in politics extended well beyond the
Realpolitik of English military, diplomatic, and commercial interests.
It was in fact his vividly ideological commitments which spurred him
to concern himself with the novel economic limits on which the nation's political and moral health had now came to depend. The policies which he recommended were certainly eminently Machiavellian
in their ruthlessness. If England wished to remain a strong, glorious,
and independent nation, it had very few options. It must strive for
commercial empire through its domination of the seas; it must retain
and exploit the captive markets of its own territorial control, whether
in Ireland or in the West Indies, and must restructure its domestic
industries in accordance with the rules of international price competition. There is no reason to doubt Davenant's sincerity when he argues
in principle for a free constitution, for freedom in the international
arena, or for the well-being of the English laboring classes. But those
who hoped or were obliged to live off the market, he realized, had to
accept its dictates and win by its own rules. A ruthless abandonment
of institutions and industries which were not viable by the standards
of the international markets was now part of any modern statesman's
virtù.

Davenant's strategy for averting decline in the face of lower wage
economies was plainly understood by at least some contemporaries,
and it evoked vigorous controversy. A particularly vehement clash
developed between Davenant, self-appointed guardian of the virtue
of English commerce, and a dominant member of the newly ap-

pointed Board of Trade, John Pollexfen,[126] a colleague of John Locke
and Abraham Hill, who actually held the office to which Davenant
aspired.[127] Pollexfen launched a frontal attack on Davenant in his
*England and East-India Inconsistent in Their Manufactures: Being an
Answer to a Treatise, Intituled An Essay on the East-India Trade by the
Author of The Essay of Ways and Means.* Davenant took up the
challenge and made the debate public, answering in print at length.[128]
He pilloried Pollexfen as an unreconstructed protagonist of mistaken
notions of money and trade balances.[129] This rhetorical strategy,
though effective, was not entirely justified. In "Foreign Trade is beneficial to England," Davenant named his opponent openly on the first
page, charging that "after the trial of 100 years" Pollexfen still refused
to acknowledge "that extended trade enriches this nation."[130]
Davenant deployed the latest results of political arithmetic to demon-

---

[126] Pollexfen sat on the old Committee of Trade and Plantations in 1675 and was a very
active and influential member of the Board of Trade from 1696 to 1705. For a
description of the workings of the Board of Trade and its attendance records see I.
K. Steele, *Politics of Colonial Policy. The Board of Trade in Colonial Administration, 1696–1720* (Oxford, 1968), Part I, "King William's Board of Trade," pp. 3–41.

[127] Davenant had an important role in the fierce debates around "the setting up the
Council of Trade." In late 1695 he wrote a "Memoriall concerning a Council of
Trade" submitted to and discussed by the Privy Council. The plan, promoted by
Harley and Shrewsbury, influenced the final proposals worked out by the whole
House of Commons sitting as a committee. The competing plan was the quasi-
republican project of a directly elected nationally representative merchant council.
Davenant's memorandum is preserved among the Harley papers (BM Harleian MS
1223) and was partially published in R. M. Lees, "Parliament and the Proposal for a
Council of Trade, 1695–6," *English Historical Review* 54(1939), 38–66. Some of this
material found its way into Davenant's discourse "On the Protection and Care of
Trade" in *Discourses on the Public Revenues and on Trade, Part II, Works,* vol. 1,
pp. 394–459.

[128] The entire *Discourses on the Public Revenues and on Trade, Part II* was designed to
answer Pollexfen's criticism, the discourse on foreign trade being beneficial, and on
the East India trade in particular, openly attacked Pollexfen's views, clearly trying
to neutralize the latter's influence on the Board of Trade and hence on the government's legislative program.

[129] Davenant caricatured Pollexfen, "once a dealer to Portugal, now in an eminent
post, and the only oracle of some people in these matters," as a person who
"maintains dogmatically," i.e., without sufficient empirical proof, that "gold and
silver is the only or most useful treasure of a nation," "Foreign Trade is Beneficial,"
Works, vol. 1, pp. 353–4. See also pp. 383–9 for an extension of this criticism and a
discussion of the irrelevance of sectional balances as opposed to the national aggre-
gate balance of trade. Note, however, that Davenant did not charge Pollexfen with
being a representative of sectional merchant interests. His folly was rather mistak-
ing the national interests and trying to sell to the "landed interest" a commercial
policy based entirely on the marketing of Britain's native products and industry.

[130] Ibid., p. 345.

strate that England's past trading strategy had been successful. But Pollexfen's criticism caused him real anxiety,[131] since the former's emphasis on the inevitable uncertainties and potential human costs of the strategy of preemptive capitulation to the dictates of international markets cast doubt on the wisdom of England's pursuing a still more aggressive foreign trade strategy in the future.

Pollexfen firmly accepted some of Davenant's more prominent assumptions and fully realized that an entrepôt trade in East India goods, if it was profitable at all, could readily benefit the nation as a whole, that the inland consumption of home manufactures was no way to generate a cash surplus, that England was an expensive and luxurious country, and that the high price of English woolen products made them virtually unsalable. But he objected strongly to Davenant's proposal to restructure English domestic manufactures in the quest for competition by concentrating solely on medium- and high-price woolen products aimed almost exclusively at the export markets and supplanted in its own home market by cheap imports from India:

That our Woollen Goods consumed at Home do not inrich the Nation, and that a high Price on our Woollen Manufactures may hinder the Sale of them, is agreed; but that we must therefore send our Money to India to purchase the Manufactured Goods made in those parts to be spent at Home, and Abroad, in the room of our own, in order to bring down the Price of them, by making Wooll and Labour cheap, are false conclusions drawn from true Principles.[132]

Not only were Davenant's conclusions misconceived in Pollexfen's view; they revealed the cranky logic of a projector. Despite Davenant's assumptions, Europe had ceased to be a seller's market for English woolen goods for some time past, and English export prices were already cut to a minimum, which left room for little, if any, profit. Since the Indian textiles undercut even this miserable level of prices, any further reduction would require drastic expedients:

For unless our Wooll fall to nothing, and the Wages of those that work it up to 2d. per Day, and Raw Silk and Silk Weavers Labour proportionable, the India Goods will occasion a stop to the Consumption of them; because those from India must otherwise be Cheapest, and all People will go to the Cheapest Markets. which will affect the Rents of Land, and bring our Working

[131] "On the Protection and Care of Trade," *Works*, vol. 1, pp. 458–9.
[132] John Pollexfen, *England and East-India Inconsistent in Their Manufactures*, London, 1696, p.20.

People to Poverty, and force them either to fly to Foreign Parts, or to be maintained by the Parishes.[133]

Beside pointing to the devastation that permitting Indian textile prices to dictate English price and wage levels would necessarily cause, Pollexfen also pointed out a weakness in Davenant's positive proposals for economic restructuring. Even if Davenant's strategy worked, it would necessarily take some time to become fully operational. The English had first to lower prices, and then to undercut all European wool producers with or without the aid of East India imports, and then to reestablish themselves as sole suppliers. Only at this stage could they dictate prices once again and raise these to a profitable level. In view of this inevitable time lag, Pollexfen argued:

We should also have been told how the Landed Men and Poor should subsist whilst the Expriment was making, and how in case this Project should not take, we should retrieve what we may lose by trying it, and how we should regain the Expence of them at Home, after the East-India Goods have gotten Possession by an uninterrupted usage.[134]

To restructure industry in accordance with Davenant's proposals, into a single efficient textile industry, would involve a yet further time lag. Silk and linen production must first be discontinued and the products imported more cheaply in exchange for woolens. But what was appreciably less clear was the eventual impact these charges would have on levels of domestic employment:

The Author seems to be of Opinion that Silk and linnen may do well in process of time, when England shall come to be more Peopled, and when a long Peace hath increased our Stock and Wealth; but the Author doth not tell us how the People we have shall live in the mean time, nor of any probability how our Stock or Wealth shall increase, nor how we shall then set up again, promote or incourage such Manufactures, if we should now permit them to be destroyed . . . nor what incouragement will be left for the increasing of People if the Manufactures be destroyed.[135]

Pollexfen fully realized that Davenant's strategy aimed to meet the challenges of Machiavellian *virtù*, anticipating a major danger and countering it well in advance, if necessary by extreme measures. But he also saw that persuading a country that it "must singly depend on

[133] Ibid., pp. 17–18.
[134] Ibid., pp. 20–1.
[135] Ibid., p. 32.

the Markets Abroad" in the hope of prevailing in the resulting price competition was to recommend a most hazardous policy. How could Davenant place such trust in markets? How could anybody be so sure that there would be "any Market or Buyer" for his products at any given time in the future? What if "it should be our misfortune to be disappointed by the increase in such Fabricks in other places, or disuse in the Expence of them"? No doubt one must bear such misfortunes with as much patience as one could muster and do one's best to minimize the damage which they inflicted. But voluntarily to open up one's home market to international market forces and actively to dismantle whole sectors of one's own home industry in anticipation amounted to presuming that "the best way for a Man to preserve his Life, were to Cut his own throat."

Davenant himself, as we have seen, was only too aware of the hazards of attempting to diversify:

It is the Prudence of a State to see that Industry and Stock be not diverted from things profitable to the whole, and where a Nation is a certain known gainer, to be turn'd upon Objects unprofitable, and perhaps dangerous to the public or new Inventions, in which it cannot be determined in many years whether we get or lose, or how the Ballance stands.[136]

In response, Pollexfen firmly rejected the strategy of shedding industries in anticipation of international market pressures and aimed instead to expand employment and increase the nation's wealth through encouraging domestic labor, "the chief cause of Riches." It was best to support every occupation that was "useful to afford a livelihood to the vast Number of People that have their sole dependence thereon;"[137] and "the having of many sorts of Manufactures of our own is not onely the best way to have Variety to send abroad, but to prevent our being in want of such Commodities, that there may be no Temptation for their being Imported."[138] In the case of linen, the raw material could be grown at home, and raw silk could also be imported cheaply. With both kinds of textiles, labor was the main component of their eventual value.

Pollexfen's strategy was to imitate the apparently successful past policies of those countries which now dominated the industries in

[136] Ibid., p. 54. Davenant's argument is in *East India Trade, Works,* vol. 1, p. 107.
[137] Pollexfen, *England and East-India Inconsistent in Their Manufactures,* p. 52.
[138] Ibid., p. 54.

question. It was no good to argue that linen and silk were "not the genuine off-spring" of England. Industrial policies had to be reexamined too, since "many Manufactures," he argued, "in this and several Countries, from a small beginning, have come to great Perfection, and therefore ought to have all incouragement given to it [*sic*]."[139]

On this basis he challenged both Davenant's support for free trade and his attempt to model England's trade on the Dutch design for a free commercial society. England was not as frugal as Holland and so needed more laws and more careful tutelage, including perhaps sumptuary laws. Could it really hope to adjust itself to complete freedom of trade? What were the proper limits of international market exchange? If East India imports were to be admitted freely, did this imply that it was right to give free admittance to every other foreign product? Did it imply the free import of any foreign product which could undercut domestic producers, including corn? Did it make it reasonable to import Irish wool in order to favor the export of English woolens to putatively lucrative foreign markets? Did it imply opening up the entire East India trade? Did it imply repealing the Act of Navigation? Pollexfen firmly rejected the view that military necessities forced England to open itself without restriction to international trade. France had shown that it was possible to carry the burdens of war without embracing such a promiscuous commercial liberty, a liberty which could easily lead to the destruction of a country's own domestic industries. By firm pursuit of precisely the opposite policy, encouraging its own manufactures and promoting its fisheries, France had given an example for every nation to follow.

The real force of Pollexfen's argument lay in its insistence on the uncertainties involved in any strategy of acceding to the dictates of international markets. Against Davenant's drastic advocacy of abandoning any form of home production which could not face international competition Pollexfen stressed the freedom of maneuver available to political leaders on their own home territory. But there remained a third possible strategy. Both Davenant and Pollexfen fully accepted the theory of price formation which underlay the conception of market power. Both accepted that wages formed the decisive component of prices, that they were extremely inelastic,

[139] Ibid., p. 30.

and that they must be taken essentially as given when devising economic strategies for a government. This assumption was soon to be challenged, however, by a novel strategy which aimed to provide employment and high wages for the country's population, while remaining internationally competitive by transforming the structure of existing processes of production. The principal exponent of this new strategy was Henry Martyn.[140] What Martyn advocated was embrac-

[140] Henry Martyn, *Considerations Upon the East-India Trade* (London, 1701). Martyn's life is not well known, and in the nineteenth century McCulloch cast doubt on his imputed authorship. Most of our supporting information comes from various editors of Addison and Steele's *Spectator* (some of it is rehearsed in P. J. Thomas, *Mercantilism and the East India Trade* [London, 1926], Appendix B, "The Authorship of the *Considerations upon East India Trade,"* pp. 171–3). Steele himself named Mr. Henry Martyn as a contributor to the *Spectator*. John Nichols, the late eighteenth century editor of the *Spectator* (8 vols., London, 1788–9) attributed to Martyn No. 180 (1711), signed as Philarithmus, and also with the letter "T." "T" also appeared in numbers 200 (in which Steele acknowledged that the argument was based on a hint in an essay, or letter, from Philarithmus). Addison in No. 221 remarked that many believed that "T stands for the Trader or Merchant," and Nichols then suggested that Steele was referring to his friend Martyn in most cases when he referred to the figure of Sir Andrew Freeport in the *Spectator* essays. The attributions of Nichols were endorsed by D. F. Bond, the *Spectator's* modern editor, arguing that the author of Nos. 180 and 220 was "doubtless" Henry Martyn. See *The Spectator*, ed. by D. F. Bond (5 vols., Oxford, 1965), vol. 1, p. lii; vol. 2, pp. 208 and 283. No. 232 (which in the different editions is signed X, Z, or was left unsigned), discussing the views of Sir Andrew Freeport, is the most important of these pieces, presenting a bold argument about the division of labor and the connection between wages and prices, strongly reminiscent of the assertions found in the *Considerations*. The internal evidence thus convincingly supports the conjecture of the *Spectator* contributions and the *Considerations* coming from the same hand. Martyn's, *alias* Sir Andrew Freeport's, politics appears to be that of a radical Whig or commonwealthman (Nos. 131 and 269); Steele was a friend of both Henry Martyn and his brother and called at least one of them "Brother Whigg Martyn," in a letter to Mrs. Steele, August 24, 1710, *The Correspondence of Richard Steele,* ed. by Rae Blanchard (London, 1941), p. 265. Not surprisingly in 1713–4 Martyn was Charles King's chief collaborator on the Whig periodical *The British Merchant, or Commerce Preserved,* which battled with Defoe's *Mercator* in aiming at the rejection of the commercial clauses of the Treaty of Utrecht, particularly the free-trade agreement with France proposed by the Tory administration. In the reconstruction of the administration following the accession of George II, Martyn succeeded Davenant in the position of Inspector General of Imports and Exports in November 1714. In 1720 the *Considerations* were republished, unrevised but under a slightly different title, *The Advantages of the East-India Trade to England Considered*. Martyn died in 1721. For discussions of the *Considerations* see William J. Barber, *British Economic Thought and India 1600–1858. A Study in the History of Development Economics* (Oxford, 1975), where the entire chap. 3, is devoted to Martyn's work; Marcus Arkin, "A Neglected Forerunner of Adam Smith," *South African Journal of Economics*, 23 (1955), 299–314; and from the perspective of protoindustrialization theory, Maxine Berg, "Political Economy and the Principles of Manufacture" in M. Berg, P. Hudson, and M. Sonenscher, *Manufacture in Town and Country before the Factory* (Cambridge, 1983).

ing the principles of the division of labor as the key to efficient production, reorganizing production by applying it without inhibition and greatly extending – perhaps even virtually removing – the existing limits to political action.

Martyn brought to bear a unique perspective on the logic of international markets. The capacity of poorer or more efficient countries to undersell the English on international markets was seen by most interested contemporaries as an inevitable calamity for which the country's economy and morale had simply to be prepared as best they could. Martyn, by contrast, saw this enforced deindustrialization, the decimation of old trades and industries, not as a forthcoming disaster, but as a potential blessing which might eventually lead a country facing such commercial attack to higher glory and achievement than it had attained before. That wages in India were significantly lower than in England was simply a brutal fact of life. The flood of Indian textiles onto the English market was simply a classical instance of competitive underselling, but the East India trade was a very special case of international competition. It was in no sense the result of an aggressive Indian attack on Britain's commerce. Because of their distant location, the Indians were able to undersell the British only by the good offices of British importers themselves. It was the British merchants who rendered it possible to surmount the almost insoluble difficulties which India would otherwise have encountered had it attempted to dump its own low-cost products on English markets. The destruction of the portion of the English textile industry which found itself in direct competition with Indian imports was a consequence of Britain's own activity, a self-inflicted national wound.

But Martyn did not see this destruction as an index of complete insanity or a demonstration of the profoundly corrupt political preparedness to permit unemployment and misery among English home producers for the benefit of the profiteers of the East India Company.[141] He did not deny the damage which would be inflicted on

---

[141] D. C. Coleman, in his "Mercantilism Revisited," *Historical Journal,* 23 (1980), p. 783, argued that instead of seeing Martyn's ideas as a contribution to the inexorable rise of free-trade economics, one should rather consider it in the context of his support to the New East India Company created by the Whig government to embarrass the old company which had Tory leanings. Though Coleman's critique of Joyce Appleby's interpretation in *Economic Thought and Ideology of Seventeenth-Century England* (Princeton, 1978), pp. 168, 262, has some force, one should not

English manufacturing: those industries whose wage costs exceeded those of their Indian competitors plainly faced decimation. But he insisted that this very economic destruction itself created the painful impetus required to transform England's economy for market success in the future. Customers bought Indian textiles in such large quantities because they were cheaper than those of equivalent English products and of at least as high quality. Such consumption was the aim of producing textiles in the first place. To provide a broader range of customers with cheaper goods was the proper purpose of economic policy. One did not produce for production's sake or simply to maintain people in employment. What consumers needed was low prices and good value. Unquestionably, "the Indian are a great deal cheaper, than equal English Manufactures."[142]

The same quantity of Silk, or Cloth, or Callico, or other Manufacture, will cloath as many Backs, and Value of 'em will feed as many Bellies, whether procur'd by the Labour of one, or by the equal Labour of three. . . . if the Riches of the Kindom are not greater, they are not less for being procur'd by fewer Hands.[143]

To maintain more people in employment than was absolutely necessary to meet the needs of consumption was wrongheaded in principle. On that presumption even free gifts of goods which are now produced with great effort at home would be a menace to be refused. In such policies of job saving there was no coherent criterion for ever calling a halt. Cheap imports were just like any labor-saving device in their consequences:

If to make work for the People, a Law is made this Year to destroy the Trade of the East-Indies, some other such Law will be wanted the very next. We may well hope that in time the Navigation of the Thames, of every other River, will be destroy'd, that many may be imploy'd in the Carriage, which is now perform'd by few. By degrees, not an Art or Engine to save the labour of Hands, will be left in England.[144]

reduce historical interpretations to trivialities either. The intellectual continuity between Davenant's and Martyn's thought on the role of the East Indian trade are quite clear, despite the fact that one had connections to the new, the other to the old company. The short-term constellation of East India company politics lost their relevance by 1720 too, when Martyn's pamphlet was reissued.

[142] *East-India Trade*, p. 2.
[143] Ibid., p. 34.
[144] Ibid., p. 58.

To pursue a policy of protecting employment, in Martyn's eyes, would halt the entire process of economic development. To retain people in employment at the cost of uncompetitive pricing was self-defeating even in its own terms. "To imploy more Hands than are necessary is the way to make our Manufactures too dear for Foreign Markets." The loss of export markets would in its turn entail loss of work. And then, "when we shall be reduc'd to plain Labour without any Manner of Art, we shall live at least as well as the Wild Indians of America, the Hottentots of Africa, or the Inhabitants of New Holland.[145]

Martyn saw that England had already reached a stage of civilization in which attempting to reverse the pattern of economic development would entail a catastrophic fall in living standards. His emphasis on the contrast between the fate of the modern laborer and that of primitive peoples brought the arguments of Locke's celebrated analysis of property firmly to bear on the debate on the merits and disadvantages of the East India trade. Echoing the fifth chapter of Locke's second *Treatise of Government,* he insisted that

among the wild Indians of America, almost every thing is the Labourer's, ninety nine Parts of an hundred are to be put upon the account of Labour: In England, perhaps the Labourer has not two thirds of all the conveniences of Life, but then the plenty of these things is so much greater here, that a King of India is not so well lodg'd, and fed, and cloath'd, as a Day-labourer of England.[146]

To refuse to import Indian textiles did not merely prevent the day laborer from being better clothed. Since lower textile prices would require him to spend less on clothing, he could also with the same wages feed himself better as well. To obstruct this outcome by prohibition and protectionism was wholly indefensible.

What then would be the consequences for these civilized day laborers, once they permitted themselves to benefit from cheap Indian imports? Competition would certainly exert pressure on the labor costs of British products. Industries in direct international competi-

---

[145] Ibid., p. 58.
[146] Ibid., pp. 72–3. For an extended interpretation of this idiom in the formation of political economy from Locke to Smith see I. Hont and Michael Ignatieff, "Needs and Justice in the Wealth of Nations" in Hont and Ignatieff (eds.), *Wealth and Virtue: The Shaping of Political Economy in the Scottish Enlightenment* (Cambridge, 1983).

tion would try to cut their labor costs by cutting wages. And since Martyn supposed there to be a de facto national wage rate, he hoped that a reduction of wages in those industries would cause a lowering of wages throughout the country. As a consequence,

. . . some English Manufactures will be intirely lost by the importation of the like, at less prices from India; some that were imploy'd in those, will betake themselves to other Manufactures, and (as it always happens in a great increase of Labourers,) they will be forc'd to work at less Wages, and by taking less Wages themselves, they will force down the Wages of other People; the abatement of Wages will be universal.[147]

The contraction in the textile industry would therefore improve England's international competitiveness by lowering wage rates throughout the economy, and the resulting increase in exports would serve the economy as a whole. Far from merely filling the coffers of exporting companies or transferring wealth from the manufacturing to the trading sector through wage cuts, the resulting surge in exports would benefit the whole population. Employment would become much more secure. In the long run workers too would gain, as other products followed in the wake of cheaper textiles and benefited from the fall in labor costs. Nominal wages would for the most part be lower than before, but they would buy at least the same quantity of goods.

Martyn himself did not fully endorse this argument, seeing it as based on an idealization of the market's working and as failing to take account of the uneven impact of falls of labor costs on the prices of other products. It was a mistake to generalize from the price behavior of highly labor-intensive products, like fine textiles, to that of agricultural products, and especially to that of staple foods. The primary "necessaries" had only a limited labor content and thus had very little downward price flexibility. Because of this price rigidity, "the Labourer will be oblig'd to work more for Wages enough to buy the same conveniences of Life,"[148] and the supreme advantage promised by a civilized society of high living standards for laborers might rapidly disappear. There was, therefore, a real danger that if "the East-India Trade shall abate the price of Labour without abating the rest of the value of Things, it will render the price of Labour less in propor-

[147] *East-India Trade,* p. 9.
[148] Ibid., p. 63.

tion to the whole price of Things, it will consequently abate the Labourer's share of Things."[149]

In this case the suspicion of those opponents of the East India trade who sought to protect the day laborer's existing share in national consumption seemed all too justified. Rather than creating a buoyant economy to benefit all, to fight price competition by cutting wages would only lead to heavier workloads and gradual impoverishment for the laborer.

This was what a purely market model would have predicted, but, as Martyn emphatically emphasized, it was not what actually happened. Just as food prices were relatively insensitive to wage costs, in the real world existing wage levels also had a tendency to stick. "I am very ready to believe," he wrote,

> that the East-India Trade, by the importation of cheaper, must needs reduce the price of English Manufactures; nevertheless it is a Matter of Fact, that the wages are not abated. As much Wages are given to the Plough-man, to the Seaman, to the Weaver, to all kind of Labourers as ever heretofore; so that the East-India Trade by reducing the price of Manufactures, has not yet abated Wages.[150]

However, this in turn implied even greater dangers. If wages failed to drop, the day laborer's share in national consumption would be maintained at the high level which it had historically achieved: Indeed, it would be raised still higher, since wage earners could now benefit from the cheap textile prices. But the country as a whole would become even less competitive on international markets. Instead of prompting an expansion in both markets and employment, the competition created by the cheap imports would create a dual economy. While wages remained high for some, others would simply lose employment altogether. The rigidity of wage rates would have bleak consequences overall. "Few do the Business of many, but then the rest are forc'd to stand still; few possess themselves of all the Riches, and leave nothing for the rest of the People."[151]

At first sight this situation presented a distressing dilemma. High wages, insofar as they represented real purchasing power, were intrinsically desirable. But historically, achieved wages appeared to hold

[149] Ibid., p. 64.
[150] Ibid., p. 65.
[151] Ibid., p. 33.

their own level, irrespective of the viability of the economy. Hence high wage levels in an established manufacturing country must be accepted as an inescapable fact of life. Martyn did see one way of eluding the terms of the dilemma. Only a restructuring of the production process itself could enable such a manufacturing country to escape being undercut by cheap wage producers, because only such a restructuring could sever the link between wages and prices.

If the same product could be produced in less time or with less labor, then, Martyn argued, "the price of it must be less tho' the Wages of Men should be as high as ever."[152] In manufactured products the labor cost amounted to most of the price:

Wool is not dearer than so much cotton, Raw-silk, or other the unwrought Produce of India; wherefore, whatsoever the English exceeds in price the Indian Manufacture, the difference is not from the dearness of the unwrought Produce of England; this is not dearer, the Labour only that makes the English is dearer than the Labour that produces the Indian Manufacture; the whole difference of the price betwixt both Manufactures, is caus'd by dearer Labour.[153]

Hence for

any English Manufacture perform'd by so many Hands, and in so long a time, the price is proportionable, if by the invention of an Engine, or by greater order and regularity of the Work, the same shall be done by two thirds of that number of Hands, or in the two thirds of that time; the labour will be less, the price of it will be also less, tho' the Wages of Men shou'd be as high as ever.[154]

The first part of this solution was obvious enough. Dutch examples had shown that "a Saw-mill with a pair or two Hands, will split as many Boards as thirty Men without this Mill; . . . Five Men in a Barge upon a Navigable River, will carry as much as an hundred times so many Horses upon the Land," and the examples could be multiplied. Clearly, "Arts, and Mills, and Engines, which save the labour of Hands, are ways of doing things with less labour of less price, tho' the Wages of Men imploy'd to do them shou'd not be abated." But what would happen to all those whose labor was displaced, particularly if it was true that their reemployment would inevitably be hindered by the rigidity of wage levels? Those who were forced out of

[152] Ibid., p. 65.
[153] Ibid., pp. 82–3.
[154] Ibid., p. 66.

the textile and other manufactures would be unskilled for any other form of work. They would "betake themselves" to only "the most plain and easie" forms of work, "for plain and easie work is soonest learn'd, and Men are more perfect and expeditious in it."[155] How was it possible for them in such "plain and easie" and newly learned work also to earn high wages and still produce cheap goods for which a real market existed?

Martyn's solution to this paradox lay in the introduction of "Order and Regularity in Manufactures," or to use Adam Smith's later terminology, in the division of labor. Under the traditional manufacturing regime "the same Weaver is also to Card and Spin, and make the Loom, and Weave, and Dress, and Dye the Cloth."[156] Yet if each of these processes were to be made "his proper business, which shall be his whole and constant imployment," then he "must needs be more skilful and expeditious at his proper business."[157] Martyn's favorite example was one of the most highly skilled trades of his time, watchmaking:

A Watch is a work of great variety, and 'tis possible for one Artist to make all the several Parts, and at last to join them all together; but if the Demand of Watches shou'd become so very great as to find constant imployment for as many Persons as there are Parts in the Watch, if to every one shall be assign'd his proper and constant work, if one shall have nothing else to make but Cases, another Wheels, another Pins, another Screws, and several others their proper Parts; and lastly, if it be the constant and only imployment of one to join these several Parts together, this Man must needs be more skilful and expeditious in the composition of these several Parts, than the same Man cou'd be if he were also to be imploy'd in the Manufacture of all these Parts.[158]

[155] Ibid., p. 68.
[156] Ibid., p. 68.
[157] Ibid., p. 69.
[158] Ibid. This crucial argument appeared in *Spectator* No. 232 (November 26, 1711) attributed to Sir Andrew Freeport: "The Price of Labour may be reduc'd by the Addition of more Hands to a manufacture, and yet the Wages of Persons remain as high as ever. The Admirable Sir William Petty has given Examples of this in some of his Writings: One of them, as I remember, is that of a Watch, which I shall endeavour to explain so as shall suit my present Purpose. It is certain that a single Watch could not be made so cheap in Proportion by one only Man, as a hundred Watches by a hundred; for as there is vast Variety in the Work, no one Person could equally suit himself to all the Parts of it; the Manufacture would be tedious, and at last but clumsily performed: But if an hundred Watches were to be made by a hundred Men, the Cases may be assigned to one, the dials to another, the Wheels to another, the Springs to another, and every other Part to a proper Artist; as there

In the new manufacturing process "the less is left to the skill of single Persons" the better, leaving not only manufacturing but even assembly work firmly in the hands of specialists. Under these conditions products could be made better and more rapidly. The increase in productivity alone could serve to reconcile high wages with low product prices. Martyn himself was at pains to emphasize the limiting condition of this model. There must be sufficient demand for the products themselves to achieve the high volumes of production needed to generate high wages. This entailed considerable inflexibility in the variety of models which the new manufacturers could hope to produce economically. Martyn demonstrated this with the vital example of shipbuilding, generally seen as the prime instance of the cooperation of several artisans to produce a single complicated product. As Martyn realized, "It is one kind of skill to make the Keel, or Ribbs, or Planks, or Beams, or Rudders, or other Parts of a Ship of One hundred Tons, and another to make the same parts of a Ship of Five hundred; and in the same manner, the composition of Parts of different Scantlings and Dimensions must needs be different."[159] To really benefit from "the greater Order and Regularity of Work," from the improvement in quality and the saving of time in shipbuilding it was essential that "the Demand of Shipping shall be so great, as to make constant imployment for as many several Artists as there are several different Parts of Ships of different dimensions."[160]

The example of shipbuilding was crucial for Martyn. England was an island, and it was natural to see the future of the English as lying in maritime trade and fishing. Both of these required ships, preferably well and cheaply built. But although Martyn's discussion up to this point concentrated on explaining how a country with old established

---

would be no need of perplexing any one Person with too much Variety, every one would be able to perform his single Part with greater Skill and Expedition; and the hundred Watches would be finished in one-fourth Part of the Time of the first one, and every one of them at one-fourth Part of the Cost, though the Wages of every Man were equal." (*The Spectator*, ed. D. F. Bond, vol. 2, p. 404). The argument of Petty referred to here can be found in his essay "Concerning the Growth of the City of London" (1683), originally published in his *Essays in Political Arithmetick*. See Hull (ed.), *Economic Writings*, vol. 2, p. 473. It is sometimes argued that Martyn was a mere plagiarist of Petty's ideas. In the *Spectator* articles the debt to Petty was meticulously documented in each case.

[159] *East-India Trade*, p. 70.
[160] Ibid., pp. 70–1.

manufacturing could escape decline in the face of sharp price competition from low-wage Asian countries, in the field of shipbuilding a new, and in some respects antithetical, problem had arisen. If England wished to undertake large-scale shipping and to build ships for this, it must reckon with the very low prices of the Dutch shipbuilders. The Dutch, however, for Martyn were the very ideal of "order and regularity of work" in action. Although their workers enjoyed high wages, through their buying of raw materials in the cheapest markets and working with high productivity, it was hard to see how they could be defeated competitively in their own leading manufacture, shipbuilding, by another European country already laboring under the pressure of high wage rates.

The only way to undersell them would be to move production to where the raw materials were the cheapest, eliminating the costs of transport, and perhaps to a country where the wage rate was simply lower than it was in Europe. For England, as Martyn saw it, this would mean building ships in great volume in the North American colonies. Timber, tar, and other materials for the hull were sufficiently cheaper there to balance the costs of imported iron, sails, and rigging, which could be made only in England. Not only were materials cheaper. In addition, "the wages of Negroes are not so great as of the Dutch builders; the annual service of a Negroe might be hir'd for half the Price that must be given to one of these."[161] With new techniques even the Negro could build perfect and advanced ships:

To single Parts of Ships, single Negroes might be assign'd, the Manufacture of Keels to one, to another Rudders, to another Masts; to several others, several other Parts of Ships. Of which, the variety wou'd still be less to puzle and confound the Artist's Skill, if he were not to vary from his Model, if the same Builders wou'd still confine themselves to the same Scantlings and Dimensions, never to diminish nor exceed their Patterns. And of Ships for the same kind of Trade, and for ordinary and common use; when once a good Model can be found, why shou'd the same be often chang'd? . . . And, thus a way is shewn to build in our Plantations by the hands of Negroes, to render a Work of such variety plain and easie, to enable Negroes to build with as much skill as those in Holland.[162]

---

[161] Ibid., p. 117.
[162] Ibid., pp. 116–7.

The inflexibility of this process need represent no disadvantage. Though large ships and naval vessels were built individually to particular specifications, and thus could not be fitted into this technology, the issue here was rather the production of much simpler ships for the fishery, which needed them in great quantity. The Dutch could build their fishing ships cheaply, Martyn pointed out, because "the model of their Busses is seldom chang'd, so that the Parts of one would serve as well for every Buss" and the assembly could proceed "with mighty expedition." The consequences might seem a trifle conservative, but in the case of fishing barges, that is, "ships for the same kind of Trade, and for ordinary and common use; when once a good Model can be found," asked Martyn, "why shou'd the same be often chang'd?"[163]

For Martyn the price competition which governed the world of trade was a realm of constant change and flux. Once "things are successfully invented to do a great deal of work with little labour of Hands," the competitive process must just go on:

. . . every man must be still inventing himself, or be still advancing to farther perfection upon the invention of other Men; if my Neighbour by doing much with little labour, can sell cheap, I must contrive to sell as cheap as he. So that every Art, Trade, or Engine, doing the work with labour of fewer Hands, and consequently cheaper, begets in others a kind of Necessity and Emulation, either of using the same Art, Trade, or Engine, or of inventing something like it, that every Man may be upon the square, that no Man may be able to undersel his Neighbour.[164]

The new production processes transformed society at large. Every cost had to be minimized and every inefficiency rooted out. Transport costs must be cut to a minimum. By trade, profits would be cut back both internally and externally by concentrating on a high volume of sales. If this were done, then finding markets would be no real problem. Diminishing prices could make every sort of product available to an ever wider public, because the new manufacturing methods virtually created their own markets. There were no immediate limits to a continuous expansion of work for those forced out of their traditional employment by labor-saving technology:

[163] Ibid., p. 116.
[164] Ibid., p. 67.

. . . every individual Man in England, might be imploy'd to some profit, to do some work which cannot be done without him; at least, the contrary is not evident, as long as England is not built, beautify'd, and improv'd to the utmost Perfection, as long as any Country possesses any thing which England wants . . . some of these things might be appropriate to England; English Labour might be exchang'd for others; these things wou'd be imployment enough for all, and a great many more than all the People of the Kingdom' tho' every one were imploy'd to the best advantage.[165]

For Martyn, therefore, the English East India trade, far from being a grotesque policy of self-defeat prompted by the misguided activities of selfish merchants, was a catalyst for change which could stimulate a thorough modernization of the entire country, rendering England a successful commercial rival even to the Dutch. The East India trade exposed the English economy to "necessity" and underlined the imperative of effective competition, of "emulation." This was an advantage, since all inventions were the "effects of necessity and emulation."[166] to rise to such challenges was the sole way to prevent decline and the loss of the civilized living standard of the country's laborers, which had been achieved with such pains. There was no point in preserving inefficient industries, and no need to fear that the virtuous must suffer in the process. No industry could be undercut by others if it was truly efficient, but to keep employment by protecting one's own domestic market was a true recipe for impoverishing the economy. It would be "as well that the People shou'd stand still, as that they shou'd be imploy'd to no profit,"[167] which must eventually lead simply to pricing England out of international markets. To create employment for its own sake was no remedy for the displacement of labor resulting from weak international competitiveness. "A People," Martyn argued dismissively, "wou'd be thought extravagant and only fit for Bedlam, which with great stir and bustle shou'd imploy it self to remove Stones from place to place, at last to throw 'em down where at first they took 'em up."[168]

Not only must such processes eventually engender terminal decline. They must also guarantee the missing of new opportunities for industrial change. "Idleness, vain Labour, the unprofitable imploy-

[165] Ibid., pp. 54–5.
[166] Ibid., p. 67.
[167] Ibid., p. 76.
[168] Ibid., pp. 52–3.

ment of the People, which might be imploy'd to profit, is the loss of so much profit."[169] The only policy open to a manufacturing country intent on living from international markets and on preserving its riches was thus to accept the need for constant change. The only way forward was to look for new profits by making old products cheaper or developing new products. Just to stand still was not an option which history allowed.

It would be a mistake to regard Martyn's elegant solution to England's economic problems as a narrowly economic response to a political dilemma. It is true that he had a keener sense of the location of the economic constraints on political action in the new situation. But to see the issue as one of preserving the civilized way of life and material well-being of the majority of the population in the long run was to see it just as firmly as a political question. The reference to Locke's analysis of property was in no sense out of place in this pamphlet on the East India trade. The issues which it raised were weighty ones and at the center of the great emerging syntheses of political economy.[170]

One should not forget, however, that Martyn's view, like that of Locke himself and also those of Davenant and Pollexfen, was very much a view from the English metropolis. For an altogether more searching and critical (if less practicable) vision of the significance of the dilemma of commercial rivalry and popular economic welfare, it is necessary to look instead to the Scottish periphery, and in particular to the highly distinctive viewpoint of Andrew Fletcher of Saltoun.[171]

The republican and neo-Machiavellian dimensions of Fletcher's thought have long been stressed by John Pocock, and in more recent years other scholars, notably Nicholas Phillipson and John Robert-

---

[169] Ibid., p. 56.

[170] See Hont and Ignatieff, "Needs and Justice in the *Wealth of Nations*," and Hont, "The 'Rich Country–Poor Country' Debate in Scottish Classical Political Economy" in Hont and Ignatieff, *Wealth and Virtue*.

[171] There is no modern biography or comprehensive assessment of Fletcher's life and thought. The basic facts, the opinions of his contemporaries, and the flavor of various Fletcher mythologies can be found in the two older accounts of his life by G. W. T. Ormond, *Fletcher of Saltoun* (Edinburgh, 1897), and W. C. Mackenzie, *Andrew Fletcher of Saltoun. His Life and Times* (Edinburgh, 1935). Fletcher's collected pamphlets were published in eighteenth-century Scotland in 1732, 1737, and 1749. There is no modern scholarly edition, but see the accessible popular presentation of D. Daiches, *Selected Political Writings and Speeches* (Edinburgh, 1979), to which all the page references refer.

son,[172] have emphasized the unique depth and subtlety of his diagnosis of the economic, social, and political challenges that Scotland faced before its full union with England was consummated in 1707. What has not as yet been captured satisfactorily is the unique fusion of his analysis of Scotland's internal economic and political problems with his keen understanding of the changing structure of international relations underlying the Scottish predicament.[173] It was this fusion that provided not merely the grounds for the intensity with which he opposed the Union itself, but also the stimulus to the range and vigor with which he searched for an alternative framework for remedying Scotland's ills. The best presentation of this viewpoint is to be found in his complex and elusive pamphlet *An Account of a Conversation Concerning the Right Regulation of Governments for the Common Good of Mankind*.[174]

A full analysis of this fundamental work is beyond the scope of the present chapter, but it is essential to underline the main elements of the position which Fletcher defended in this dialogue.[175] In it he savaged the bland promise that the Union would be likely to favor the development of Scotland's economy, insisting that poor countries inevitably suffered in competition with wealthier communities more

---

[172] See J. G. A. Pocock, "Neo-Machiavellian Political Economy: The Augustan Debate over Land, Trade and Credit" in *Machiavellian Moment,* pp. 426–36; Nicholas Phillipson, "Culture and Society in the 18th Century Province: The Case of Edinburgh and the Scottish Enlightenment" in L. Stone (ed.), *The University in Society* (2 vols., Princeton, 1975), vol. 2, pp. 407–48; Phillipson, "The Scottish Enlightenment" in R. Porter and M. Teich (eds.), *The Enlightenment in National Context* (Cambridge, 1981), pp. 19–40; Phillipson, "Politics, Politeness and the Anglicisation of early Eighteenth-Century Scottish Culture" in R. A. Mason (ed), *Scotland and England, 1286–1815* (Edinburgh, 1987), pp. 226–46; and John Robertson, "The Scottish Enlightenment at the Limits of the Civic Tradition" in Hont and Ignatieff, *Wealth and Virtue,* pp. 137–78; Robertson, *The Scottish Enlightenment and the Militia Issue* (Edinburgh, 1985); "A. Fletcher's Vision of Union" in Mason, *Scotland and England,* pp. 203–25.

[173] Two earlier works of Fletcher, *A Discourse Concerning Militias and Standing Armies; with relation to the Past and Present Governments of Europe and of England in particular* (London, 1697), and the *Discorso delle Cose di Spagna* (Naples [in fact Edinburgh], 1698) together show his exceptionally clear grasp of the transformations in the seventeenth-century political world.

[174] With the subtitle *In a letter to the Marquiss of Montrose, the Earls of Rothes, Roxburgh and Haddlington, From London the first of December 1703* (Edinburgh, 1704), in *Selected Writings,* pp. 105–37.

[175] The dialogue was with the Scottish Earl of Cromarty and the senior English country party politicians Sir Edmund Musgrave and Sir Edward Seymour. Seymour was earlier an MP for Exeter and was primarily responsible for the leadership of the campaign for suppressing the Irish woolen trade.

from the limits of their productive skills and their premodern social structure than they benefited from their lower wage costs[176] and pointing challengingly to the poverty and stagnation of Wales over the preceding centuries of its political incorporation within the English Crown.[177] Without genuinely independent political authority to protect its interests, Scotland would find itself at the mercy of a purely market dynamics which it could do nothing to alleviate and subjected to the most relentless pressures of impoverishment as well as cultural corruption.[178] As the casual brutality of England's destruction of the Irish woolen industry just a few years earlier had demonstrated beyond challenge, Scotland could not have the slightest confidence that those who controlled the machinery of the English state and the parliamentary factions would hesitate for a moment to crush the interests of Scottish producers wherever these encroached upon the English national interest.[179] To form a union with England, so far from guaranteeing rising commercial prosperity and enhanced popular well-being in Scotland itself, would place the Scottish people at the mercy of English state interest and destroy their existing economy, cultural integrity, and capacity for autonomous political and social initiative.

[176] Cromarty, a supporter of the Union took a leaf out of the Irish debate and endeavored, Fletcher claimed, "by many arguments to show that our country would be the place, where all manufactures, as well of the use of the whole island, as for exportation, would be made by reason of the cheapness of living, and the many hands that Scotland could furnish." (*Account of a Conversation*, p. 119).

[177] Ibid., p. 120. This argument hit hard at the Anglo-Irish commonwealthmen who having learned a lesson in the woolen prohibition debates became convinced that the only way for their community based in a poor country to obtain the rights of free trade was to join with the English and the Scottish in a full and equal union. See Molesworth's famous preface to François Hotman's *Franco-Gallia* (London, 1721): "If we had not the example of those Masters of the World, the Romans, before our eyes, one would wonder that our own Experience (in the instance of uniting Wales to England) shou'd not convince us, that altho both Sides would incredibly gain by it, yet the rich and opulent Country, to which such an Addition is made, wou'd be the greater Gainer." (p. xx).

[178] The true promises of free trade could be estimated, Fletcher pointed out, if one paid attention to the theory of empires. The wealth of every empire, as Davenant and others suggested, would always gravitate toward the center, preserving the advantage of the imperial seat over the periphery. The province's benefits from the general circulation of goods and money would be cancelled by the monopolistic and centralizing nature of metropolitan markets. "A distinct sovereignty," Fletcher argued, "always enables a people to retain some riches and leaves them without excuse if they do not rise to considerable wealth" (*Account of a Conversation*, p. 118).

[179] See the opening motto of this chapter, taken from ibid., p.120.

More strikingly still, Fletcher insisted, these grim national prospects were simply a particularly stark and revealing indicator of the
harsh logic of military and commercial conflict among the European
rivals for the dominance of world trade.[180] Commerce assumed the
shape of war, he insisted, precisely because it was now considered not
only to be a means of obtaining foreign luxuries or of making the
common people more prosperous, but to be the foundation of military greatness and national glory. This transformation of older notions of the national interest placed quite new demands upon political
imagination. Peaceful commerce must be understood in terms of mutual interests, the interest of the international community, the interest
of mankind. But politics, the defense of the national interest, was
invariably conceived in terms of distinct societies and hence provided
no means for taking into account the rights, virtues, and interests of
others. The requirements of international society, the interests of
mankind as a whole, were simply beyond the horizon of politics:

Not only those who have ever actually formed governments, but even those
who have written on that subject, and contrived schemes of constitution
have, as I think, always framed them with respect only to particular nations,
for whom they were designed, and without any regard to the rest of mankind.
Since, as they could not but know that every society, as well as every private
man, has a natural inclination to exceed in everything, and draw the advantages to itself, they might also have seen the necessity of curbing that exorbitant inclination, and obliging them to consider the general good and interest
of mankind, on which that of every distinct society does in a great measure
depend. And one would think that politicians, who ought to be the best of all
moral philosophers, should have considered what a citizen of the world is.[181]

---

[180] As Musgrave put it in the dialogue; " We must not rely too much upon our own
speculations, or think the world can ever be rightly governed; but must take things
as they are, and consider the interest of the society in which we live. And if any
profitable trade be in the possession of our neighbours, we may endeavour to
dispossess them of that advantage for the good of our own society." Later he added,
"You do not consider that things just in themselves are not always so in relation to
government; that the condition of human affairs necessarily obliges those that
govern to attend the good and interest of the whole of society, and not to be
overscrupulous in doing exact justice to particular persons; especially if their interest should happen to be different from that of the community. And for this reason,
those countries which are most remote from the seat of the government ought not
to expect equal participation of liberty and immunities with those that lie at less
distance. For if they should enjoy the same privileges, the subjection of such
nations could not be secured." Ibid. (p. 126).
[181] Ibid., p. 132.

Fletcher had no doubt of the prospective fate of a world in which each state's interest and political agency were decided without regard to the general good of mankind. A world divided among violent, unjust, unnatural governments following the dictates of their best "advantage" in trade was not a world of *doux commerce* but of intensified general wars. Modern wars, as Fletcher and his antagonists agreed, had become "universal wars," engulfing "all Europe and America," along with "a great part of Asia and Africa."[182] Only a comprehensive and simultaneous reconstitution of the domestic political orders and the international relations of European societies could rescue international trade from the moral distortion and malignity which the geopolitical struggles of Europe's great powers had inflicted upon it.

International order could be preserved only if the European nations were organized into extended military alliances of roughly equivalent power.[183] Fletcher was not utopian enough to project a complete cessation of potential military aggression. But the systematic conflict that stemmed from commercial competition could be avoided only if no nation could hope for permanent advantage through aggression, if military conquest were indeed impossible. To regulate these less bellicose relations Fletcher envisaged an adaptation of some of the federative institutions of the Greek and Tuscan city-states, a system whose only recent examples were the Swiss Confederation and the United Provinces of the Netherlands.[184] He imag-

---

[182] Ibid., p. 129.

[183] This part of Fletcher's proposal, in the spirit of his earlier investigation of Spanish and French aspirations for universal monarchy in the *Discorso della Spagna*, followed a grand European tradition represented by the *Le nouveau cynée*, Sully's *Grand dessein,* or later the Abbé de Saint Pierre's *Projet de traité pour rendre la paix perpetuelle en Europe* and Rousseau's critique of it. See John Robertson, "Fletcher's Vision of Union" in Mason, *Scotland and England,* pp. 203–25.

[184] The incapacity for conquest was a well-known feature of the type of federal leagues such as the United "States" of the Netherlands, as Sir William Temple at one point called them. Talking about the military capability of the Dutch confederacy, Temple reminded his readers that, "the frame of this State (as of most great machines made for rest not for motion) is absolutely incapable of making any considerable enlargements or conquests upon their neighbours; which is evident to all that know their constitution." See his "A Survey of the Constitution and Interests," *Works,* vol. 2, p. 224. Fletcher's model was not drawn from the federalist theories in the law of nations, although Pufendorf, whose works he possessed, was a great supporter of such ideas. See his *Of the Law of Nature and Nations in Eight Books,* tr. B. Kennet, 3rd ed. (London, 1717), bk. 7. chap. 5. secs. 16–21. Rather, Fletcher was operating within the neo-Machiavellian tradition, moving from Machiavelli's best model for

ined a world of large defensive alliances built on successive layers of federal arrangements, a multiple union of unions.[185] Only political communities whose governmental institutions were structurally organized to protect the interests of their own citizens and which enjoyed the political and military independence that were prerequisites for this purpose were compatible with a system of international trade that respected in practice the rights of all human beings as well as nations "to the fruits of their own labour." The societies over which these more virtuous governments would preside would not display the corrupt dynamism of the England or France or Spain of Fletcher's day. They would lack their sinister courts, their repressive standing armies, and their huge unhealthy urban centers. In contrast to the military aggrandisement and the hectic rivalry for world domination to which these latter states were now as compulsively committed, the smaller and more autarkic communities which Fletcher advocated would also relate to one another, both militarily and diplomatically, in a less menacing and humanly wasteful fashion. The federal governments which were "the best to preserve mankind, . . . from great and destructive wars," were also the best to contain the "corruption of manners" and to guarantee "every part of the world that just share in the government of themselves which is due to them."[186] Fletcher did not imagine that the difference between poor and rich nations would thereby disappear. But within such a carefully balanced international

an empire, Rome, to the second best, the model of the Tuscan federation of city-states (see *Discorsi,* II.5.), thereby remaining a Machiavellian, but nonetheless correcting Harrington's and Davenant's adherence to the model of Rome and the notion of empires for expansion. Harrington knew of the option of taking the Achaian league, Switzerland, and Holland as a model, and recognized Machiavelli's admiration for such "equal leagues" but was not in favor of it (see *Oceana,* pp. 180, 324, 332.

[185] See Montesquieu's definition of federal societies on the model of equal leagues. Such a "république fédérative" was "a convention by which several bodies politic consent to become citizens of a larger state that they want to form. This is a *society of societies* who form a new one," *The Spirit of Laws,* bk. 9. chap. 1. Nugent's 1754 translation was quite imprecise in its phrasing, talking about a "kind of assemblage of societies." The problems of this translation and the blurred distinctions behind it are discussed by Martin Diamond, "The Federalist's View of Federalism" in *Essays in Federalism,* published by the Institute for Studies in Federalism (Claremont, Mass., 1960), pp. 21–66. For an excellent survey of the history of federative ideas in Europe see Koselleck, "Bund, Bundnis, Federalismus, Bundesstaat" in O. Brunner, W. Conze, and R. Koselleck, *Geschichtliche Grundegriffe. Historische Lexikon zur politisch-sozialen Sprache in Deutschland,* 6 vols., (Stuttgart, 1972–89), vol. 1, pp. 631–2.

[186] *Account of a Conversation,* p. 132.

order the rich would no longer be able to suppress the poor, and international trade would revert to its original godly design of satisfying the mutual needs of nations living under different climates and in regions with varying natural advantages.

In contrast with the English theorists of national greatness and virtue, Fletcher broke radically with the assumptions of Machiavellian politics, with their obsessive focus on the "mighty power of the Roman commonwealth" and their commitment to civic virtue as instrument of imperial expansion. In a trading world, competition had made the ancient Roman idea of benignly administered provinces simply incredible. "Whoever contrives to make a people very rich and great," Fletcher charged, "lays the foundation of their misery and destruction, which in a short time will necessarily overtake them."[187] What was now needed was a new conception of civic virtue which firmly repudiated the goals of imperial aggrandisement and sought instead to secure national political communities which had some real hope of proving "durable and lasting." Fletcher denounced all forms of constitution that lacked adequate provision for restraining "the desire of enlarging their dominions." Institutional restraints against the human desire for dominion were as indispensable among states as they were in the relations among individual citizens. For all the evident utopianism and the short-term practical irrelevance of his proposals, it was Fletcher's dark vision which offered the deepest analysis of the political dilemma of commercial competition for a territorial society of the early eighteenth century.

Today, as in 1704, there are two drastically discrepant images of the nature of international trading relations. One of these, classically formulated a century later in David Ricardo's doctrine of comparative advantage, sees international commerce without hesitation as a mutual exchange of (eminently self-interested) benefits that enhances the long-term interests of all participants and that is in its essence a true system of natural liberty.[188] The other, powerfully expressed by

---

[187] Ibid., p. 133.

[188] See David Ricardo, *On the Principles of Political Economy and Taxation* [1817], ed. P. Sraffa and M. H. Dobb, *The Works and Correspondence of David Ricardo,* vol. 1 (Cambridge, 1951), pp. 133–4: "Under a system of perfectly free commerce each country naturally devotes its capital and labour to such employments as are most beneficial to each. This pursuit of individual advantage is admirably connected with the universal good of the whole. By stimulating industry, by rewarding ingenuity,

Fletcher and echoed at intervals ever since by intellectual and practical champions of the weaker participants in international commerce,
sees it instead as a tense and unsteady field of force, constructed and
sustained in every instance by the disciplined, if sometimes intricate,
application of coercive power to the invariable advantage of the rich-
est and most powerful nations.[189] The foundations of these alternative
visions are now three hundred years old. The imaginative tug of war
between the two of them still lies at the very center of the understanding of modern politics.[190] Neither of these two evocative and drastic
images captures the economic limits on modern politics. None of us
has a genuinely convincing idea how to go beyond them. Rich nations
still fear those whose wages are lower. The poor still see themselves
as mere provinces living under the sway of rich metropolitan centers.
When, as William Temple noticed, the "Noblemen and Gentlemen"
countries turned to trade and usurped the traditional role of the free
states and cities specialized in commerce, a new era began. We are
still searching "for the right regulation of governments in the interest
of mankind" in the politics of distinct societies inexorably tied together in the erratic workings of the world economy.

and by using most efficaciously the peculiar powers bestowed by nature, it distrib-
utes labour most effectively and most economically: while, by increasing the general mass of productions, it diffuses general benefit, and binds together, by one
common interest and intercourse, the universal society of nations throughout the
civilised world. It is this principle which determines that wine shall be made in
France and Portugal, that corn shall be grown in America and Poland, and that
hardware and other goods shall be manufactured in England. Each country naturally devotes its capital and labour to such employments as are most beneficial to
each."
　　According to Robert Gilpin it is this Ricardian statement of the gains from trade
through comparative advantages and the harmony of interest doctrine which under-
lies the modern liberal view of international economic relations. See his *The Political Economy of International Relations* (Princeton, 1987), p. 174.
[189] Fletcher formulated his dilemma in terms of metropoles and provinces. The core–
periphery model of the world system offered by Immanuel Wallerstein and others
follows him in this tradition of seeing the international economy in terms of an
empire. Wallerstein and his school have written voluminously on this topic. For a
trenchant statement of the methodological perspective see his "A World-System
Perspective on the Social Sciences" in *The Capitalist World-Economy. Essays by
Immanuel Wallerstein* (Cambridge, 1979), pp. 152–1964. For an overview of these
options see Gilpin, *The Political Economy of International Relations,* pp. 65–117.
[190] See Robert Keohane's searching piece in this volume. (Chapter 5).

CHAPTER 3

The political limits to premodern economics

J. G. A. POCOCK

To speak of "the economic limits to modern politics" suggests that the modern state operates in a context, and within limits, set for it by modern economics; that there are economic limits to what the state can do. What, then, were things like before there were modern economics? Could "the state," or some other kind of political structure, do more than it can now that modern economics have arisen to condition it? I intend to show that this was by no means the case: that the efficacy of modern politics, its power and perhaps also its justice, have increased concurrently, though not exactly proportionately, with the increase in the efficacy of economic(s) arrangements: and particularly, with the increased efficacy of market mechanisms in human society. This is a major development in social history, and like all such developments it is attended with problems. We may be able to advance our understanding by some consideration of the way things used to be before they became what they are now.

Before I proceed with this subject, I had better explain the way in which I shall be presenting it. I look at the general history of society from the viewpoint not of an economic or even a social historian, but of a historian of social theory; a historian, that is, of the ways in which people have tried to understand and present the things that were happening to them in society. Professor Dunn has recently reminded us[1] that the history of social relations and the history of social perceptions never quite collapse into a single history; and without going too far into a difficult and partly irrelevant problem, it is worth pointing

[1] John Dunn, *Rethinking Modern Political Theory: Essays, 1979–83* (Cambridge University Press, 1985), p. 2.

121

out as a reason for this that the perception of a society by its inhabitants and its perception by a subsequent historian – which includes his
perception of their perceptions – are never conducted from exactly
the same point of view. We are fairly sophisticated historians and
social scientists; but historians and social scientists in a hundred years'
time (if there are any) will not perceive us quite as we perceive
ourselves, partly because they will know things we do not and will
have forgotten things we do know, but also because they will be
addressing problems and making assumptions other than those which
are occupying our minds now.

It is therefore a temptation to the historian to suppose that he knows
a past society better than it was known by those living in it; that what he
knows is reality, and what they knew only ideology. This is a ridiculous
piece of arrogance on his part, if only because experience is one of the
bases of knowledge; but from this it follows that he cannot altogether
share their perceptions of their society and even when he knows what
these were cannot take them as gospel in constructing his historian's
perception of that society and those living in it. He has to learn from
their perceptions, understand why they had them, and find means of
translating them into perceptions of his own. This is why a historian
like myself, who specializes in doing the latter sort of thing, must
become in some respects rather like a historian of literature, but of
literature considered as a source of social information.

I am dwelling on all this because my intention here is to explore
"the political limits to premodern economics" by examining what
people in some premodern societies had to say on the subject, or
rather on a variety of subjects which we may group together under
the phrase constituting my title (which is itself a modern phrase); that
is, by examining aspects of their value systems, their ethical and social
theories, and their perceptions of what to them were matters of practical concern. In many ways these premodern people lived in a mental
world unlike ours, in which what mattered was not setting economic
limits to politics or political limits to economics, but practical and
theoretical concerns structured in quite different ways. In seeing this
we can at least hope to understand ourselves better by realizing that
our mental world emerged from a quite different one.

So once upon a time there were no modern economics; what did
the world look like to people living without them? The trouble with

such a question is that there was truly no "*once* upon a time" about which you can ask it. What we mean by "modern economics" came into being about two hundred years ago in a few societies of Europe and America; and before that time in the West, and both before and after it in the rest of the humanly inhabited planet, there existed such a variety of human societies and social perceptions as to beggar the imagination. All attempts by historical sociologists – and there have been many – to construct antitheses between "modern" and what they all too often call "traditional" society break down when one recognizes the fact that "traditional society" is meant to include about 98 percent of recorded history and a far higher proportion of unrecorded history. The number of traditions required to constitute so much history must have been so vast that it becomes extremely doubtful whether the word "traditional" means anything whatever. It is used – and I shall not be using it very seriously – in an attempt to fix the characteristics of certain societies as they were before the rise of (1) the modern bureaucratic state and (2) modern national and international market mechanisms. A large part of the argument in which we find ourselves arises from the fact that these two great phenomena appeared at about the same time and for closely connected reasons. But when we talk about societies as they were before these appeared, we are in practice usually talking about societies in the premodern West, and it is a dangerous thing to try and extend our generalizations to the rest of the humanized planet. Japanese and other non-Western historians are now at work on the history of their societies before "modern economics" overtook them, and we had better attend to what they have to tell us. I shall not attempt to report on what they have to say, but I do want to make you aware that I am not doing this. Like any other Occident-bound historian, I shall be talking almost exclusively about premodernity and modernity in the history of the West. My only excuse is that I am conscious of having this limitation.

I have not yet finished with the word "traditional." It has very complicated origins, one of them being a distinction drawn by the Greek philosopher Aristotle in the time of Alexander the Great, when he addressed himself to questions of property, consumption, and wealth. He distinguished between what he called *oikonomika* – from which we form our word "economics" – meaning the management of a household, and something else which he called *chrema-*

tistika – meaning the acquisition of wealth. Aristotle was well aware, of course, that "households," which could be quite large families of masters and slaves, engaged in exchange relationships with each other, and that judicious management of exchange would increase the household's wealth. But there is in his thought a certain tendency to prefer – to give priority to – the notion of a household producing much of what it consumes and engaging in exchange with a view to increasing its efficiency as a consuming and producing mechanism; he certainly took it as settled that it was higher and nobler for a free man to be a consumer than a producer. Though he lived in a city which grew rich and powerful by trading Aegean oil for Black Sea grain, he did not think of households or cities as driven by a profit motive to expand their operations; if he knew this was happening, he thought of it as of contingent and not necessary importance.

From this there follow very important juristic, ethical, and philosophical consequences. Aristotle defined justice as distributive, and Roman lawyers over the next thousand years developed systems of jurisprudence in which it was defined as concerned with questions of mine and thine – *meum et tuum* – and of giving to each his own, *suum cuique.* This means, of course, that the tribunal, not the market, is the original home of possessive individualism, and that it is the imperial authority of the sovereign which defines the individual by defining his property. All juristic thought is about the necessity of right and authority to one another, and uses the same word, *jus,* to define each of them. But it means at the same time that we are looking at a world in which *chrematistika* are a good deal less important than *oikonomika,* and *oikonomika* – our "economics" – a good deal less important than jurisdiction. What matters to the household, and to the individual, is less the maximization of its efficiency as a producing-consuming mechanism than the definition and protection of its property. Economics, we may say, are still subordinate to property. The great "political economists" – we must return to that phrase – of the eighteenth century had no difficulty in pronouncing that a system of law which protected the individual's property was a prerequisite of the growth of a system of commerce and enterprise. What rendered them unique in history – and they knew it – was that for the first time the growth of commerce was becoming so important that defining something as property was becoming hard to distinguish from defining it as commodity. Yet the terms are not identical, and to understand the world before economics we must learn to think of them separately.

In such a world economics were subordinate to property, and it followed that politics, in a proper use of the term, were subordinate to jurisdiction. The great territorial sovereignties of premodern times – the Roman Empire, its Arab and Turkish successors, the kingdoms of Europe, the Confucian bureaucracy, the Tokugawa *bakufu* – were strictly speaking empires rather than polities. In the Western world at least, they exercised *imperium* or sovereign authority, which they used to centralize and control the administration of justice over vast areas; their juridical structures consisted of the codes of law they elaborated and the relations among magistrates, of whom one – the prince – must exercise *summum imperium,* which these codes defined. Our term for such structures of centralized and bureaucratized jurisdiction is "the state," but it is important to note that in the speech of early modern Europe, "the state" often meant not the structure controlling justice so much as the structure which made war and determined the policies that went with it. This is why we are able to say that "the state" ought to be subject to the "law"; and what disturbs us about the modern state is less that justice has become bureaucratized – it almost always has been – than that war and policy have. But if the great territorial empires were not precisely "states," they were not polities either; and under premodern conditions it is hard to talk of the relations of politics to economics, because the terms have not yet developed to the point where it is appropriate to do so. *Politika* to Aristotle meant the affairs of the *polis,* or city-state, and this was less a territorial jurisdiction than a community, commonwealth, or republic of citizens trying to live together in a moral equality based on the common possession of power and constantly finding themselves obliged to display both the equality and the power in war against neighboring populations. It will become important later in this chapter to see how modern politics and economics have developed in relation to the place of war in human life. For the present we need note merely that ancient politics were concerned with regulating a common morality and a common heroism, and displayed very little sense that *oikonomika* were important enough to interest them. If the city did not regulate the affairs of the household, it was not out of belief that the wealth of the city required leaving the household alone.

This is a point at which I should turn back to investigate the concept of a "traditional society" – though I have warned you that I do not like the term – less as it appears in the *polis* than in what I have been calling the "empire." If we imagine a world of highly localized areas, or markets, relating local producers to local consumers, with only a minimal development of exchange relationships between these areas and only a minimal apparatus of government necessary to control these relationships, we shall be imagining something not unlike the "natural" condition of society, or "state of nature," envisaged by the English philosopher John Locke. Locke was saying that a world of local settlement communities, doing no more than occupy the land and exchange its products among them, would have only neighborly disputes to settle and little need of any law to settle them by, other than the "law of nature," which each neighbor could understand and enforce for himself. In such a society there would be little role for complex systems of enacted and interpreted jurisprudence, or of centralized and bureaucratized systems of *imperium* to administer them; the individual would find his property, his rights and obligations, and to that considerable extent his social self, defined for him less by the decisions of the *polis* or the jurisprudence of the empire than by the law of nature expressed in the customs or traditions of the local community. If we imagine that community as one less individualized than Locke may have supposed it as being, and more as a patriarchal, familial, or tribal community, then its customs and traditions would assign each individual his place in the tribe and inform him that it was part of the order of nature that he should occupy it. The adjudication of disputes among neighbors would be simply a matter of restoring each to his place in a "natural" or "traditional" order. In this sense, the notion of a "traditional society" may therefore owe a good deal to the Lockean "state of nature."

It was with the invention of money as a medium of exchange, Locke observed, that appetites increased, that appropriation of surpluses became possible, and – above all – that actions and disputes became effective over wider territorial areas, thus generating the need for civil government. There was a relation between the velocity of exchange, the size of the market area, and the area of civil government, or what we call "the state." This is the point at which Locke became engaged in a theory of "political economy," in the sense that he was supposing the growth of a territory definable as both a national market and a national sovereignty, in which human relations were regulated by patterns of monetarized exchange, themselves regulated by jurisdiction, administration, and legislation on the part of a sovereign *imperium*. Locke was not alone in supposing this, nor was supposing it of any crucial importance to the politics of England in the 1680s, since both the national government and the national market had been effectively unified for several hundred years. Changes were beginning to happen in Locke's world, however, which would make this theoretical synthesis of an altogether new kind of importance.

Locke, notoriously, found no need whatever to abandon at this stage the concept that the law of civil government was fundamentally a law of nature. The growth of monetarized exchange relationships necessitated a much more active jurisprudence, a sovereign and legislating government; it obliged humans to become juristically, governmentally, and as we should say politically active in ways that they had not been before; but it did not annul the relationships that had subsisted among them in the strictly natural economy, and it did not mean that either the new relationships or the new government that regulated them did not belong to nature or to natural law. Money, we might almost say, did not abolish nature but perfected it. It was a consequence, of course, that the entrepreneur might justify the use of his property as an exchangeable commodity by appealing to the natural right he had to dispose of his property as an extension of his self; but it is another consequence that the extension of sovereign empire might still appear little more than a territorial extension and consolidation of what we call "traditional society." How far the empires of antiquity grew in consequence of the extension of monetarized exchange – "Whose image and superscription is this?" asked Jesus of Caesar's tribute money – might be worth investigating. It has certainly been possible to argue that the territorial empires and kingdoms were juridical and mercantile consolidations of communities in each of which the relations between inhabitants continued to be those of "traditional society," of the household, and of what Aristotle (and perhaps Locke) still meant by "economics" or *oikonomika*. Insofar as that term continued to refer to the household, it referred to an item of the order of nature and meant something very far removed from "political economy" or modern "economics." It can be argued that premodern territorial "states" claimed to rule by natural law and maintained the order of nature – employing such ideologies as scholastic Aristotelianism in Europe or neo-Confucianism in Tokugawa Japan – until such time as their inhabitants were overtaken by the politicoeconomic process identified by Locke, and the national market and the national government in combination swept away "traditional society," replacing it by social relations and personal identities constantly created and re-created by the dynamic forces of economics and politics, and transferring them from a world of nature to a world of history. Students of both European and Japanese social and intellectual history claim to identify such a process, taking place alike in the world of social relations and the work of concepts.[2]

So, it is said, we have been pushed out of a world of nature, in which our moral and social relationships are part of the order of the world in which we live, and into a world of history, in which they are constantly being remade by political and economic processes for which we must take responsibility even though we cannot control them. Modern politics and economics are part of the process of this historicization, and from my point of view it does not matter much whether the state regulates the economy or leaves it to the invisible hand. We can resist this line of argument only if we are prepared to believe (as some still are) that there is still a natural law operating through historical change, and that this natural law authorizes the workings of the market. There is, furthermore, what I shall term a possessive-individualism[3] thesis, according to which all this has come about primarily through the effecting of a move from *oikonomika* to *chrematistica* – from a state of affairs in which "economics" meant "household management," or controlling the doings of the small local communities of which I spoke earlier, to one in which "economics"

---

[2] The classic account of the process in European thought is that of Friedrich Meinecke, *Die Entstehung des Historismus* (in English as *Historism: The Rise of a New Historical Outlook,* London and New York, 1972); in Japan, that of Masao Maruyama, *Studies in the Intellectual History of Tokugawa, Japan* (Princeton, N.J.: Princeton University Press; Tokyo: Tokyo University Press, 1974).

[3] C. B. Macpherson, *The Political Theory of Possessive Individualism: From Hobbes to Locke* (New York: Oxford University Press, 1962). See also Joyce Appleby, *Economic Thought and Ideology in Seventeenth-Century England* (Princeton, N.J.: Princeton University Press, 1976).

meant the management of a national market kept in being by the individual's drive toward the acquisition of wealth. Proponents of this thesis argue that it is the growth of an individualist, acquisitive economy which has sparked the growth of the modern state and pushed us from a world of nature, in which what mattered was the just distribution of goods according to natural law, into a world of history, in which the relations of production are constantly transforming our lives and our selves. We have to decide how far this transformation can be managed by collective action within the structure of the state – that is, by "politics" in the modern meaning of the word. A powerful group among proponents of this thesis argues further that in the process we have lost control of our selves and the ways in which we are being shaped, on the grounds that the movement from *oikonomika* to *chrematistika* permits us to define the individual self only as one who claims rights and exerts them, or as one who maximizes needs and seeks to satisfy them, and that neither of these definitions of the self is adequate to the richness and complexity of actual moral and social life or permits us to manage it with sufficient regard to our moral selves. There are those who reply that the production and regulation of new goods and new conditions under which our selves may live satisfies our need for a more intensive moral life, and satisfies it in history rather than in nature.

In the remainder of this chapter I shall try to argue that this thesis (or model, or paradigm) of a shift from distributive to acquisitive economics is not fully adequate to explain what has been happening over the past two or three hundred years; not because it does not serve to describe many of the things which have been happening, but because it does not provide an adequate history of the ways in which the self has been described and defended during that period. An advantage of presenting my argument in this way is that it will enable me to return to my original title and explore some ways in which the concept of "politics" limited, or rather dominated, thinking about the productive and distributive foundations of life in the premodern world, as well as some ways in which it was itself enlarged and helped enlarge the understanding of "economics," as both these words moved toward being used in their modern senses. Up to this point, let me repeat, I have been talking about "government" rather than "politics," about the sorts of ruling activity which were known by such names as *jurisdictio, gubernaculum,* "governance," and *reggimento:* the activities of the sovereign authority in affairs of justice and affairs of state. To us it is natural to use the word "politics" when speaking of such things; but times can be found when *politika* meant the same as it had meant to Aristotle – the affairs of citizens conducting a community of moral action which was at the same time a community of heroic action. One of the fundamental premises of Western thought has been that "man is by nature a political animal," a being to whom it is part of his nature, part therefore of his self, to engage in *politika* and live if he can in a *polis*. The definition of the self has therefore been in part a political definition; the self whom some moralists have seen as deprived and lessened in the move towards a chrematistic society has been in part a political self. Here is a real and important sense in which "politics" can be said to have set limits to premodern "economics"; before the latter was ever heard of, the former had defined the moral universe in which it would have to operate.

To stress that heroic action was a component of this universe is a way of stressing the importance once possessed in the definition of the self by arms bearing and war.[4] Until at earliest a hundred years ago, it was taken for granted by all that the citizen must be also a warrior, and of course there are plenty among us who take it for granted still. For those of us who, in our abhorrence of modern war, wish to deny the necessity of this equation, it is a problem that most theories of political liberty state it as impossible that the individual should be a free citizen unless he bears arms and knows how to use them; as the most relevant of constitutional documents puts it, a well-regulated militia is necessary for the security of a free state. In Greco-Roman antiquity the hoplite or *quiris,* in the Middle Ages the knight or yeoman, under early-modern conditions the militiaman or minuteman based his political identity on the possession and use of arms. Feudalism was simply an interlude during which the free warrior needed a horse as well as a shield and spear, and for complex historical reasons usually possessed this equipment as a vassal or free dependent of another man. The productive infrastructure of the possession of arms was normally the possession of land, which guaranteed the arms bearer both his arms and the freedom to exercise them for

[4] J. G. A. Pocock, *The Machiavellian Moment: Political Thought and the Atlantic Republican Tradition* (Princeton, N.J.: Princeton University Press, 1975).

himself, and these in turn guaranteed that he possessed not only rights, but a voice to claim and regulate them: in other words, political individuality. This concept was older than feudalism, but so far compatible with it that it generated a certain nostalgia for feudalism among early-modern men. It does not require a society of masters and slaves, lords and serfs, or barons and vassals; but we may call it "feudal" in the technical sense that those who work the land, or control the labor that works it, possess the arms that ensure them the rights of proprietors and the share in self-government that makes them political beings. The concept of freedom thus arising, apparently archaic and irrelevant to the technology of the modern battlefield, has more to do with our modern thinking about politics than we sometimes realize.

It is hardly too much to say that the modern theory of political economy was born in the eighteenth century out of the breakdown of the underspecialized social world in which landowner, warrior, and citizen could be one and the same.[5] This identity mattered more in theory than in practice; the wars of the seventeenth century were fought by landless and masterless mercenaries, the underclass of urban and peasant society; but as these were transformed into standing armies of regimented professionals, maintained in both peace and war by states which for the first time possessed the fiscal and bureaucratic resources to make armies part of their structure, European and American theorists recognized two momentous changes that were occurring. In the first place, the individual was losing the capacity to use his own weapons and use them in the assertion of his political personality; whether the classes that lost this capacity were Polish nobles or American frontiersmen (or Indian tribesmen) was a separate though major issue. In the second place, this was coming about because the state now possessed a structure of credit, taxation, and coinage in which capital could be invested and the income used to pay the armies; it was not Locke's theoretical construct, though Locke himself took a hand in building it, but something different. The problem of capitalism for eighteenth-century theorists was not whether or how the state (or natural law) should regulate the investment of private capital in private enterprises, but whether and how private or

---

[5] J. G. A. Pocock, *Virtue, Commerce and History: Essays on Political Thought and History, Chiefly in the Eighteenth Century* (Cambridge University Press, 1985).

joint-stock capital should be invested in the war-making and govern-mental power of the state. In proportion as this happened, the mean-ing of the term "politics" must shift from the relations among citizens, defined as arms bearers and landowners, to the relations among rul-ers, representatives, and investors in a capitalist and war-making economy and empire. The United States was an empire, long before 1898, and found no difficulty in saying so.

This is the reason that classical republicanism – the theory of *politika* and *oikonomika* – came to be of such importance in the eigh-teenth century. It was (if you like the word) nostalgic, in the sense that it seemed to define the characteristics of a kind of political indi-vidualism from which the world was moving away; but it was by no means confined to expressing the nostalgias of declining landed aris-tocracies. The great democratic revolutions at the end of the century were in many ways aimed at restoring the warrior republics of antiq-uity. *Aux armes, citoyens! formez vos bataillons;* and make sure you don't turn into Napoleon's Imperial Guard in the process, as anyone with the slightest knowledge of Roman history can predict you will. A well-regulated militia being necessary for the security of a free state, the right of the people to keep and bear arms shall not be abridged. There is going to be a United States Army, but the state militias will check its dangers so long as they consist of volunteers owning their own rifles, and only on this uniquely underpopulated continent can empire expand without professionalizing the legions of Caesar Augus-tus. The framers of the Second Amendment knew of no handguns except dueling pistols, and Kentucky rifles were much closer to what they were thinking about; but I have read a British account of what occurred on a battlefield near New Orleans, and if my informant is to be believed, the riflemen caused them very little distress. The Penin-sula veterans stood grimly in reserve and watched inexperienced storming columns being smashed by grape from Jackson's and (I suppose) Lafitte's artillery.[6]

I am talking now of things we do not like to remember. Machine guns and barbed wire, bomber aircraft and tanks, nuclear technology and revolutionary guerrillas have given a bad name to the equation between autonomous citizen and patriotic warrior; yet it is very hard

[6] G. C. Moore Smith (ed.), *The Autobiography of Sir Harry Smith* (London, 1901).

to understand the history of politics, economics, and freedom without it. The point is that classical warrior politics continued to make their own kind of sense in the midst of financial and technological change all through the eighteenth century and made their own contribution to the birth of modern political economy. The Scottish fathers of the science were thinking only in a secondary way about the problem of whether the state should regulate the economy or leave it to the invisible hand of market forces – though that problem has its own history and I will turn to it before I conclude. What concerned them far more deeply was the problem of specialization, or division of labor: the process, occurring in history as they saw it, whereby social beings concentrated their energies on increasingly specialized and subdivided tasks, thus generating (they knew) an enormously more effective production and distribution of goods, but at the same time (they feared) enormously more narrow privatized and conditioned social personalities, human beings decreasingly capable of enjoying the increasing goods or of exercising the moral freedoms of citizens. The Scottish theorists recognized two crucial moments in the history of this deeply ambivalent process; and both were crises in the history of politics classically understood – understood, that is to say, by means of the assumption that freedom required the citizen to be a warrior and the warrior to be a proprietor.

The first moment had occurred in classical antiquity, when the Roman republic, having destroyed its enemies, was destroyed by its own soldiers. The extension of empire required the legionaries to become long-service professionals, serving in camps which were far from the cities; they therefore ceased to be citizens and became the storm troopers of their own generals in setting up a military despotism. Once they ceased to be citizens, however, the decay of their military virtue was only a matter of time, and the decline and fall of the Roman Empire was a reflex of the decline and fall of the republic.[7] The original specialization and division, therefore, the original sundering of the classical political self, had been the specialization

---

[7] The classical early-modern sources for this interpretation include Machiavelli, *Considerazioni sopra la Prima Decade di Tito Livio* (c. 1521); Montesquieu, *Considerations sur les causes de la grandeur des Romains et de leur decadence* (1734); Edward Gibbon, *History of the Decline and Fall of the Roman Empire* (1776–88); Adam Ferguson, *History of the Progress and Termination of the Roman Republic* (1783, 1799).

which divided soldiers from citizens and military from political capacity. It was this specialization, thought the maverick Scottish philosopher Adam Ferguson, which must on no account be permitted to recur in modern society.[8]

But Rome had risen and declined in an economically primitve society. It was the lack of an adequately organized internal market, thought all the Scottish philosophers including Ferguson, which accounted for the entire process. With the advent of money, the warrior peasant got into debt and had no way of avoiding debt slavery except going out with the legions to conquer new lands and capture new slaves to work them. Had there been a better market, he might have stayed at home to work off his debts as an industrious yeoman and generate an economy of industrious tradesmen into which the legionary might have been absorbed at the end of his military service. The specialization which separated soldier from citizen had been disastrous precisely because it had occurred in an underspecialized economy.[9] The history of Rome was, in a sense, an exemplification of the Lockean paradigm, an example of what happened to government once money had been invented; though it should be added that the Scottish historians seem to have thought rather little of Locke's economics, his politics, or his history.

The second crucial moment was occurring in their own time and was constituted by the concurrent rise of a commercial society, unified by patterns of investment and exchange, and a professionalized army under the state's control; the disproportion between the military power of government and the military weakness of the people had never been so great as it now was, at precisely the time when it was recognized that the purpose of government was to protect the people in their property, which was one reason Hume thought the latter function might well be discharged by an absolute monarchy.[10] But it had been recognized at the end of the seventeenth century that professional armies arose and flourished when commercial society became so efficient at the production and distribution of goods that individuals preferred to devote themselves to these processes, leaving

[8] Adam Ferguson, *An Essay on the History of Civil Society, 1767,* ed. Duncan Forbes (Edinburgh: Edinburgh University Press, 1966), p. 230.

[9] Ferguson's *Progress and Termination* is the best eighteenth-century exposition of this thesis.

[10] Duncan Forbes, *Hume's Philosophical Politics* (Cambridge University Press, 1975).

their defense in the hands of professional soldiers and (it might follow) their government in the hands of professional administrators. At the end of the feudal period, in short, the problem of specialization recurred in the form it had taken at the end of the republican period. It was Adam Smith who deepened the whole analysis by linking the specialization of the professional soldier with the division of labor which enhanced the processes of production. Many single-skilled operatives, he pointed out, combined to produce technologically sophisticated products without themselves becoming sophisticated technologists. Of these products the military musket was as good an example as any, and the least skilled operative involved in its production and use was the private soldier who worked it in the drilled regiments of European warfare; he needed to know no more than how to obey words of command and pull a trigger.[11] Hence, we may observe, the historical symbolism of the possibly mythical American frontier rifleman; like the hoplite or the longbowman before him, he was a plebeian warrior skilled enough in a technology he could own for himself to operate as an individual on the battlefield or in democratic politics. Unfortunately, it was to be the role of the rifle to help restore the superiority of massed defensive firepower and bring us by stages to New Orleans, Cold Harbor, and the Somme. Iraq and Iran, it seems, were diligently repeating the process in the war of the Persian Gulf.

None of this troubled the dreams of the Scottish philosophers; nor did they diagnose the democratic revolutions as attempts to get arms back into the people's hands, while bringing under popular control the financial as well as the military structure of the eighteenth-century state. Among Thomas Paine's most original propositions is his perception that a national debt is perfectly compatible with an arms-bearing democracy; he insisted that it was only aristocratic control that corrupted debit financing.[12] But the Scotsmen, living in and accepting an aristocratically governed society, were in no doubt that a landed elite was still competent, and necessary, to govern an increasingly commercial society and control the nonbenign aspects of its increasing specialization. The eighteenth-century private soldier was too unskilled a

---

[11] Adam Smith, *An Inquiry into the Nature and Causes of the Wealth of Nations* (1776; Glasgow edition, New York: Oxford University Press, 1976–9; Liberty Classics reprint, 1981), vol. 2, pp. 699, 707–8.
[12] See Pocock, *Virtue, Commerce and History,* pp. 288–9.

military proletarian to be himself of much danger to the liberties of his fellows, so long as he was officered by the nobility and gentry of the country; what was dangerous about him was that he drained off the military capacity of his fellow citizens and thus lessened their political capacity. This danger was the price to be paid for so enormous an advance in comfort, civilization, and morals that the process could not possibly be reversed, and should not be; but it was a danger, and to meet it patrician rule, thought Smith and Ferguson – democratic rule, thought Paine and Jefferson – was still a necessity.

I have been emphasizing the military component in eighteenth-century social theory as a deliberately dark and uncomfortable way of making the point that – at the level of theory, which is where I am operating – the political limits to premodern economics took the form of a doctrine of the unspecialized and multicompetent self, which came increasingly into conflict with economics as the latter became more modern. It is not comfortable to realize that the classic expression of this doctrine lay in the assertion that a man (and not a woman) must be both soldier and citizen, that keeping, bearing, and using the weapons of death were considered essential to the unity of the self. We do not want to believe this after a century of unimaginable warfare which has given heroism a bad name, but it is a fact of history that this has been cardinal doctrine, and the implications of the fact go beyond the horrors of war. We rebel against the assertion that the highest development of humanity leaves us nothing to be or do except speak in the assembly and do combat on the battlefield, and that the most powerful modern exponent of this thesis, Hannah Arendt, was a woman seems to us odd, to say the least. But the philosophers of the eighteenth century (most of whom were males) rebelled against this assertion as heartily as anyone could. They thought it cramping, restrictive, harsh, and barbarous; they were keen critics of classical antiquity; they thought the Romans doomed by the lack of an internal market to devastate the world and destroy themselves, and the great Republic not all that different from a Tartar horde. They were entirely clear – and said it again and again – that in the process whereby commerce had replaced conquest (which was their way of putting it) human beings had become increasingly capable of producing goods, moral as well as material, and exchanging them with one another on a scale and with a variety never known before, and that this had made the human personality capable of developing needs of its own and means of satisfying them, depths of sentiment and sympathy with its fellows, which made the antique hero – even the antique artists and philosopher – look stiff, archaic, and incredibly limited. It is profoundly wrong to think that neoclassical social theorists were nostalgic for antiquity; they were harshly critical of it and knew themselves to be moderns.

But antique man had possessed one characteristic which it was dangerous to have lost. He had been a citizen, capable of joining with his fellows to make decisions governing his own life in all the things that mattered. His commitment to the warrior ideal – his heroism – had been the outward and visible sign of his political capacity and of the unity of will and capacity which only political life could produce in human beings. The capacity to keep and bear arms had been given up into the hands of professional soldiers, only rather recently – almost within the lifetime of the Scottish philosophers – and an effort to restore it to democratic possession was about to emerge. (The Scottish philosophers, dismayed by their own people's inability to defend themselves in 1745 and anxious to establish a militia in Scotland, were part of that enterprise.)[13] What lay behind this, more significantly than behind their nascent criticisms of the industrial process, was a profound appreciation of the huge civilizing power, and the huge moral danger, of specialization of function and division of labor. In the last analysis, it was this which had made possible the diversification of goods, of human needs and ways of satisfying them, and of human types and personalities themselves which made modern society utterly different from ancient society and a great deal more sympathetic and attractive (these are themselves eighteenth-century adjectives). But there was a counterdanger which simply would not go away. The specialization which made all this diversification possible might be producing an increasing number of human personalities so highly specialized that they were capable of doing and enjoying only one thing, and so were incapable of enjoying the vast diversity of modern society or contributing to it. There might be a moral, as well as material, poverty in the midst of plenty. The Scots who worried about a possible excess of specialization were not thinking exclusively

---

[13] John Robertson, *The Scottish Enlightenment and the Militia Issue* (Edinburgh: John Donald, 1985).

about the pinmakers and proletarians and morlocks[14] at the bottom of the industrial pyramid; they feared the effects of this moral impoverishment at elite social levels as well, and this once again explains the importance in their thoughts of the ancient citizen, with his union of political and military capacity. They were not naive or romantic seekers after heroism, but they asked insistently whether a society which renounced heroism altogether could retain its freedom. The irony is that heroism was about to go into mass production, with results not altogether beneficent to freedom; but that only means that the problem has not gone away. Meanwhile, the Scottish philosophers were beginning to ask whether the assertion of rights or the protection of one's property, the maximization of one's needs, or the refinement of one's manners, even the pursuit of happiness itself or the free and open-ended choices apparently offered in a consumer society, satisfy the self's need for a moral and political unity within itself. It is typical of the strange reversals of meaning which constantly happen in the history of words that the qualities which indicate the presence of this unity were once spoken of as the "liberal virtues," and that we now use the term "liberalism" to denote a society and a scheme of values in which it is precisely these virtues which are constantly said to be lacking or at risk.

"The political limits to premodern economics," then, can be said to indicate a scheme of values in which the ideals of the ancient *polis* first functioned in the absence of a modern economics and then articulated in the form of a trenchant and enduring criticism the dangers presented to them by its rise. The infrastructure of these ideals in the worlds of matter and power may be found in the premodern state's lack of a monopoly of coercive force, and the conditions which obliged it to leave the means of homicidal coercion in the hands of proprietors – whether feudal or not – thus constituting them as political beings. But this means that the *polis,* and the idea of the *polis,* flourished in the relative weakness of the state, a premodern politics in the absence of a premodern economics. In turn, this strongly suggests that modern politics and economics arose and flourished together, that the national state and the national market are not antithetical but symbiotic (as John Locke may be said to have perceived).

---

[14] The Eloi and Morlocks of H. G. Well's *The Time Machine* (1895) are a social Darwinian science-fiction projection of the specialization of labor.

To speak of the mutual limitations of economics and politics, then, requires us to execute a complex shift from a conceptual politics founded on the values of the ancient *polis* to another founded on the values of the state, and apparently modern in character. But there is a difficulty here, whether we are talking of values or of practice; what we call "the state" is not exclusively modern in character, but can be seen as the historical descendant of what I described earlier as "the empire," that is, the territory governed by the jurisdictional and administrative authority of a monarch. There is a sense in which we need to return to this structure and its language, and trace the concurrent growth of the national market and the national jurisdiction, considering this to be the process of which ancient politics were used to keep up a constant and telling criticism. The growth of the term "political economy," occurring so prominently among eighteenth-century theorists, is a valuable index to this process, since it states, unequivocally if by implication, that "economics" is no longer the management of the *oikos,* or household, but of the state, while "politics" is no longer the conduct of the *polis,* or city, but of the managed territorial jurisdiction which we name "the state."

If we ask how the adjective "political" came to be used as it is in this phrase, part of the answer must lie, I think, in the history of certain words like the English "policy" and the French *"police,"* which may be ultimately derived from the Greek *polis* but have come a long way from it. "Policy" appears as the title of a fifteenth-century English poem, *The Libel of English Policy,* which exhorts the king to use his authority to discourage the export of necessities, including bullion, in exchange for luxuries; however archaic its economics, the poem clearly declares that the realm is a market, which may enjoy a favorable or unfavorable balance *and* that "policy" denotes both the problems and the management of this state of affairs. The king and his commonwealth will be stronger or weaker, better or worse, in consequence of their management of it. *"Police"* appears in the title of a French royal officer of the seventeenth century, the *prévôt de la police,* whose duty was to see that the great street produce markets of Paris were kept clean and decent – *poli* – and that prices were not allowed to fluctuate too widely. In consequence, the word *police* came to be used to denote both the art and science of urban administration – this is why we call our law enforcers policemen –

and the art and science of ensuring that rural produce was brought into the cities and a national market maintained. This is how Adam Smith uses the word, adapted into English. To say that the function of a state police is to ensure the free workings of a national market seems odd to us, but would not have seemed at all odd to our ancestors in the eighteenth century. Jurisdiction must be national, and so must the market. There were revolutions to ensure the breakdown of internal trade barriers and unify the state, if the monarch would not do it.

All this sounds to us like mercantilism, and we think of Adam Smith as the great apostle of the view that the free flow of goods within the national community – *police* – and between one national unit and another – policy – did not need the intervention of the state but was better left to the workings of free-market forces. We set Smith in opposition to his English predecessors like Sir William Petty, who had founded a science called "political arithmetic," the study of demographic, productive, and distributive data as these made the nation richer or stronger, or his German contemporaries who were calling the same science "statistics," the quantification of data by the state for its own purposes. In such terminology we can see the term "political" moving away from its Greek meaning to denote the activity of agents within a state which is adding policy and *police* to its older concerns with jurisdiction and war. But Adam Smith and his associates did not come to halt these processes and aimed neither to abolish the term "politics" nor to restore it to its classical significance. On the contrary, they continued to call themselves "political economists," and Edmund Burke once called them "economical politicians"; more strikingly still, Smith called his great treatise *An Inquiry into the Nature and Causes of the Wealth of Nations* – not *of Individuals*. It is nations which will increase in wealth if they leave individuals to pursue their own interests and abstain from using *police* to regulate the market or policy to expand the state's jurisdiction in the creation of unnecessary empires. But this does not mean that either *police* or policy will disappear, only that they must from now on be conducted with a vastly enhanced prudence; and it does not mean that the association between wealth and power is to disappear. To the first Chinese and Japanese visitors to nineteenth-century Europe, it was self-evident that the free-market economies of the Westerners were what made them powerful and aggressive states.[15] "Politics" now denoted the conduct of the policy and *police* of such states, expanding their internal and external power in consequence of their engagement in market processes they did not attempt wholly to control. To the individual – above all to the intellectual – it meant his involvement in the life of such a state, which expanded its power by recognizing his freedom, but no longer treated (if it ever had) his participation as defining his moral personality or minded very much what sort of moral personality he had. He had to decide whether he felt liberated or alienated by this indifference, which is why the term "liberalism" is now used as a term of reproach, both by conservatives, who fear that it is not libertarian enough, and by radicals, who fear that it is not liberating enough.

[15] Benjamin I. Schwarz, *In Search of Wealth and Power: Yen Fu and the West* (Cambridge, Mass.: Belknap Press, 1964).

CHAPTER 4

On some economic limits in politics

FRANK HAHN

A preface

When the subject matter of this essay was first suggested to me I found it interesting, but it was quite unclear how the question "What are the economic limits to modern politics?" could be made sufficiently precise to call forth a grammatical answer. As I set about thinking and reading, some kind of order came to be imposed on the question – indeed, so much so that the answers seemed almost inevitable. What I had not bargained for was that I would not at all like the answers. Indeed, they bear a close family resemblance to propositions found in Hayek's *Road to Serfdom* (1944), a book which in my youth I detested. Yet it seems that recent work on agency and information has strengthened rather than weakened the force of Hayek's arguments. I still hope that there are counterarguments which I have neglected or flaws in my own reasoning, for in this case my inclinations and findings are in conflict. The reader is invited to consider what follows with a critical eye in the knowledge that the author would not be displeased to find that he has been mistaken.

I

We must eat and drink to live. If follows that arguments designed to convince us that the good life can be led only in arid deserts are intrinsically uninteresting as political arguments. Much of political theory and discourse is concerned with the good society which facilitates the good life. A simple first question is not whether the "good" really is good (although *that* is important) but rather whether it is feasible. If we can show that this or that proposal is not feasible, then we have shown it to be uninteresting as politics (although it might be interesting in other ways – for instance, as poetry or reflections on the human condition).

It is, however, rare that a feasibility test is so simply concluded as in the case of a proposed good society in which we cannot eat and drink. Indeed, the test of feasibility is complex and subtle and I fear rarely conclusive. Certainly in the hands of coarse politicians it has often been used to discredit opponents on grounds which go from incoherence to silliness. This is particularly so when "economic" feasibility is the test. Here intellectual incompetence often combines with self-interest to produce an unlovely mess. To avoid the worst of the traps I propose to start in a rather abstract and arid way, but only briefly.

In the first instance I want to distinguish between two quite different kinds of feasibility, which I call *transition feasibility* and *equilibrium feasibility*. At any moment we live in a particular society. Let us call it A. We are to consider a good society. Call it G (which is different from A). Transition feasibility questions ask: Is it possible to make the transition from A to G? Equilibrium feasibility asks: Is G feasible? These two questions are quite different, but it may well be that a negative answer to *either* is sufficient to rule out G. The distinction I am proposing is the main one I shall want to make, but I have found that it is not quite fine enough, for often we are urged to accept G and told that the transition can be made in a certain way and within a more or less limited period of time. Questions concerning the feasibility of such proposals I shall call questions of practical feasibility. A proposal of G may thus be found transition feasible while the actual transition proposal does not meet the test of practical feasibility.

It would be nice to be able to say that this is the end to classification. But one must face the obvious fact that proposals may be infeasible in any one of the senses I have given in different ways. For instance, a proposal that in G the nuclear family has been abolished while the young happily care for the old raises questions of our psychological possibilities. Yet the proposal that in G factory production has been abolished but the material conveniences of life have not raises quite different feasibility considerations. Obviously no precise categorization will be possible, and ideally the various aspects of feasibility should be considered together. But I am unable to do that, and I shall therefore concentrate on *economic* feasibility. I shall give this a definition which may seem somewhat odd. Feasibility questions will be classified as economic if there is a prima facie case that a professional economist in that capacity would have a special expertise in considering them. This sounds evasive, and it is. What it evades is tiresome definitional questions. What it accomplishes is an emphasis on the limited nature of both question and answer.

It goes without saying that, insofar as political proposals are logically coherent, feasibility questions must be answered on the basis of what we now know of the world. This may be thought disabling, but it is not. A proposal shown to be infeasible on our present knowledge can be ruled out as politically uninteresting unless the proposer can convince us that he has knowledge which we do not have. But knowledge may not be as straightforward as this suggests. Our knowledge will often be of the following kind: This and this is extremely unlikely (or likely). That is, it will be in the form of, say, a probability distribution. It is in the nature of this sort of knowledge that probability distributions may differ among people. Thus some may attach a high probability to genetic engineering being possible within the next ten years, others a low one. Discussion may bring about convergence but not necessarily identity.

It is the form of our knowledge and not its temporal dependence which causes difficulties. We often cannot declare a proposal to be feasible or infeasible but only give our degree of belief in one or the other eventuality. The question "Is this proposal feasible (in any of the ways given)?" may thus not have an answer. Whenever this is the case I shall speak of *uncertain* feasibility, whether it is of the transitional or equilibrium variety. However, it should be noted that even in these cases it may be possible to be definite as when we say, "It is not feasible to act on the belief that feasibility is certain."

I have used the phrase "politically uninteresting" in relation to infeasible proposals. This may be disputed. For instance, there have recently been a number of books devoted to the political interest of utopias, which do not depend on the latter's feasibility. One may think of these as ideal states – just as a perfect vacuum is an ideal state – which serve to organize our thinking even if the states are "ideal" in the sense of "infeasible". This view clearly has some merit, as does perhaps the advice that our aim should exceed our grasp. But I shall here be thinking of G not as a theoretical, but as a practical goal of political action and argument.

II

I now want to be more concrete. This I find easiest in the context of a well-known infeasibility proposition which in its modern form owes a good deal to economists. The proposition is this: "If the good society gives considerable weight to liberty, then it is neither transition feasible nor equilibrium feasible to depart from a private property market economy."

It seems, alas, necessary to spend some time on the notion of "liberty" before I proceed. This is, of course, a well-trodden path, and one could simply follow John Stuart Mill (1982) (as Hayek does) or Isaiah Berlin (1969) (which however would leave the concept somewhat flabby). But I want to argue that for my present purposes the portmanteau concept of liberty is too abstract and ill defined to be usable.

Suppose we want to rank situations A and B in which an individual may find himself by the relation "no less liberty than." So if we write $A \ L \ B$ we interpret it as saying that this individual has a much (or more) liberty in A as he has in B. One criterion on which such an ordering could be based is that the set of choices open to the agent in A includes the set of choices open to him at B. If we adopt this view, then we must rest satisfied with a partial order since there will be many situations for which no set of choices is a subset of another. But a partial order will not do. For example, if private property is abolished, some choices are preserved but others may be added: for instance, a choice of not competing with others. Moreover, such an ordering treats all choices alike – it does not value them. Recall what has been said concerning the liberty of the poor to sleep under bridges.

Suppose next that individual agents have a complete ordering of social states by the criterion L. It might then be thought that from this we could derive a social ordering by L. To this there are at least two objections. First, since it is not at all obvious that Arrow's axioms do not apply here as in the familiar case, such a social ordering may be impossible (Arrow 1951). Second, it is not obvious that such an ordering would be relevant even when possible, for it may be part of G that it has brought it about that individuals are different in their preferences and liberty ordering than they now are. To this must be added that it may well be held that liberty of a certain kind is what people should want, which is not the same as what they now want. For instance "socialist man" is not Mr. Rupert Murdoch. I return to this matter again later.

From all of this I conclude that liberty is one of those aggregating concepts (like GNP) which is not suitable for more than a first rough survey and certainly not suitable for my present enterprise. (For instance, economists know the chasm which lies between comparisons of GNP and comparisons of welfare.) Subaggregates like "economic liberty," "personal liberty," and "political liberty" go some of the way but not far enough. For the analysis of feasibility there is no alternative to enumeration. One needs to know what choices are given and freely made in G and which choices are not given and cannot be made. It may then be open for us to say that there is less or more liberty in G than in the present society, but for feasibility we need to say nothing of the kind. For we are interested in only two questions: Are the choices enumerated as available in G compatible with G being an economy without private property and markets? And could G maintain this economic structure if it were to permit other choices which one may regard as desirable from the point of view of liberty? It is important to remember that these are two different questions. But I shall have to return later to argue that the questions may not be properly phrased.

Let me now be quite specific and consider Hayek's arguments in his *Road to Serfdom*. This book was designed to show that socialism with liberty was neither transition nor equilibrium feasible. The argument will be very familiar (Milton Friedman 1963, has, if nothing else, seen to that). Agents in their actions are governed largely by private concerns and projects. A capitalist market economy, as Adam Smith was among the first to note, ensures that the privately motivated activities of many agents results in an efficient use of a society's resources and an allocation which reflects the private concerns of individuals. In addition, the institution of private property permits political independence of some sort to individuals and in various ways limits the power of the state. In an economy which is not a private property market economy, efficient production requires central direction of economic activity. Individuals are no longer able to make choices according best with their private interests. Choice must be replaced by command. To command requires power, and power feeds on itself (corrupts). Those who can command resource use will soon command other spheres like education, art and science. Moreover, it is not possible to have those who command chosen by the commanded. The transition to such an economy – say, by the mixed or regulated economy – is characterized by a successive narrowing of economic choices and subjection to bureaucratic direction. It is thus no more possible to combine the transition with liberty than it is to do so in the end state. Thus it is not feasible, and so not coherent, to aim at a socialist society with liberty.

It is clear that some of these arguments fall outside those concerned with what I have called economic feasibility. It is also apparent that the argument as here given has just that lack of precision in referring to liberty which I have said it would be desirable to avoid. I will accordingly proceed by a series of steps.

Let us say that a socialist society is one in which private individuals do not own the means of production. That means that such individuals cannot choose how to use them by virtue of ownership, nor are they entitled to the return from their use. But someone must choose how to use them, and someone must decide on the destination of the returns from their use. Moreover, somehow the accumulation of the means of production must be determined.

The first suggestion, much discussed in the thirties by, for instance, Lange (1936, 1937) and Lerner (1944) and more recently by Hurwicz and others, is that socialism should mimic perfect competition capitalism. This it does by instructing managers to behave like perfect competitors. This proposal derives from what is known as the second fundamental theorem of welfare economics. I shall not state it here but observe that it assumes that the center has aggregated all private information so that it knows all private production possibilities and all preferences. This is an uninteresting assumption. If it is not met, then the center must elicit truthful private information and that requires it to provide incentives for truth telling. In the latter, one of course includes truthful revelation of attitude to work and performance of what has been revealed. All this has two consequences: The distribution of income will now be, at least partly, tied to the incentive need and there will be losses in economic efficiency. To this one must now add that the whole proposal rests in any case on a profoundly unsatisfactory underlying model which has nothing to say on the Schumpeterian element of innovation and enterprise. To provide for these, further incentive problems would arise with further consequences for income distribution.

The end result of this kind of market socialism is that it will not differ much from redistributive modern capitalism, except that citizens may have little say in the choice of distribution. Not only would confiscation of the means of production simply replace the former owner by the manager, but the latter would require incentives related to returns to make proper use of them and to accumulate them at the proper rate. There is in this market socialist society no intrinsic reason why it should not be combined with political democracy except that privatization of the means of production would be excluded as a political choice. There would be some small loss of liberty, but it would be hard to argue it would be incompatible with liberty.

But, in fact, this kind of market socialism is not really feasible. The computational complexity as well as the innumerable messages between the center and individuals which it requires simply rule it out of court. Moreover, by retaining a strong connection between performance and reward, it negates the underlying socialist motives for not permitting private ownership of the means of production. For instance, it would be necessary to reward the proper use and accumulation of resources, and that is precisely what gives rise to "exploitation" in a capitalist society. This is quite different from centrally withholding from labor some of the fruits in order to accumulate. In that case the withholding does not benefit any particular private person.

The alternative to mimicking the market is a command economy. A society with such an economy must find a substitute for the incentives of a market economy. Hayek argues that it must substitute fear and coercion. Even so, since these instruments are imperfect substitutes and since the centre will still lack all the information it needs, it will not be a very efficient economy. This in turn will necessitate dealing with discontent from failed aspirations and so repression of political means of voicing discontent. So the project of socialism with liberty seems equilibrium infeasible.

For a number of reasons this conclusion is premature. Let us first enquire whether socialism with *no less liberty* than under capitalism is equilibrium feasible, which strikes me as a more interesting question.

In a capitalist economy workers either work or starve or work well or are dismissed. In a socialist economy it may be that one either works or works well or goes to prison. It is quite unclear how liberty on that score is to be compared. In a capitalist economy there may be more choice of where to work and what to work at. But even in the socialist command economy the sheer difficulty of allocating workers by command and training them in different skills by command is likely to leave similar choices available. The difficulties of central supervision will probably ensure that the choice of work effort is retained. Yet the choice among consumer goods is likely to be much richer in a capitalist society because the command economy will be highly monopolistic and lack the incentive to search out consumer preferences. A loss of liberty there. Against this one might put the absence of choices of secure employment under capitalism, whereas all socialist employment may be secure. Under capitalism one can choose to strive for wealth; under socialism, for power.

One can go on enumerating and comparing in this way. After some time it becomes clear that the central and decisive issue is the connection between a command economy and political choices, not economic choices, which remain open. By this I mean choices which concern a share in public decision and public advocacy. An argument from economic organization to political circumstances is available, but it cannot be claimed to entail inevitability.

The argument may go something like this. A coherent command economy must pay attention to intertemporal consistency of plans. So, of course, must large companies in a capitalist economy, but even the largest of these accounts for only a relatively small fraction of GNP. Mistakes made by the many will differ and so to some extent cancel. This is not true of mistakes made at the center, which for rather obvious reasons will tend to be highly correlated. The economic costs of allowing free periodic and political choice of government may therefore be very large, not only because of the increased

uncertainty of planning but because of the likely high costs of resulting intertemporal inconsistency of plans. This, it seems to me, will
certainly result in pressures inimical to free political choice.

To this one must add the much more obvious point that the command economy requires centralized power of a high order as well as a
central bureaucracy. There are strong inductive reasons for believing
that this must lead to a reluctance to put existing political power to a
periodic political test. Since there may be political opposition nonetheless, it will tend to be suppressed.

As I have already said, all of this leads to uncertain equilibrium
infeasibility of socialism with liberty. However, the weight of history
and of the plausibility of some of the arguments does suggest that he
burden of establishing feasibility is on the liberty-loving socialist.

I must now return to a difficulty which I have already hinted at:
Are we asking the right questions? One of the contentions of those
who advocate a socialist society is that it will be one in which human
nature will, to some extent at least, have been transformed. Strong
egalitarianism will be compatible with people giving of their best
because envious and competitive capitalist trends will have been eliminated. The removal of the "alienation" of a capitalist society, where
human relations are obscured, will cause much greater weight to be
given to the "common good" and much less to the self. It is therefore
only in the transition from capitalism, while "socialist man" is in the
making, that his choices and so his liberty will need restricting. In
socialist equilibrium people will choose what otherwise would have to
be commanded. So while transition infeasibility of socialism with
liberty may be granted, a demonstration of equilibrium infeasibility
fails.

This line of argument reveals a weakness in my earlier treatment of
liberty. Enumeration of choices available in A and G may not clinch
or even be relevant; for prohibitions may be what economists call
"slack." That is, they may not restrict any choice the agent actually
wants to make, and commands may simply tell one to do what one
has already freely chosen to do. Thus a prohibition against eating my
mother does not truly restrict my choices, while a command to engage
in economic research leaves me unaffected. This line of argument
may lead us to the view that Uncle Tom had no less liberty than his

master since he wanted to serve and love him and that capitalist man's liberty is illusory when viewed by socialist man.

To deal with this new difficulty one must either appeal to immutable essentials of all human beings or to moral categories of the good (and free) human being. I am quite unsure whether either of these moves will save the day when it come to feasibility. Certainly there seem to be no agreed propositions one could deploy. So has the whole exercise run into the sand?

I think not. Suppose we agree that socialist man will put the "common good" above his private good. This then leaves the obvious question of how he is to know when he is acting in the common good. Certainly in his economic actions the agent will often be quite uncertain. Should he train as a dentist or as an engineer? Should he produce wheat or barley, should he work hard and neglect political activities and so on? Moreover, although he may put the common good first, it is quite unclear why socialist man should agree on what it is both generally and in any particular. From this it seems to me to follow that socialist man must often act on command in a way which he might not have chosen to act. The transformation of human nature does not dispose of the need to coordinate economic activity in a concrete way, and though we have some idea of the way in which this can occur as a result of self-interested free choice in a market economy, we have no idea of how it is to be achieved by free choice of agents seeking the common good.

An analogy may be a group of patriotic men, so often to be seen in war films, on a mission to destroy an enemy installation. They all want to destroy it and they are all selflessly interested in doing so. But this will be manifested both in having a commander and in agreeing to obey him; for at each juncture of the mission there might otherwise be disagreement on how to accomplish it and no obvious way of coordination and resolution. To make the free choice to obey another seems self-evidently a free choice to restrict one's liberty. The voluntariness of the choice seems irrelevant to that conclusion, although it is relevant to the question of whether, having made it, the soldiers are satisfied with it.

The analogy is, of course, too favorable to the case for socialist man and his liberty; for in the example common good is clearly defined, which can hardly be so for the common socialist good. But it suffices for the main conclusion that, while socialist man may voluntarily submit to the commands of others, it cannot be the case that he does not thereby restrict the choices which he might have wanted to make. He may be happier but hardly as free as capitalist man.

I now want to emphasize that I base this conclusion on economic considerations. There is no plausible way in which economic activity can be coordinated by the free decisions of men and women guided by the common good as they perceive it. To achieve such coordination requires consideration of trade-offs between elements of the common good. This in turn requires knowledge of what it is possible to trade and on what terms. It also requires unanimity as to the rate at which trade-offs are determined by the common good. This knowledge cannot be available. Hence choices must be delegated. In a capitalist economy the trade-offs compatible with self-interest are known and the actual possibilities are given by the market.

I can also now revert to an earlier argument. Since we do not know whether the transformation which is desired in human nature will or can take place, it must be at best that uncertain equilibrium feasibility can be claimed. That in turn must mean that to persuade himself and others of the virtues of socialism requires that capitalist man be persuaded, and so one needs his valuation of liberty and his attitude to the risk of losing some of it. By that I mean that capitalist man must attach positive probability to finding that he (or his children) are still capitalist man in a socialist society. If so, the required restriction of his choices will be more severe than if a transformation had taken place. Therefore, the circumstance that socialism with desired choices being freely open is only uncertainly equilibrium feasible may suffice for national unwillingness to be a socialist.

The question of socialism with liberty is, of course, too large and its elements too complex to allow more than telling as opposed to clinching arguments. I chose it nonetheless because it is important and in some way raises all the most pressing issues in a discussion of economic feasibility. However, there surely were too many trees to discern the wood and I now make an attempt to rectify this.

Any society which produces goods in some considerable abundance and variety requires a division of labor among different individuals and groups of individuals. As Adam Smith observed, people can specialize when they have the opportunity to exchange their specialized product for others. They may also have to engage in such exchange in order to produce. Somehow this exchange and production must be coordinated. A market economy is one way of doing that and a question is whether it is the only way or the most agreeable or efficient way. But the first point is simply that the job must be done if we value a reasonable abundance and variety of goods.

Though an actual market economy does the job, it does it imperfectly. There are monopolies and there are fluctuations and there are some goods it cannot provide at all because they are public goods. All of these blemishes and difficulties provide occasions for public policy and so politics. Some of them also lead to well-known claims that capitalism is in itself not equilibrium feasible – that is, it should be looked at as a transition, albeit a rather long-lived one. Some of the arguments supporting such a claim are interesting and suggestive, while others are demonstrably false. But this is so well trodden a field that I shall not add my own footprint.

What is of interest is the politics which is founded on a dissatisfaction with capitalism and with its institution. The driving motor of the system is self-interested greed, and any slackening in this motive may lead to stagnation and decay. Typically it generates considerable inequalities of income and spectacular inequality of wealth. The market for labor turns men and women into objects, and work itself becomes a main source of alienation. The factory system and increased mechanization maintain and fuel that alienation. The legal and political systems as well as education are designed to maintain and strengthen the status quo and reflect the interests of those most interested in maintaining it. Finally, capitalism is voracious in its consumption of irreplaceable resources and uncaringly destroys our environment. In a recent book, John Dunn (1984) called capitalism 'unlovely' and worse and felt it to be sufficiently obvious not to require comment. And, of course, he was justified since one or the other of capitalist society's ills will be recognized by many – specially by readers of books on politics.

III

The question, however, is not whether these complaints have substance but whether it is possible to avoid the ills by some other arrangement without falling into worse ones. I have already discussed the lack of precision and coherence which results when motives of greed are replaced by a desire for the common good, even if such a replacement is possible. One may point to early kibbutzim as examples in which this was accomplished. But it must be remembered that they were small elements in a predominantly capitalist society. Moreover, the loss of liberty, such as of where and when to work and whether and how much education to provide for one's children, was perceived as sufficiently great as to lead to drastic modifications in some kibbutzim and the collapse of others. Yugoslavia is perhaps a better example of a society that has attempted to do without capitalist man's motives and to reduce the alienation of work. Evidence seems to suggest that, although there has been some success with the latter, no notable victory has been won in the former. Moreover, Yugoslavia is known neither as an economically very successful country nor for being lavish in liberty.

None of this amounts to a demonstration that escape from the ills in question is infeasible. But it suggests that there are some hard economic imperatives which have to be overcome. For instance, worker-run and -owned firms may reduce the alienation from work of the workers concerned. As a group, however, they must act in what they, perhaps after debate, consider to be the group's interest or they must be commanded or they may try and fathom the common interest.

If they act in their own interests and are part of a market economy, then that may be a perfectly feasible arrangement, but its improvement over the capitalist mode is debatable. For instance, if the workers have property rights in their firms, they will be inclined to exploit whatever market power they have and may also keep other workers from joining them. Since growth in material comforts requires ongoing changes in industrial structure, ways will have to be found to close some firms and start others. But workers who run firms may well be a potent special-interest group politically, and unless all workers own shares, the share-owning workers may behave as badly or as well as capitalists do now. They will seek protection from change and from the risks of closure. If, however, workers do not own their firms, then management by workers requires goals and some direct relation between performance and effort. No drastic departure from present arrangements would occur.

If workers are commanded, then it is not clear that anything has been achieved. If they, somehow, all decide to act in the common good, old problems of coordination which I have already discussed reappear. The cost in goods and so on foregone may be very high.

So syndicalist solutions are either infeasible or not self-evidently an improvement. The real difficulty here as with other proposals seems to be this. The old injunction that we should love each other or at least care for each other is of little relevance to most economic decisions that one takes in any society with a reasonably elaborate division of labour. Politics of "love for others" or of "the good and full man or woman" must somehow fill the lacuna if citizens are to be provided with material plenty. In pseudo-market structures this cannot be done without at least a tension between the noble injunction and the need to have economic agents respond to signals of private advantage or disadvantage. Alternatively one needs centralized commands which not only exact a cost in economic performance but are likely to put considerable strain on one's resolve to love and care. It simply is economically infeasible to arrange economic affairs on the noble principles alone. It is transition infeasible because the lack of economic coordination will lead to the abandonment of the experiment before it has got very far. On all of this the history of attempts at creating utopian society, if not governed by self-interest (admittedly on a small scale and embedded in others), is instructive.

One therefore inclines to the view that the uncertain feasibility of large-scale improvements by radical change makes the politics of amelioration more attractive and interesting. So how much is it possible to tinker with capitalism? One, of course, observes that in the past hundred years or so there has been a great deal of tinkering already. There are inheritance taxes and progressive income taxes, there are subsidized industries of all sorts, many industries are regulated and there are public welfare provisions in most capitalist societies. In addition there are ongoing attempts to regulate the economy as a whole by means of fiscal and monetary policy. The question is whether these changes which have already taken place and those which may yet be proposed will make capitalism itself infeasible. Everyone knows that President Reagan had nightmares about this and that Mrs. Thatcher continues to have them to the present day.

But let me begin with the easier matter of ineffectual tinkering. As a first example take the proposal, certainly made by many politicians, to raise compulsorily the wage of those whose pay is unacceptably low. The purpose presumably is that people in those occupations should enjoy a higher income. But with the exception of situations in which labor to some firms is in inelastic supply because it is highly immobile and the firm enjoys some monopoly power, it is pretty certain that they will not be employed or far fewer of them will be employed. The policy will fail in its purpose because this is not a feasible way of redistributing income. A very similar objection applies to the widely adopted policy of rent control. Its consequences are a redistribution to an arbitrarily selected group, namely of those who have accommodation already; it will certainly reduce the supply of rented accommodation and it will misallocate what there is. For instance, couples whose children have grown up will be reluctant or unable to move to smaller accommodation. If the aim of the policy was equity and justice, then this aim is not achievable by the policy.

A great many political platforms include incoherent elements of this kind. They are often the result of intellectual laziness and often of stupidity. They are costly if implemented. But they raise no interesting feasibility problems.

More interesting is the question of how far egalitarian policies can be pursued under capitalism without destroying it. The evidence on the immediate and obvious matter of incentives is ambiguous. It is not clear that there is a simple relation between absolute reward and performance rather than between relative reward and performance. Certainly the economist's model of the supply of effort is in many ways unpersuasive since attitudes to work and reward are almost certainly richly influenced by the social setting. One can think of many reasons why relative rewards, that is, relative to others, rather than absolute rewards, are central to the incentive question. Rewards are not just a means of transforming work into consumption, but indicators of social esteem and a source of self-esteem. Keynes (1936) argued that it is only the rank order of rewards rather than the absolute gaps which are important for incentives. If he was right, then much smaller inequalities than we have at present would be compatible with capitalist incentives.

Neither theory nor evidence can at the moment settle this matter. Rawls's (1972) instruction to maximize the worst-off individual's welfare insofar as this does not reduce what there is to give is not really operational. For what it is worth one can report that a more traditional approach, in the style of Bentham, based on the traditional theory of work has led to surprisingly flat income tax schedules (Mirrlees 1971). The difficulty for the egalitarian is that one cannot redistribute by means of lump-sum taxes, that is, by means which do not interfere with the margin between effort and reward. So at this level all one can conclude is that a decentralized economy will impose limits on egalitarian ambitions.

However, there is a somewhat subtler point to be made. May it not be that the capitalist ethos and the egalitarian ethos are incompatible? If I am persuaded that inequalities in income or wealth, or substantial inequalities in these, are morally repugnant, then I shall not be induced to take risks and make efforts simply because they will yield me a relatively high reward. An egalitarian ethos is more likely to produce flower children than captains of industry.

Suppose, for instance, that dentists are relatively scarce. In a market economy this is likely to be reflected in the high earnings of dentists. This in turn would induce some students to switch from medicine or veterinary studies to dentistry, and in due course there would be more dentists. But egalitarian-minded students could hardly be expected to make the switch for those reasons, and an egalitarian society would in any case have taxed away the scarcity rents of dentists. So either there are no signals to students because of the policy or, if there are signals, they do not induce an appropriate response. An egalitarian ethos even without an egalitarian policy can plausibly be supposed to put an effective spanner into the capitalist machine. If that is correct, then all the problems of economic coordination which I have already discussed will have to be faced. One should be much less concerned by vociferous complaints about redistributive taxation than by its cheerful acceptance. The latter would be a danger signal that limits of a properly functioning decentralized economy are being approached.

The egalitarianism I have been discussing concerns income and wealth. The politics of egalitarianism, however, is often muddled, as is the economics. Take, for instance, the desire that there be equality of esteem. Most incentives that most societies provide, if they provide incentives at all, turn on the possibility that some individuals will be offered the opportunity to be esteemed more than are others. For instance, this is as true of academics as it is of businessmen, and it was as true of Roman soldiers as of Roman Senators. Indeed, one is tempted to bowdlerize and say that if everyone is esteemed equally, then no one is esteemed at all. But for my present purpose what is important is that in capitalist economies income is an element of esteem, although there is no reason to suppose that it is the sole element. But it is variations in that element which allow the most obvious means of economic coordination. Economists are muddled because they generally do not regard esteem by others or self as a motive at all. Political theorists often seem muddled because they start with a rather abstract desideratum of esteeming people equally as people but fail to specify concretely either the elements in esteem or their possible social and economic function.

The dangers to the feasibility of capitalist society by a weakening of the specific capitalist elements of esteem are well exemplified in Britain. Here the weakening is not so much due to egalitarian motives as to the diverse notions of gentlemanly or even aristocratic virtues. This thought is a commonplace among those commenting on the British scene and I shall not elaborate. But it is worthwhile remembering that, for instance, a widespread aesthetic revulsion from the materialism of capitalist esteem hierarchies can have serious economic consequences.

Dr Johnson may have been too optimistic when he gave it as his opinion that a man is never so innocently engaged as when he is pursuing money. I take him to mean that if we do not pursue money we may be pursuing something more dangerous like power. But that is not my main contention. My main contention is that when a man is not pursuing money it is not at all clear how his pursuits can be harnessed to the coordination of economic activity and to the innovating necessities of growing prosperity. It would be silly to think that this ignorance on my part constitutes a claim that it cannot be done in any other way. What it does suggest, I think, is that there are serious problems of economic feasibility which go far beyond the question of whether high marginal tax rates do or do not discourage effort.

A noticeable omission in the discussion so far is the international dimension. It would take me very far afield to treat that at all comprehensively. I shall accordingly confine myself to one particular matter which it seems to me important to understand.

Trade among countries is not the same as that between agents in one particular country in this important respect: There are relatively few countries, whereas there are many agents in any one country. Countries have governments, and since there are relatively few of them, it becomes possible, and so appears desirable, to act strategically. In the domestic market economy transactions to some extent become anonymous and individuals do not find themselves engaged in transactions in which responses of opponents have to be anticipated and conjectured. There are obvious exceptions to this rule, but the distinction I am making does not greatly depend on the exceptions.

Governments in the nature of things are endowed not only with political but also with market power. They can impose tariffs and quotas, they can stop the movement of capital into and out of their countries and they have political favors and disfavors which they can trade. In certain important respects a country may find itself in the same position as does a domestic monopolist and use that power to bring about a redistribution of world income in its favor. It is well understood by economists and game theorists that this game of governments with relatively few players may have outcomes which make the citizens of all the countries worse off than they need be, given the international distribution of resources and skills.

A famous example is that of trade between two countries A and B in which A's production is relatively more labor intensive in production than B. If trade is opened up between these two countries (where previously there was none), it can often be true that real wages in country B will fall. That may make B's government reluctant to allow such trade. But in fact it could by taxation policy ensure that after trade everyone in B was at least as well off as before trade and some are better off. (I do not dot the *i*'s here – there *are* exceptions to this result.) Citizens of A would also be better off. But the political necessities may make it impossible for B to follow this policy, and indeed if there is substance to the economic theory of politics, electoral considerations may rule it out of court. Similar arguments apply to tariffs and quotas – they lead to an outcome for the *world* which is Pareto-inferior for the world, although, given the constraints on policy, not necessarily for the country imposing them (see, e.g., Dixit and Norman 1980). (Once again I am not stating this as a theorem, that is, I am not listing all the circumstances in which this is a true statement.

However, I believe the onus of showing the circumstances to be such as to negate the propositions is on those who wish to show this.)

For all these reasons one is led to the view that something akin to antitrust policy is required internationally. That is, one requires rules of conduct for governments. The trouble, of course, is that it is unclear how any such rules can be enforced. Indeed, in the nature of the case they would have to be self-enforcing, by which I mean that the cost to any country (or coalition of countries) of deviating from them exceeds the benefits of deviation. One must ask not only whether such rules (e.g., like those of the General Agreement on Tariffs and Trade) are self-enforcing but also whether it is possible to reach the "best" of self-enforcing rules among those which are feasible.

All of this is one aspect of the larger political question of how countries can live with each other without unnecessrily harming each other. In federal countries such as the United States, what could have been countries have become states, and as far as I know, trade among them has always been virtual "free trade." Notice, however, that Washington is the place where battles over the distribution of income to states are fought. They can be fought without dissolving the federation for many reasons, including historical ones and the fact that there are relatively few "countries" involved.

It is at this point that I return to my brief. International trade has inevitable consequences for the international distribution of welfare. Schemes for a "federal world" or even a "federal Europe" would, before the growth of a federal identity and perhaps patriotism, have to pay central attention to self-enforcing adherence based either on a previous national identity or on brute force. The transition feasibility is doubtful but hardly impossible. If overcome, one would still have to pay attention to the complexity of the task and so to the need for decentralization. It would also be a very long time before a federal government could cease to use fiscal and other means to redistribute income between what had been national states. If there are obstacles to the eventual feasibility of such an arrangement, they are more likely to be political, historical and social than economic. Rather the reverse. Economists have at least since Ricardo's time described a free-trade world in which national identities were irrelevant and only the location of (presumed immobile) resources mattered. Certainly a federal world economic market system with fiscal redistributions can be envisaged without bumping against economic constraints. But that leaves other questions of feasibility undiscussed.

As it is, the shoe is on the other foot, for the question may be asked: Is a free-trade world equilibrium feasible? To this question the answer must be in much greater doubt because of the difficulty of self-enforcing agreements and the motive of exploiting a government's strategic advantages in their absence.

I want to conclude by clarifying and simplifying two general strands of all the arguments I have produced. These are the economic imperatives flowing from imperfect and dispersed information and from the motives of individual agents.

Since an individual's capacity to receive and process information is quite limited, it is important that we economize in the informational requirements of economic coordination. Such an economy is easier to achieve with self-regarding motives than it is with others, for instance the motive of acting in the common good. It is not correct to suppose that an economy of information is possible by substituting command for incentive. On the contrary, the order of complexity grows with centralization. To this must be added the need for those that command to be able to verify that their commands have been carried out. For quite similar reasons it will be the case that an egalitarian ethos will increase the informational requirement of an agent who is to play his part in the coordination of economic activity.

Coordination of economic activity is not a very well defined concept, and I have really been appealing implicitly to some well-known economic ideas. Certainly societies can get along with massive coordination failures, as one can easily verify. By coordination failures I have the Pareto concept in mind. That is, the well-being of every citizen is lower than it could be, given knowledge and answers. Arguments of infeasibility therefore turn into a kind of political sociology. That is, one holds that massive coordination failures will, by creating dissatisfaction, lead to massive political changes – as for instance in China. But political sociology is not an exact science (any more than economics is), and such predictions cannot be treated as laws. So all infeasibility arguments except the most primitive with which I started are uncertain.

But that does not make them unimportant. Rather the contrary. Uncertain feasibility is itself an element which serious politics must take into account. It certainly has prudential implications. It also makes clear demands on honesty. Political discourse following these demands will be phrased in the language of probability. That should make it not only more honest but also of greater worth.

The economic limits are only one category of limits on politics. I suspect that there are important political limits on politics as well. By this I mean the limits to acquiescence to political change and limits to coercion. These limits are not in my brief. However, they as well as their economic counterpart share the feature that they are limits set by ignorance and complexity. This ignorance and complexity have consequences at the level of the individual citizen as well as that of the politician. These in turn ensure that political intentions rarely lead to intended outcomes. That is one reason why I have always found political enthusiasm as difficult to understand as religious enthusiasm. Indeed, the latter is easier since its consequences are so evidently beyond verification.

This leaves one important matter which I have mentioned fairly often but not examined in any detail. It concerns public goods in the widest sense. It is not sufficiently appreciated by noneconomists that it is not feasible to rely on a market economy for an acceptable supply of these goods. It is true that if we could have property rights in clean air, we would not require antipollution legislation or regulation. But we cannot have such rights. It is not easy to see how to make individuals who refuse inoculation responsible for the infections they spread to others. There is no obvious way in which the layman can assess the qualities of an uncertified doctor. And so on and so on. Indeed, economic life abounds in externalities, that is, effects of private actions on others, which are the hallmark of the public-good problem and are simply an indication that we do live in society. A society which neglects the provision of public goods not only will be unpleasant but may itself not be equilibrium feasible.

It is important to understand that private interest and private information are quite inadequate here. Consider as an example the question of health insurance. Suppose that someone is not insured (because he prefers to spend his money elsewhere) and that he has a heart attack. We have two choices: We can let him die or save him though he is uninsured. A society which habitually makes the first choice is not one many of us would care for, although I am told that such a choice is sometimes made in America. If the second choice is made, we encounter the difficulty of moral hazard: Self-regarding agents will not insure because they know they will in any case be looked after. Here there is a case for compulsory insurance.

There are, of course, thousands of examples of this kind. For instance, it is not true that the private and social benefits of literacy coincide. It is not the case that private information on many goods from pharmaceuticals to motor cars is as good as the pooled information of society. The private interests of the speculative builder are rarely straightforwardly in the social interest. If one looks, one finds that everywhere the invisible hand is pulling the wrong levers as well as some of the right ones.

The politics of ignoring all these cases strike me as equilibrium infeasible – that is, if this ignoring takes place in the context of political democracy. The exceptions are too numerous and too important not to be reflected in political programs. And indeed the history of Western capitalist societies confirms this. The real question then is whether the political hand can be expected to deliver what the invisible hand cannot. I do not have the expertise to answer this question. All I can say is that I hope it can.

In summary, politics is concerned with actions which in an important sense are cooperations. Cooperation is difficult and it requires the participants to know what to do and, if they are free, to want to do it. Forced cooperation is mostly inefficient. Economics has shown how often cooperative results can be achieved noncooperatively. But that is not always the case, and there are important exceptions. A combination of the invisible and political hands seems feasibly to lead to a tolerable outcome. Political schemes which are more ambitious (and perhaps thereby more appealing) are mostly not feasible because they neglect the requirements both of information and of motivation. In the case of the latter I do not appeal to original sin but to the incoherence and lack of specificity in the injunction to do good to everyone rather than to my neighbor.

References

Arrow, K. J., *Social Choice and Individual Values*, Wiley, New York, 1951.
Berlin, I., *Four Essays on Liberty*, Oxford University Press, New York, 1969.

Dixit, A., and V. Norman, *Theory of International Trade,* James Nisbet, Edinburgh, 1980.

Dunn, J., *The Politics of Socialism,* Cambridge University Press, 1984.

Friedman, M., and R. D. Friedman, *Capitalism and Freedom,* University of Chicago Press, Chicago, 1963.

Hayek, F. A., *The Road to Serfdom,* Routledge & Kegan Paul, London, 1944.

Keynes, J. M., *The General Theory of Employment, Interest and Money,* Macmillan, London, 1936.

Lange, O., "On the Economic Theory of Socialism," *Review of Economic Studies, 3* (1936) and *4* (1937).

Lerner, A. P., *The Economics of Control,* Macmillan, New York, 1944.

Mill, J. S., *On Liberty,* ed. G. Himmelfarb, Penguin Books, Harmondsworth, 1982.

Mirrlees, J. A., "An Exploration in the Theory of Optimum Income Taxation," *Review of Economic Studies, 38* (1971), p. 175.

Rawls, J. *A Theory of Justice,* Clarendon Press, Oxford, 1972.

CHAPTER 5

International liberalism reconsidered*

ROBERT O. KEOHANE

World politics both creates opportunities for modern governments and imposes constraints on the range of actions that it is feasible for them to pursue. One way to think about these opportunities and constraints is to analyze the operation of the contemporary international political–military system, or the world political economy, and to consider how these systems affect state action. Much of the modern study of international relations is devoted to this task. Yet another perspective on the impact of world politics on states can be gained by asking how perceptive observers of politics have reflected on these issues in the past. This approach, which looks to the history of political thought for insights into contemporary international affairs, will be pursued here.[1] Although the form and intensity of the constraints and opportunities created by the contemporary world system are different from those in earlier centuries, the impact of international politics and economics on state action has been evident for a long time, and has occasioned a great deal of sophisticated commentary.

At some risk of blurring differences between thinkers of broadly

[1] For the classic modern work in this vein, see Kenneth N. Waltz, *Man, the State and War* (New York: Columbia University Press, 1959).

*The author is grateful for comments on earlier drafts of this paper to Professors Vinod Aggarwal, Michael Doyle, John Dunn, Ernst B. Haas, Stanley Hoffman, Nannerl O. Keohane, Joseph S. Nye, Susan Moller Okin, and Kenneth N. Waltz. Further valuable suggestions were received when such a draft was presented to the Harvard-MIT study group on international institutions and cooperation during the fall of 1986 and to a discussion group at the Center for Advanced Study in the Behavioral Sciences during the fall of 1987.

similar inclinations, three major Western schools of thought on this subject can be identified: Marxist, realist and liberal. Each has been influential, although it is probably fair to say that realism has been the creed of Continental European statesmen for centuries, and that since World War II it has been predominant in the United States as well. Marxism has remained the doctrine of a minority in Western Europe and a mere splinter group in the United States, although in the Soviet Union and elsewhere it has, of course, attained the status of official truth. Liberalism has been heavily criticized as an allegedly naive doctrine with utopian tendencies, which erroneously ascribes to the conflictual and anarchic international realm properties that only pertain to well-ordered domestic societies.[2] Although the most sophisticated critics of liberalism have often borrowed important elements of it – Carr perceived a "real foundation for the Cobdenite view of international trade as a guarantee of international peace"[3] – and Morgenthau put much of his faith in diplomacy,[4] – self-styled realists often dismiss the insights of liberalism as naive and misleading.

This essay takes issue with this common denigration of liberalism among professional students of international relations. My argument is that liberalism – or at any rate, a certain strand of liberalism – is more sophisticated than many of its critics have alleged. Although liberalism is often caricatured, a sophisticated form of liberalism provides thoughtful arguments designed to show how open exchanges of goods and services, on the one hand, and international institutions and rules, on the other, can promote international cooperation as well as economic prosperity. Liberalism makes the positive argument that an open international political economy, with rules and institutions based on state sovereignty, provides incentives

---

[2] On British and American thinking, see Arnold Wolfers and Laurence W. Martin, eds., *The Anglo-American Tradition in Foreign Affairs: Readings from Thomas More to Woodrow Wilson* (New Haven: Yale University Press, 1956). For the most influential English-language critiques of liberalism in international relations, see E. H. Carr, *The Twenty Years' Crisis, 1919–1939* (London: Macmillan, 1st edition, 1939; 2nd edition, 1946); Hans J. Morgenthau, *Scientific Man Versus Power Politics* (Chicago: University of Chicago Press, 1946); and Waltz, *Man, the State and War.*

[3] E. H. Carr, *Nationalism and After* (New York: Macmillan, 1945), p. 11.

[4] See Hans J. Morgenthau, *Politics Among Nations* (New York: Knopf, 4th edition, 1967).

for international cooperation and may even affect the internal constitutions of states in ways that promote peace. It also makes the normative assertion that such a reliance on economic exchange and
international institutions has better effects than the major politically-
tested alternatives. I do not necessarily subscribe to all of these
claims, but I take them seriously, and I wish to subject them to
examination in this chapter.

The first section of the chapter briefly examines Marxism and realism, the principal alternative traditions to liberalism in international
relations theory. I ask what answers writers in these two traditions
provide to three questions, two empirical and one normative:

1. What are the "limits to modern politics" in the advanced industrial
   democracies imposed by the state system and the world political
   economy?
2. How do the state system and the global system of production and
   exchange shape the character of societies and states?
3. Are the patterns of exchange and of international rules and norms
   characteristic of contemporary capitalism morally justifiable?

Second, I consider liberalism in some detail, distinguishing three
forms that liberal doctrines of international relations have taken. I
argue that a combination of what I call commercial and regulatory
liberalism makes a good deal of sense as a framework for interpreting
contemporary world politics and for evaluating institutions and policies. Such a sophisticated liberalism emphasizes the construction of
institutions that facilitate both economic exchange and broader international cooperation.

The third and final section considers the normative judgments
made by liberals about the capitalist international political economy
that they have fostered since World War II. I emphasize that even
sophisticated liberalism is morally questionable, since the international political economy defended by liberals generates inequalities
that cannot be defended according to principles of justice. Nevertheless, on balance I uphold the view of liberals themselves, that liberal
prescriptions for peace and prosperity compare favorably with the
politically tested alternatives.

Marxism and realism

Marxism

Contemporary Marxists and neo-Marxists hold that the external limits to modern politics result principally from the world capitalist system of production and exchange. One of the major manifestations of the impact of the capitalist system is the power of transnational capital, which is expressed both through the operation of transnational corporations and the impacts of transnational capital flows, especially capital flight. Business has a privileged position over labor not merely because of the internal characteristics of the capitalist state, but because capital is more mobile than workers: It can easily leave jurisdiction in which government policies are markedly less favorable to it than elsewhere. The mobility and power of transnational capital thus constrain the internal policies of governments, particularly their economic and social welfare policies.

Capitalist governments have created international institutions: informal arrangements for policy coordination as well as formal international organizations such as the World Bank and the International Monetary Fund. This means, according to Marxist writers, that the probusiness bias exerted by the mobility of transnational capital is reinforced by the need of governments, whether of Left or Right, for support at critical moments from other governments and from international economic institutions. As Ralph Miliband has argued:

> Capitalism is now more than ever an international system, whose constituent economies are closely related and interlinked. As a result, even the most powerful capitalist countries depend, to a greater or lesser extent, upon the good will and cooperation of the rest, and of what has become, notwithstanding enduring and profound national capitalist rivalries, an interdependent international capitalist "community."[5]

Not only does world capitalism impose limits on modern politics, the location of a society in the international division of labor profoundly affects its character as a state. Theda Skocpol declares that "all modern social revolutions must be seen as closely related in their causes and accomplishments to the internationally uneven spread of capitalist eco-

[5] Ralph Miliband, *The State in Capitalist Society* (New York: Basic, 1969), p. 153.

nomic development and nation-state formation on a world scale."[6] Domestic class struggles are shaped in considerable part by the position of a country in the world capitalist system – this is as true for imperialist states as for dependent ones. Furthermore, global class struggle may appear as nationalist or ethnic struggle in particular countries: "The fundamental political reality of the world-economy is a class struggle which however takes constantly changing forms: over class consciousness versus ethno-national consciousness, classes within nations versus classes across nations."[7] Marxists argue that the political coalitions that are formed within countries cannot be understood without comprehending both how the capitalist world political economy functions and how particular countries are inserted within it.

On the normative value of capitalism, Marxist arguments are of course familiar: Capitalism is an exploitative system that oppresses poor people, especially those on the periphery of the world system, and that generates war. Its rules are designed to perpetuate exploitation and oppression, not to relieve them. The sooner they are destroyed by revolutionary action, bringing into being a vaguely defined, but assertedly superior new order, the better. Fortunately, since capitalism contains the seeds of its own destruction, its development, however exploitative, contributes to the conditions for socialism.

Realism

For realists, limits on state action result primarily from the power of other states. World politics lacks common government and is therefore an arena in which states must defend themselves or face the possibility of extinction. The necessity of self-help, however, entails competitive efforts by governments to enhance their own security, which create a "security dilemma," defined as a situation in which "many of the means by which a state tries to increase its security decrease the security of others."[8] The power that states wield is derived ultimately not only from population, natural resources and in-

---

[6] Theda Skocpol, *States and Social Revolutions* (Cambridge University Press, 1979), p. 19.

[7] Immanuel Wallerstein, *The Capitalist World-Economy* (Cambridge University Press, 1979), p. 230.

[8] Robert Jervis, "Cooperation Under the Security Dilemma," *World Politics,* vol. 30, no. 2 (January 1978), p. 169.

dustrial capacity, but also from organizational coherence, the ability to extract resources from society, military preparedness, diplomatic skill, and national will.[9] The external limits on modern politics, for realists, operate largely through political–military competition and the threat thereof.

Such competition also forces states to rely on themselves to develop capacities for self-defense.[10] By creating threats, the state system helps to create states organized for violence: The Spartas and Prussias of this world are in part results of political–military competition. Realists follow Otto Hintze, who declared around the turn of the century, "It is one-sided, exaggerated and therefore false to consider class conflict the only driving force in history. Conflict between nations has been far more important; and throughout the ages, pressure from without has been a determining influence on internal structure."[11]

Marxists would reply that in the modern era conflict among nations has resulted principally from the contradictions of the world political economy, in particular from inequality and uneven development. But for the realists, it is not inequality among states that creates conflict; indeed, a world of equal states could be expected to be particularly warlike, even if there were no capitalist exploitation. Hobbes argued that, in the state of nature, the natural equality of men leads to conflict by creating "equality of hope in the attaining of our ends," which leads to conflict when both desire the same goods. "In the condition of mere nature," he argues, "the inequality of power is not discerned but by the event of battle."[12] Hobbes implies that a virtue of establishing independent states is that this equality disappears, leading to more security as a result of the fact that unequal combat has more predictable results than combat among equals. A contemporary realist, Robert W. Tucker, has argued that trends toward greater equality are likely to lead to a "decline of power" and a more disorderly international system.[13]

---

[9] For a classic listing, see Morgenthau, *Politics Among Nations,* chap. 9.

[10] For a discussion of "self-help" as a defining characteristic of world politics, see Kenneth N. Waltz, *Theory of International Politics* (Reading, Mass.: Addison-Wesley, 1979), chap. 6.

[11] Felix Gilbert, ed., *The Historical Essays of Otto Hintze* (New York: Oxford University Press, 1975), p. 183.

[12] Thomas Hobbes, *Leviathan* (1651, chaps. 13, 15; Library of Liberal Arts Edition, Indianapolis: Bobbs-Merrill), pp. 104, 118.

[13] Robert W. Tucker, *The Inequality of Nations* (New York: Basic, 1977), p. 175.

From realism's standpoint, liberalism's flaw is less moral than explanatory: not its countenance of exploitation but its reliance on incentives provided by economic exchange and on rules to moderate state behavior in a condition of anarchy. A judgment on the validity of this criticism must await our exploration of liberalism's analysis of the limits imposed by the international system on state action.

The insufficiency of realism and Marxism

The insights that states are constrained by capitalism and by the state system are clearly true and profound. They are necessary elements of our understanding of the economic and military limits to modern politics. Yet the constraints pointed to by Marxist and realists, taken separately or in combination, are hardly sufficient to determine state action. If they were, realists or Marxists would have been more successful in devising accurate predictive theories of world politics. We would not observe variations in cooperation from one time period to another, or issue by issue, that were unexplained by the dynamics of capitalism or by changes in international structure.[14] Yet we do observe such variations in cooperation. And we also encounter international institutions, whose actions are not well explained simply by the social forces or states on which Marxism and realism focus their attention.[15]

This suggests that any claims to theoretical closure made by Marxists or realists in moments of theoretical enthusiasm should not be taken very seriously. Neither Marxism nor realism constitutes a successful deterministic theory, and the most thoughtful Marxists and realists have always recognized this. Marx taught that "men make their own history, but they do not make it just as they please."[16] Hans J. Morgenthau devoted much of his life to instructing Americans on how they should act in world politics to attain peace as well as power;

[14] International structure for neorealists such as Waltz comprises three elements: the central principle of anarchy, the similarity of the units composing the system, and the distribution of power among them. See Waltz, *Theory of International Politics,* chap. 5.

[15] For a sustained discussion of this point, see Robert O. Keohane, *After Hegemony: Cooperation and Discord in the World Political Economy* (Princeton: Princeton University Press, 1984).

[16] Karl Marx, *The Eighteenth Brumaire of Louis Napoleon,* second paragraph (1852), reprinted in Lewis Feuer, ed., *Marx and Engels: Basic Writings on Politics and Philosophy* (Garden City, N.Y.: Doubleday, 1959), p. 320.

he especially stressed the role of diplomacy. Toward the end of *War and Change in World Politics*[17] Robert Gilpin argues that "states can learn to be more enlightened in their definitions of their interests and more cooperative in their behavior" (p. 227), and he calls on "statesmen in the final decades of the twentieth century to build on the positive forces of our age in the creation of a new and more stable international order" (p. 244). Kenneth Waltz acknowledges explicitly that state behavior depends not just on international structure but on the internal characteristics of states and that the decisions of leaders also make a difference.[18]

The absence of a successful deterministic theory of international relations is fortunate for us as agents in history, since determinism is an unsatisfactory doctrine for human beings. In an era when the fates not only of our species but of the biosphere seem to depend on human decisions, it would be morally as well as intellectually irresponsible to embrace deterministic accounts of world politics. The avoidance of nuclear war is not guaranteed by the existence of capitalism or the state system, any more than its occurrence is rendered inevitable by these structures. Nor do international political and economic structures either guarantee or entirely preclude economic growth or the more equitable distribution of income in Third World countries, although, as will be seen below, they may render the latter difficult to obtain. In combating both war and poverty, there is considerable scope for the effects of conscious human action: Neither Pangloss nor Cassandra provides an accurate guide to issues of war and poverty in the contemporary world.

Avoiding nuclear war and promoting equitable Third World development both require interrnational institutions. So do such tasks as retarding nuclear proliferation and protecting the global environment. Managing economic interdependence requires an unprecedented degree of international policy coordination, which the forces of power and world capitalism hardly bring about automatically. Neither class struggle nor hegemonic rule alone offers us much hope of coping successfully with these issues.

In contrast to Marxism and realism, liberalism is not committed to an ambitious and parsimonious structural theory. Its attempts at

[17] Cambridge: Cambridge University Press, 1981.
[18] Waltz, *Theory of International Politics,* p. 122.

theory often seem therefore to be vaguely stated and to yield uncomfortably indeterminate results. Yet liberalism's theoretical weakness can be a source of strength as a guide to choice. Liberalism puts more emphasis on the cumulative effects of human action, particularly institution building, than does either Marxism and realism; for liberals, people really do make their own history. Liberalism may therefore offer some clues about how we can change the economic and political limits to modern international politics.

Liberalism as a theory of international relations

As Michael Doyle points out, "there is no canonical description of Liberalism."[19] Some commentators equate liberalism with a belief in the superiority of economic arrangements relying on markets rather than on state control. This conception of liberalism identifies it with the view of Adam Smith, David Ricardo and generations of classical and neoclassical economists. Another version of liberalism associates it more generally with the principle of "the importance of the freedom of the individual."[20] From this classic political perspective, liberalism "begins with the recognition that men, do what we will, are free; that a man's acts are his own, spring from his own personality, and cannot be coerced. But this freedom is not possessed at birth; it is acquired by degrees as a man enters into the self-conscious possession of his personality through a life of discipline and moral progress."[21]

Neither the view of liberalism as a doctrine of unfettered economic exchange nor its identification with liberty for the individual puts forward an analysis of the constraints and opportunities that face

---

[19] Michael W. Doyle, "Liberalism and World Politics, " *American Political Science Review,* vol. 80, no. 4 (December, 1986), p. 1152.

[20] Michael W. Doyle, "Kant, Liberal Legacies, and Foreign Affairs," Part I, *Philosophy and Public Affairs,* vol. 12, no. 3 (1983), p. 206. A parallel definition, focusing on political freedom, is offered by Stanley Hoffmann, "Liberalism and International Affairs," in Hoffmann, *Janus and Minerva* (Boulder: Westview Press, 1986).

[21] R. G. Collingwood, "Preface" to Guido de Ruggiero, *The History of European Liberalism,* tr. R. G. Collingwood (Boston: Beacon, 1959), pp. vii–viii, quoted by John Dunn, *Rethinking Modern Political Theory* (Cambridge University Press, 1985), p. 158. The use of the word, "man," rather than "person," in this quotation reflects a limitation of the thinking of classical liberalism, with the notable exception of John Stuart Mill, as well as of other schools of political thought before the late twentieth century: Women are not regarded as the political equals of men, and labor and nurturing by women, which have traditionally been instrumental in the development of children's personality, are ignored.

states as a result of the international system in which they are embedded. Instead, the emphasis of liberalism on liberty and rights only suggests a general orientation toward the moral evaluation of world politics.

For purposes of this chapter, therefore, it is more useful to consider liberalism as an approach to the analysis of social reality rather than as a doctrine of liberty.[22]

I will therefore regard liberalism as an approach to the analysis of social reality that (1) begins with individuals as the relevant actors, (2) seeks to understand how aggregations of individuals make collective decisions and how organizations composed of individuals interact, and (3) embeds this analysis in a worldview that emphasizes individual rights and that adopts an ameliorative view of progress in human affairs. In economics, liberalism's emphasis on the collective results of individual actions leads to the analysis of markets, market failure, and institutions to correct such failure; in traditional international relations theory it implies attempts to reconcile state sovereignty with the reality of strategic interdependence.

Liberalism shares with realism the stress on explaining the behavior of separate and typically self-interested units of action, but from the standpoint of international relations, there are three critical differences between these two schools of thought. First, liberalism focuses not merely on states but on privately organized social groups and firms. The transnational as well as domestic activities of these groups and firms are important for liberal analysts, not in isolation from the actions of states but in conjunction with them. Second, in contrast to realism, liberalism does not emphasize the significance of military force, but rather seeks to discover ways in which separate actors, with distinct interests, can organize themselves to promote economic efficiency and avoid destructive physical conflict, without renouncing either the economic or political freedoms that liberals hold dear.[23] Finally, liberalism believes in at least the possibility of cumulative progress, whereas realism assumes that history is not progressive.

Much contemporary Marxist and neo-Marxist analysis minimizes

---

[22] For this suggestion I am indebted to Andrew Moravcsik.

[23] As a large critical literature emphasizes, of course, liberalism is not power free: As E. H. Carr emphasized, liberal economic institutions have typically been undergirded by structures of power, which may be hidden by the veil of economics and therefore be more or less invisible.

the significance of individuals and state organizations, focusing instead on class relations or claiming that the identities of individuals and organizations are constituted by the nature of the world capitalist system, and that the system is therefore ontologically prior to the individual. Thus, liberalism is separated from much Marxist thought by a rather wide philosophical gulf. Yet liberalism draws substantially on those aspects of Marxism that analyze relations between discrete groups, such as investigations of multinational corporations or of the political consequences of capital flows. Both schools of thought share the inclination to look behind the state to social groups. Furthermore, both liberals and Marxists believe in the possibility of progress, although the liberals' rights-oriented vision is to emerge incrementally whereas Marxists have often asserted that their more collective new world order would be brought about through revolution.

Liberalism does not purport to provide a complete account of international relations. On the contrary, most contemporary liberals seem to accept large portions of both the Marxist and realist explanations. Much of what liberals wish to explain about world politics can be accounted for by the character and dynamics of world capitalism, on the one hand, and the nature of political–military competition, on the other. The realist and Marxist explanations focus on the underlying structure of world politics, which helps to define the limits of what is feasible and therefore ensures that the intentions of actors are often not matched by the outcomes they achieve. Yet as noted above, these explanations are incomplete. They fail to pay sufficient attention to the institutions and patterns of interaction created by human beings that help to shape perceptions and expectations, and therefore alter the patterns of behavior that take place within a given structure. Liberalism's strength is that it takes political processes seriously.

Although liberalism does not have a single theory of international relations, three more specific perspectives on international relations have nevertheless been put forward by writers who share liberalism's analytic emphasis on individual action and normative concern for liberty. I label these arguments republican, commercial, and regulatory liberalism. They are not inconsistent with one another. All three variants of international liberalism can be found in Immanuel Kant's essay "Eternal Peace," and both commercial and regulatory liberalism presuppose the existence of limited constitutional states, or republics in Kant's sense. Nevertheless, these liberal doctrines are logically distinct from one another. They rest on somewhat different premises, and liberals' interpretations of world politics vary in the degree to which they rely upon each set of causal arguments.

Republican liberalism

Republican liberalism argues that republics are more peacefully inclined than are despotisms. For Kant, a principal spokesman for all three versions of liberalism, republics are constitutional governments based on the principles of freedom of individuals, the rule of law, and the equality of citizens. In republics, legislatures can limit the actions of the executive; furthermore, "the consent of the citizens is required in order to decide whether there should be war or not," and "nothing is more natural than that those who would have to decide to undergo all the deprivations of war will very much hesitate to start such an evil game."[24] Yet as Michael Doyle has pointed out, for Kant republicanism only produces caution; it does not guarantee peace. To prevent war, action at the international as well as the national level is necessary.[25]

The association of republics with peace has often been criticized or even ridiculed. Citizens in democracies have sometimes greeted war enthusiastically, as indicated by the Crimean and Spanish-American wars and with respect to several belligerent countries, by the onset of World War I. Furthermore, many of the people affected by war have not been enfranchised in the actual republics of the last two centuries.[26] In the twentieth century, it has been difficult for legislatures to control actions of the executive that may be tantamount to war. And republics have certainly fought many and bloody wars.

Yet the historical record provides substantial support for Kant's view, if it is taken to refer to the waging of war between states founded on liberal principles rather than between these states and their illiberal adversaries. Indeed, Michael Doyle has shown on the basis of histori-

---

[24] Immanuel Kant, "Eternal Peace" (1795), in Carl J. Friedrich, ed., *The Philosophy of Kant* (New York: Modern Library, 1949), pp. 437–9.

[25] Doyle, "Liberalism and World Politics," cited, p. 1160.

[26] Susan Okin has pointed out to me that Kant excluded from citizenship women and day laborers. Many republics excluded people without property from voting until late in the last century, and women until early in this one.

cal evidence for the years since 1800 that "constitutionally secure liberal states have yet to engage in war with one another."[27]

This is an interesting issue that could bear further discussion. But my essay concerns the impact of *international relations* on state behavior. Republican liberalism explains state behavior in the international arena on the basis of *domestic* politics and is thus not directly germane to my argument here. Furthermore, as noted above, sophisticated advocates of republican liberalism, such as Kant, acknowledge that even well-constituted republics can be warlike unless international relations are properly organized. Attention to liberalism's arguments about international relations is therefore required.[28]

Commercial liberalism

Commercial liberalism affirms the impact of international relations on the actions of states. Advocates of commercial liberalism have extended the classical economists' benign view of trade into the political realm. From the Enlightenment onward, liberals have argued, in Montesquieu's words, that "the natural effect of commerce is to lead to peace. Two nations that trade together become mutually dependent if one has an interest in buying, the other has one in selling; and all unions are based on mutual needs."[29] Kant clearly agreed: "It is the *spirit of commerce* that cannot coexist with war, and which sooner or later takes hold of every nation."[30]

This liberal insistence that commerce leads to peace has led some critical observers to define liberalism in terms of belief in "a natural harmony that leads, not to a war of all against all, but to a stable, orderly and progressive society with little need for a governmental intervention."[31] The utopianism that could be fostered by such a

[27] Doyle, "Liberal Legacies," cited, p. 213. Doyle defines liberal states in a manner consistent with Kant's specifications.
[28] Another reason for this emphasis is that recent work on liberalism and international affairs, especially that by Michael Doyle, has discussed republican liberalism with great sophistication but has paid less attention to commercial and regulatory liberalism.
[29] Albert O. Hirschman, *The Passions and the Interests: Political Arguments for Capitalism Before its Triumph* (Princeton: Princeton University Press, 1977), p. 80.
[30] Kant, "Eternal Peace," cited, p. 455, italics in text.
[31] Kenneth N. Waltz, *Man, the State and War*, p. 86. Twenty years before Waltz's book, E. H. Carr argued that liberalism was essentially utopian in character, and that the liberal engaged in "clothing his own interest in the guise of a universal interest for

belief is illustrated by a statement of the American industrialist and philanthropist, Andrew Carnegie. In 1910 Carnegie established the Carnegie Endowment for International Peace, stating, as the Endowment's historian says, "that war could be abolished and that peace was in reach, and that after it was secured his trustees 'should consider what is the next most degrading remaining evil or evils whose banishment' would advance the human cause and turn their energies toward eradicating it."[32]

In its straightforward, naive form, commercial liberalism is untenable, relying as it does both on an unsubstantiated theory of progress and on a crudely reductionist argument in which politics is determined by economics. The experience of the First World War, in which major trading partners such as Britain and Germany fought each other with unprecedented intensity, discredited simplistic formulations of commercial liberalism. Yet in my judgment too much has been discredited: Commentators have identified commercial liberalism with its most extreme formulations and have thus discarded it rather cavalierly. Defensible forms of commercial liberalism have been put forward in this century, most notably in the 1930s.

At the end of that decade, Eugene Staley proposed a particularly lucid statement of commercial liberalism. Staley begins, in effect, with Adam Smith's dictum that "the division of labor depends on the extent of the market." Increased productivity depends on an international divison of labor, for countries not exceptionally well-endowed with a variety of resources. Economic nationalism blocks the division of labor, thus leading to a dilemma for populous but resource-poor states such as Japan: expand or accept decreased living standards.

The widespread practice of economic nationalism is likely to produce the feeling in a country of rapidly growing population that it is faced with a terrible dilemma: either accept the miserable prospect of decreased living standards (at least, abandon hope of greatly improved living standards), or seek by conquest to seize control of more territory, more resources, larger market and supply areas.[33]

---

the purpose of imposing it on the rest of the world." Carr, *The Twenty Years' Crisis, 1919–1939;* 2nd edition, pp. 27, 75.

[32] Larry L. Fabian, *Andrew Carnegie's Peace Endowment* (New York: Carnegie Endowment for International Peace, 1985), p. 43.

[33] Eugene Staley, *The World Economy in Transition* (New York: Council on Foreign Relations, 1939), p. 103.

This leads to a general conclusion:

> To the extent, then, that large, important countries controlling substantial portions of the world's resources refuse to carry on economic relations with the rest of the world, they sow the seeds of unrest and war. In particular, they create a powerful dynamic of imperialism. *When economic walls are erected along political boundaries, possession of territory is made to coincide with economic opportunity* [italics added]. Imperialistic ambitions are given both a partial justification and a splendid basis for propaganda.[34]

Staley's argument does not depend on his assumption about increasing population, since increasing demands for higher living standards could lead to the same pressure for economic growth. The important point here for our purposes is that in Staley's version of commercial liberalism, incentives for peaceful behavior are provided by an open international environment characterized by regularized patterns of exchange and orderly rules. Commerce by itself does not ensure peace, but commerce on a nondiscriminatory basis within an orderly political framework promotes cooperation on the basis of enlightened national conceptions of self-interest that emphasize production over war.

Regulatory liberalism

Advocates of regulatory liberalism emphasize the importance for peace of the rules governing patterns of exchange among countries. Albert O. Hirschman points out that as people began to think about interests in the eighteenth century, they began to realize "that something was to be gained for both parties (in international politics) by the adherence to certain rules of the game and by the elimination of 'passionate' behavior, which the rational pursuit of interest implied."[35] Kant regards regulation as a central principle of perpetual peace. He proposes a "federalism" of free states, although this federation is to fall short of a world republic, since a constitutionally organized world state based on the national principle is not feasible.[36]

---

[34] Ibid.
[35] Hirschman, *Passions,* cited, p. 51.
[36] Kant, "Eternal Peace," pp. 441, 445.

Kant does not go into details on how such a federation would be institutionalized, but his vision clearly presages the international organizations of the twentieth century, with their established rules, norms, and practices. A major change in the concept of regulatory liberalism, however, has taken place, since relatively few contemporary international organizations limit membership to republics. Indeed, most members of the United Nations would qualify as despotisms by Kant's criteria. Contemporary practice has created different types of international organizations. Some, such as the European Community and the Organization for Economic Cooperation and Development (OECD), are at least for the most part limited to republics, but the United Nations, a variety of global economic organizations, and regional organizations outside Europe are not. Contemporary advocates of regulatory liberalism may continue to believe that republics in Kant's sense are the best partners for international cooperation; but for a number of global problems, it would be self-defeating to refuse to seek to collaborate with autocratic states. Even autocracies may have an interest in following international rules and facilitate mutually beneficial agreements on issues such as arms control, nuclear reactor safety, and the regulation of international trade.

Kant's argument for a federation is in my view profoundly different from the conception (also found in "Eternal Peace") of the gradual emergence of peace through commerce as a natural process, implying a theory of progress. In contrast not only to Marxism and realism but also to this notion of peace deriving automatically from commerce, regulatory liberalism emphasizes discretionary human action. International rules and institutions play a crucial role in promoting cooperation; yet there is great variation in their results, depending on the human ingenuity and commitment used to create and maintain them. This emphasis of regulatory liberalism on human choices conforms with experience: the life-histories of international organizations differ dramatically. In some cases, their institutional arrangements, and the actions of their leaders, have encouraged sustained, focused work that accomplishes common purposes and maintains support for the organization: NATO, the European Community, the Association of Southeast Asian Nations (ASEAN) and the World Health Organization (WHO) are examples. Other organizations, such as UNESCO, have failed to maintain the same level of institutional coherence and political support.[37]

If we keep the insights of regulatory liberalism in mind, along with the experiences of international organizations in the twentieth century, we will be cautious about seeking to predict international behavior on the basis of "the effects of commerce." Such an inference is no more valid than purporting to construct comprehensive analyses of world politics solely on the basis of "the constraints of capitalism" or the necessary effects of anarchy. "Commerce," "capitalism," and "anarchy" can give us clues about the incentives – constraints and opportunities – facing actors, but without knowing the institutional context, they do not enable us to understand how people or governments will react. Regulatory liberalism argues that we have to specify the institutional features of world politics before inferring expected patterns of behavior. I believe that this awareness of institutional complexity is a great advantage, that it constitutes an improvement in subtlety. It improves our capacity to account for change, since change is not explained adequately by shifts in patterns of economic transactions (commercial liberalism), fundamental power distributions (realism), or capitalism (Marxism).

Nothing in regulatory liberalism holds that harmony of interest emerges automatically. On the contrary, cooperation has to be constructed by human beings on the basis of a recognition that independent governments both hold predominant power resources and command more legitimacy from human populations than do any conceivable international organizations. Neither peace nor coordinated economic and social policies can be sought on the basis of a hierarchical organizing principle that supersedes governments. Governments must be persuaded; they cannot be bypassed. This means that international institutions need to be constructed both to facilitate the purposes that governments espouse in common and gradually to alter governmental conceptions of self-interest in order to widen the scope for cooperation. International institutions provide information, facilitate communication, and furnish certain services that can-

---

[37] For a comparative analysis of eight international organizations that substantiates the importance of institutional histories and choices, see Robert W. Cox and Harold K. Jacobson, eds., *The Anatomy of Influence: Decision Making in International Organization* (New Haven: Yale University Press, 1973).

not be as easily offered by national governments: They do not enforce rules. Liberals recognize that although it is possible to cooperate on the basis of common interest, such cooperation does not derive from an immanent world community that only has to be appreciated, nor does it occur without sweat and risk.

The accomplishments of regulatory liberalism in our age are substantial. They should not be dismissed because severe dangers and dilemmas continue to face governments or because much that we would like to accomplish is frustrated by state sovereignty and conflicts of interest. The global environment would be in even greater danger in the absence of the United Nations Environmental Program (UNEP) and agreements reached under its auspices; protectionist trade wars might be rampant were it not for the General Agreement on Tariffs and Trade (GATT); starvation would have been much worse in Africa in the early 1980s without the World Food Program and other international cooperative arrangments; smallpox would not have been eradicated without the efforts of the World Health Organization. Regulatory liberalism asserts that better arrangements that constructively channel the pursuit of self-interest – or that enrich definitions of self-interest – can realistically be constructed, not that they will appear without effort. History supports both parts of its claim.

Sophisticated liberalism

Commercial liberalism stresses the benign effects of trade; in Staley's version, trade may, under the right conditions, facilitate cooperation but does not automatically produce it. Regulatory liberalism emphasizes the impact of rules and institutions on human behavior. Both versions are consistent with the premise that states make choices that are, roughly speaking, rational and self-interested; that is, they choose means that appear appropriate to achieve their own ends. Yet this premise misses an important element of liberalism, which does not accept a static view of self-interest, determined by the structure of a situation, but rather holds open the possibility that people will change their attitudes and their loyalties. As students of European political integration have shown, a combination of strengthened commercial ties and new institutions can exert a substantial impact on people's conceptions of their self-interest.[38] People cannot be expected, in general, to cease to act in self-interest ways, but their conceptions of their self-interest can change.

What I call sophisticated liberalism incorporates this sociological perspective on interests into a synthesis of commercial and regulatory liberalism. It does not posit that expanding commerce leads directly to peace but rather agrees with Staley that conditions of economic openness can provide incentives for peaceful rather than aggressive expansion. This is only likely to occur, however, within the framework of rules and institutions that promote and guarantee openness. Not just any set of commercial relationships will lead to peace: The effects of commerce depend on the institutional context – the rules and habits – within which it takes place. Furthermore, the development of commerce cannot be regarded as inevitable, since it depends on a political structure resting on interests and power.

What liberalism prescribes was to a remarkable extent implemented by the United States and its Western European allies after World War II. The United States, in conjunction with Western European governments, set about constructing a framework of rules that would promote commerce and economic growth. Consistently with the expectations of both realism and Marxism, American power was used to ensure that the rules and institutions that emerged satisfied the basic preferences of American elites. What the Europeans established differed considerably from American plans, and the construction of European institutions preceded the implementation of the global economic arrangements that had been outlined at the Bretton Woods Conference and at the negotiations leading to the General Agreement on Tariffs and Trade (GATT).[39] Yet without American prodding, it is unclear whether these European institutions would have been created; and the United States had relatively little difficulty accepting the new European institutions, which promoted basic

---

[38] The pioneering works are, Karl W. Deutsch et al., *Political Community and the North Atlantic Area: International Organization in the Light of Historical Experience* (Princeton: Princeton University Press, 1957); Ernst B. Haas, *The Uniting of Europe: Political, Social and Economic Forces, 1950–1957* (Stanford: Stanford University Press, 1958.

[39] For an impressive work of scholarship that emphasizes the European ability to obstruct American plans and implement their own, see Alan Milward, *The Reconstruction of Western Europe, 1945–51* (Berkeley and Los Angeles: University of California Press, 1984).

American goals of security and prosperity within the institutional frameworks of representative government and capitalism.

Even if the European institutions were not entirely devoted to the principles of commercial liberalism – and the European Payments Union, the European Coal and Steel Community, and the European Economic Community had many restrictionist elements – they were not sharply inconsistent with the institutions of Bretton Woods and GATT, which emphasized the value of open markets and nondiscriminatory trade. The resulting arrangements, taken as a whole, epitomized a liberalism that was "embedded" in the postwar interventionist welfare state. That is, liberalism no longer required rejection of state interventionism, but rather efforts to ensure that interventionist practices were limited by joint agreements and rules, in order to maintain their broadly liberal character and to facilitate international exchange.[40] Economic growth, promoted by international trade and investment, was expected to facilitate the growth of democratic institutions within societies, and thus to reshape states in pacific directions as well as to provide incentives for peaceful economic expansion rather than military conquest. The political complications entailed by growing economic interdependence were to be managed by an increasingly complex network of formal and informal institutions, within Europe and among the advanced industrial countries.[41]

This strategy was remarkably successful. Indeed, the benign results foreseen by such writers as Staley ensued, although it might be difficult to prove decisively that they resulted principally from institutionalized patterns of interdependence more than from the looming presence of the Soviet Union. At any rate, war and threats of war were eliminated as means of economic aggrandizement for the advanced parliamentary democracies. Futhermore, as American hegemony began to wane after the mid-1960s, the value of liberalism's emphasis on rules became more evident to those who sought to avoid a return to economic warfare and generalized conflict. International regimes such as those revolving around the GATT or the International Mone-

---

[40] John Gerard Ruggie, "International Regimes, Transactions and Change: Embedded Liberalism in the Post-War Economic Order," *International Organization*, vol. 36, no. 2 (1982), pp. 379–415.
[41] For a discussion, see Robert O. Keohane and Joseph S. Nye, Jr., *Power and Interdependence: World Politics in Transition* (Boston: Little, Brown, 1977).

tary Fund have displayed remarkable staying power, even after the power constellations that brought them into being had eroded.

Liberals have used their positive theory stressing the role of institutions to bolster their normative argument that liberal orders are to be preferred to available alternatives. It is important to note here that the liberal stress on institution building is not based on naivete about harmony among people, but rather on an agreement with realists about what a world without rules or institutions would look like: a jungle in which governments seek to weaken one another economically and militarily, leading to continual strife and frequent warfare. Liberals do not believe in the soothing effects of "international community." It is precisely because they have seen the world in terms similar to those of the realists – not because they have worn rose-colored glasses – that sophisticated liberals from Kant to Staley to Stanley Hoffman have sought alternatives. Their pessimism about world politics and human conflict makes sophisticated liberals willing to settle for less than that demanded by utopians of whatever stripe.

Evaluating liberalism: doctrine and practice

Regulatory liberalism argues for the construction of institutions to promote exchanges regarded by governments as beneficial. This is to be done without directly challenging either the sovereignty of states or the inequalities of power among them. Liberals who appreciate Marxist and realist insights are careful not to present these exchanges as unconstrained or necessarily equally beneficial to all parties concerned, much less to categories of people (such as the rural poor in less developed countries) that are unrepresented at the bargaining table. As a reformist creed, liberalism does not promise justice or equity in a setting, such as that of international relations, in which inequalities of power are so glaring and means of controlling the exercise of power so weak. It is therefore open to charges of immorality from utopians and of naivete from cynics; and depending on the context, liberals may be guilty of either charge, or of both. Liberals seek to build on what exists in order to improve it, and run the risk that their policies will either worsen the situation or help to block alternative actions that would radically improve it. Nevertheless, liberals can fairly ask their opponents to propose alternative strategies that are not merely attractive in principle, but seem likely to produce better results in practice.

Yet even if we accept the liberal argument this far, we may be reluctant to embrace liberalism as a normative theory of international affairs. Before we could do so, we would need to consider the negative as well as the positive aspects of the open international order, with its rules and institutions to guide the actions of states, that liberals favor. In particular we would need to consider the impact of such an order on two major values: peace and economic welfare. What are the effects of an open, interdependent international order on the constraints facing states, and on the ways in which states are reshaped in world politics? What is the liberal view of these constraints? How do these constraints compare with those imposed by alternative arrangements for the management of international affairs?

Liberalism and peace

As we have seen, liberalism assures states of access, on market or near-market terms, to resources located elsewhere. "In a liberal economic system," admits a critic of liberalism, "the costs of using force in pursuit of economic interests are likely to outweigh any gains, because markets and resources are already available on competitive terms."[42]

This access to markets and resources is assured by complex international political arrangements that would be disrupted by war. If the division of labor is limited by the extent of the market, as Adam Smith taught, the extent of the market is limited by the scope of international order. The more tightly intertwined and interdependent the valued interactions among states, the greater the incentives for long-term cooperation in order to avoid disrupting these ties. In international relations as in other social relations, incentives for cooperation depend on whether actors are "involved in a thick enough network of mutual interactions" and on the degree to which they benefit from these ties.[43] This does not mean that commerce necessarily leads

---

[42] Barry Buzan, "Economic Structure and International Security: The Limits of the Liberal Case," *International Organization,* vol. 38, no. 4 (1984), p. 603.

[43] Russell Hardin, *Collective Action* (Baltimore: Johns Hopkins University Press, 1982), p. 228.

to peace, or that entwining the Soviet Union in networks of interdependence will get the Soviets to stop fostering revolution in the Third World; but it is reasonable to assert that a calculation of costs and benefits will enter into state decision making, and that this calculation will be affected by the costs of disrupting beneficial ties. Thus we can find analytical support for the view, espoused by liberals such as Staley, that an open, rule-oriented international system provides incentives for peaceful behavior.[44]

The existence of an orderly and open international system may affect the balance of interests and power for societies poised between commercial and belligerent definitions of self-interest. Japan before and after World War II provides the outstanding example. Admittedly, the contrast between its behavior before World War II and since is partly accounted for by the restructuring of Japanese government and society during the American Occupation and by the dependence of Japan on the United States for defense against the Soviet Union. Nevertheless, the dominance of peacefully inclined commercial rather than bellicose military elites in postwar Japanese policymaking has surely been encouraged by the opportunities provided for Japanese business by relatively open markets abroad, particularly in the United States.[45]

Yet the picture for liberalism is not so rosy as the previous paragraphs might seem to suggest. Liberalism may indeed inhibit the use of force, but it may also have the opposite effect. Whether American liberalism was in any way responsible for the massive use of violence by the United States in Southeast Asia is still unclear: Liberal moralism may have justified the use of force, although it seems from *The Pentagon Papers* that a skewed conception of geopolitics provided a

---

[44] For a recent book that revives this thesis, in a not entirely consistent or persuasive form, see Richard N. Rosecrance, *The Rise of the Trading State* (New York: Basic, 1985). Rosecrance drifts too much, in my view, into seeing the "rise of the trading state" as a more or less inevitable trend, ignoring some of the qualifications that must be made to the thesis, as observed below.

[45] It is hard to be more specific than this about the effects of the international system without detailed empirical investigation. In general, we must guard against the temptation to overestimate the effects of international arrangements on the propensity of governments to use force. Even sophisticated international liberalism is a systemic theory which does not probe deeply into the nature of domestic political and social coalitions. The impact of the international system is only one of many factors – even if an important one – affecting the behavior of states.

more powerful motivation for action.[46] Furthermore, liberal values were crucial in providing the moral basis for the popular protests against United States military involvement in Vietnam, which eventually brought the war to an end.

Yet even if liberalism tends to be peacefully oriented, and was not responsible for the war in Vietnam, the effects of liberalism on peace may not necessarily be benign. The extension of economic interests worldwide under liberalism in search of wider markets requires the extension of political order: Insofar as that order is threatened, protection of one's own economic interests may entail the use of force. Thus a global political economy may make it difficult for leaders of a peacefully oriented liberal state not to use force, precisely by making it vulnerable to the use of force against it by nonliberal states or movements. Three examples illustrate this point:

Direct foreign investment. The United States in recent decades has intervened directly or indirectly in a number of countries in which it had substantial direct foreign investments, including Guatemala (1954), Cuba (1961), and Chile (1973). Fear of the extension of Soviet influence to the Western Hemisphere seems to have been a principal motivation for American action, but in all three cases, intergovernmental conflicts were generated by the presence of U.S.-owned companies in societies undergoing revolutionary change. In the absence of the extension of American economic interests to these countries, such interventions would, it seems, have been less likely to occur.

Control over resources. The Carter Doctrine, which raised the possibility of American intervention in the Persian Gulf, was clearly motivated by United States government concern for access to oil resources in that area. So was the movement of a large U.S. naval task force into the gulf in the spring and summer of 1987. Such military action in defense of far-flung economic interests – of America's allies even more than of itself – creates the obvious possibility of war between the United States and Iran. Soviet–American confrontation is also conceivable: Indeed, the scenarios of superpower conflict

---

[46] For an analysis of policymaking in the Vietnam War, based principally on *The Pentagon Papers,* see Leslie H. Gelb with Richard K. Betts, *The Irony of Vietnam: The System Worked* (Washington: The Brookings Institution, 1979).

arising in the Middle East seem in many ways more plausible than the scenarios for Soviet–American military confrontation in Europe.[47] The general point is that the global economic interests of liberal states make them vulnerable to threats to their access to raw materials and to markets. Liberal states may use violence to defend access to distant resources that more autarkic states would not have sought in the first place.

Air transport. Liberal societies not only extend their economic interests worldwide, they also believe in individual freedom to travel. This means that at any given time, thousands of citizens of such societies are in airplanes around the world – potential hostages or victims of terrorists. Since socialist or mercantilist governments not only have limited foreign economic interests but often restrict travel by their people, they are not so vulnerable. Reacting to their vulnerability, powerful republics may escalate the use of force, as the United States did, in April 1986, against Libya. The global extension of international activity fostered by liberalism's stress on economic openness and political rights not only creates opportunities for terrorists but also provides incentives for powerful republics to use force – even if its use is justified as defensive and protective rather than aggressive.

How do incentives for the use of force balance out against incentives against such use? The peaceful behavior of liberal governments toward one another, and their reluctance to resort to force against nonliberal states in the oil crisis of the 1970s, suggest that the current interdependent international political economy may have inhibited – or at least, has not encouraged – widespread resort to force. Barry Buzan argues that, despite this success, liberalism will lead in the long run to the use of force because it is unstable and will deteriorate.[48] The recent upsurge of terrorism reminds us that this caution is well founded. A degenerating liberal system, in which commitments and vulnerabilities exceed the capacities of liberal states to deal with them, could be exceedingly dangerous – perhaps even more so than a decaying system of self-reliant mercantilist states. But this observa-

---

[47] See Graham T. Allison, Albert Carnesale, and Joseph S. Nye, Jr., *Hawks, Doves, and Owls: An Agenda for Avoiding Nuclear War* (New York: Norton, 1985).
[48] Buzan, "Economic Structure and International Security."

tion could just as well be taken as a justification for committing ourselves more strongly to underpinning a liberal economic system with multilateral institutions supported by power, than as an argument against a liberal international system. To regard the dangers of a decay of liberalism as an argument against an open international order is reminiscent of Woody Allen's character in *Hannah and Her Sisters* who attempts to commit suicide out of fear of death!

Liberalism and economic welfare

Conservative economists find the international order favored by liberalism congenial. The international market serves as a "reality test" for governments' economic strategies. Inefficient policies such as those overemphasizing provision of welfare and state bureaucracy will do badly.[49] Eventually, the failure of these policies will become evident in slow and distorted growth and balance-of-payments problems. From this standpoint, the constraints imposed by the world economy are not properly seen as malign constraints on autonomy, but rather as beneficial limits on governments' abilities to damage their own economies and people through foolish policies. International liberalism fosters a world economy that gives timely early warning of economic disaster, rather than enabling states to conceal crises by using controls that in the long run only make matters worse. As Locke said about law, "That ill deserves the Name of Confinement which hedges us in only from Bogs and Precipices."[50]

The international political economy of modern capitalism is viewed more critically, however, both by liberals who empathize strongly with ordinary people in the Third World and by First World supporters of social democracy. It is evident to many liberals as well as Marxists that the modern capitalist world economy exerts a bias against poor, immobile people as well as against generous welfare states. Conservative economists point this out with some glee: The McCracken Report argues that "countries pursuing equality strenu-

---

[49] See, for instance Paul McCracken et al., *Towards Full Employment and Price Stability* (Paris: OECD, 1977) for an analysis along these lines by a "blue-ribbon panel" of economists.

[50] John Locke, *Second Treatise of Government* (1690), paragraph 57. Idem, *Two Treatises of Government,* edited by Peter Laslett, 2nd edition (Cambridge University Press, 1967), p. 323.

ously with an inadequate growth rate" may suffer "capital flight and brain drain."[51] The existence of international capitalism improves the bargaining power of investors vis-à-vis left-wing governments. The ease with which funds can flow across national boundaries makes it difficult for any country with a market-oriented economy to institute measures that change the distribution of income against capital.

Capital flight can have catastrophic effects on the debt-ridden nations of the Third World. As Marxists emphasize, it also constrains attempts to promote equity or nibble away at the privileges of business in the advanced industrialized countries of Europe, North America, and the Pacific. When Thatcher or Reagan sought to help business and improve profits, capital flowed into their countries – at least temporarily. When Mitterand sought to expand the welfare state, stimulate demand, and nationalize selected industries, by contrast, capital flowed out, the franc declined and his social democratic policy was eventually exchanged for austerity. An open capitalist world financial system therefore tends to reinforce itself, although, even in the face of such constraints, such countries as Sweden and Austria have been able to devise effective strategies to maintain high levels of employment and social equality. Ironically, states with strong but flexible public institutions, able to manipulate the world economy when possible and to correct for its effects when necessary, seem to thrive best in an open world political economy. For countries not blessed with such institutions, the international economic order of modern capitalism manifests a pronounced bias against policies promoting equality.[52]

International liberalism: an evaluation

The international order proposed by liberalism has a number of appealing features, particularly when a substantial number of powerful

---

[51] McCracken et al, *Towards Full Employment and Price Stability*, pp. 136–7.

[52] For an elaboration of this argument, see Robert O. Keohane, "The World Political Economy and the Crisis of Embedded Liberalism," in John H. Goldthorpe, ed., *Order and Conflict in Contemporary Capitalism* (Oxford: Clarendon Press, 1984), pp. 22–6. The best work on strategies of small states such as Austria for coping with constraints from the world economy is by Peter J. Katzenstein. See *Corporatism and Change: Austria, Switzerland and the Politics of Industry* (Ithaca, N.Y.: Cornell University Press, 1984); and idem, *Small States in World Markets* (Ithaca, N.Y.: Cornell University Press, 1985).

states are republics. Orderly exchange, within a framework of rules and institutions, provides incentives for peaceful expansion and productive specialization. International institutions facilitate cooperation and foster habits of working together. Therefore, a realistic liberalism, premised not on automatic harmony but on prudential calculation, has a great deal to commend it as a philosophy of international relations.

Yet liberalism has several major limitations, both as a framework for analysis and as a guide for policy. It is incomplete as an explanation, it can become normatively myopic, and it can backfire as a policy prescription.

Liberalism only makes sense as an explanatory theory within the constraints pointed out by Marxism and realism. Viewed as an explanation of state action, sophisticated liberalism emphasizes the difference that international rules and institutions can make, even when neither the anarchic state system nor world capitalism can be transformed or eliminated. If major powers come into violent conflict with one another or capitalism disintegrates, the institutions on which liberalism relies will also collapse. International liberalism is therefore only a partial theory of international relations: It does not stand on its own.

Normatively, liberalism is, as John Dunn has put it, "distressingly plastic."[53] It accommodates easily to dominant interests, seeking to use its institutional skills to improve situations rather than fundamentally to restructure them. Liberalism is also relatively insensitive to exploitation resulting from gross asymmetries of wealth and power. Liberals may be inclined to downplay values such as equality when emphasis on such values would bring them into fundamental conflict with powerful elites on whose acquiescence their institutional reformism depends. Liberalism is sometimes myopic as a normative theory, since it focuses principally on moderating "economic constraints on modern politics" in a way that facilitates governments' purposes, rather than directly on the condition of disadvantaged groups. To satisfied modern elites and middle classes, liberalism seems eminently reasonable, but it is not likely to be as appealing to the oppressed or disgruntled.

---

[53] Dunn, *Rethinking Modern Political Theory,* cited, p. 169.

As policy advice, liberalism can backfire under at least two different sets of conditions. First, if only a few governments seek to promote social equity and welfare in an open economy, they may find their policies constrained by the more benighted policies of others. "Embedded liberalism" represents an attempt to render a liberal international order compatible with domestic interventionism and the welfare state. As we have seen, this is a difficult synthesis to maintain. Second, liberalism may have perverse effects if the global extension of interests that it fosters cannot be defended. Decaying liberal systems may be the most dangerous of all. One way to deal with this problem of decay is to use military power to uphold the liberal order. But we may also want to consider how to make ourselves less vulnerable by trimming back some of these interests, insofar as we can do so without threatening the rule-based structure of exchange that is the essence of a liberal order. It would be foolish for liberalism to commit suicide for fear of death. But perhaps we could go on a diet, reducing some of the excess weight that may make us vulnerable to disaster. Greater energy self-reliance – endangered by the mid-1980s fall in oil prices – remains one valuable way to do this.[54]

The appeal of liberalism clearly depends in part on where you sit. Liberalism can become a doctrine of the status quo; indeed, this danger is probably greater for the nonutopian liberalism that I advocate than for the utopian liberalism that E. H. Carr criticized almost half a century ago. But realism has an even greater tendency to be morally complacent, since it lacks the external standards of human rights that liberalism can use to criticize governments in power. Realism lacks the "imaginative flexibility" of liberalism about human possibilities, and is therefore missing an ethical dimension that liberals possess.[55] Marxism is anything but complacent about the capitalist status quo, although as a moral theory the weakness of orthodox Marxism is its inability to show that the alternatives it proposes *as they are likely actually to operate in practice* are morally superior to feasible reformist alternatives. Soviet Marxists, of course, have traditionally supported the status quo in socialist states within the Soviet

[54] It could be worthwhile to ask whether there could be analogous self-protective responses to terrorism. The problem, clearly, is that the obvious solution – restricting the right of one's citizens to travel or denying them protection if they do so – conflicts with liberalism's conception that the state should protect individual rights.
[55] The phrase, "imaginative flexibility," I owe to John Dunn.

sphere of influence, regardless of how repressive their governments may be.

The strength of liberalism as moral theory lies in its attention to how alternative governing arrangements will operate in practice, and in particular how institutions can protect human rights against the malign inclinations of power holders. Unlike realism, liberalism strives hard for improvement; but unlike Marxism, it subjects proffered "new orders" to skeptical examination. "No liberal ever forgets that governments are coercive."[56] A liberalism that remains faithful to its emphasis on individual rights and individual welfare as the normative basis for international institutions and exchange, can never become too wedded to the status quo, which never protects those rights adequately.

In the end I return to the emphasis of liberalism on human action and choice. Liberalism incorporates a belief in the possibility of ameliorative change facilitated by multilateral arrangements. It emphasizes the moral value of prudence.[57] For all its faults and weaknesses, liberalism helps us to see the importance of international cooperation and institution building, even within the fundamental constraints set by world capitalism and the international political system. Liberalism holds out the prospect that we can affect, if not control, our fate, and thus encourages both better theory and improved practice. It constitutes an antidote to fatalism and a source of hope for the human race.

[56] Judith Shklar, *Ordinary Vices* (Cambridge, Mass.: Harvard University Press, 1984), p. 244.

[57] Dunn, *Rethinking Modern Political Theory,* cited, p. 169.

CHAPTER 6

Capitalism, socialism, and democracy: compatibilities and contradictions*

JOHN DUNN

Any coherent modern political theory must contain, at a minimum, three elements. It must contain in the first place an articulated conception of individual good. It must add to this, in the second place, a constitutional theory of how power can be institutionalized, not merely to acknowledge formally the status of this conception of individual good, but also to promote its effective implementation in practice. And it must round these two elements out with a third and equally indispensable element: a conception of sound economic policy that can reasonably hope to prove effective through time. Each of the elements in this inventory could do with some glossing, and no one should mistake it as, even in intention, an exhaustive list.[1] But it does, I trust, focus helpfully the three most problematic and least dispensable elements in modern political theory[2] and brings out immediately the still more problematic relations that obtain between them. One feature which is rather evidently missing from the three elements

[1] I have made some attempt to extend it in a variety of directions in John Dunn, *Western Political Theory in the Face of the Future,* Cambridge University Press, 1979; idem, *Political Obligation in its Historical Context,* Cambridge University Press, 1980, esp, chaps 8–10; idem, *The Politics of Socialism,* Cambridge University Press, 1984; idem, *Rethinking Modern Political Theory,* Cambridge University Press, 1985; and hope to make further attempts in the future.

[2] One topic it leaves severely alone (and which may yet render the entire history of political theory retrospectively absurd) is the question of whether modern state powers can in principle shoulder the burden of furnishing physical security and preventing physical hazard for their subject populations. See Dunn, "Responsibility without Power: States and the Incoherence of the Modern Conception of the Political Good," IPSA Conference, Paris, July 1985.

*This essay was first prepared for a seminar on problems of democracy organized by Philippe Schmitter at the European University, Badia Fiesolana in May 1985.

is a determinate (and essentially prepolitical) conception of a community of membership which furnishes many of the most significant components in the several conceptions of individual good held by its members, lends a natural and compelling form to the constitutional theory of how power can best be institutionalized to do justice to these conceptions, and fosters (or at least fails to militate drastically against) the devising and sustaining of dependable modes of economic policy.[3]

This omission is certainly important, but it is not simply an instance of inadvertence. Ancient political theory, the theory of ancient liberty as Benjamin Constant describes it,[4] is predominantly a theory of community making and community preservation, an exercise in the historical construction of political order. Within the theory of ancient liberty, community membership is not merely the site of the densest and most glorious of personal opportunities (an ideological assessment which was of course always open to question even in the ancient world). It was also a locus of value that enjoyed, at least in its own estimation, a clear and evident priority of esteem and significance over the contingent preferences of its individual members. There is at least one major modern tradition of political understanding (the socialist or communist tradition) which attaches a very similar priority of esteem and significance to the communal over the merely personal, and this tradition, too, has quite appropriately seen itself as a theory of community making, a theory of the creation of social, political, and economic order.[5] Its historical experiences in this venture have thus far been a trifle erratic, partly no doubt just as a result of human error, moral as well as practical, and partly, certainly, also as a consequence of the initial vagueness and

---

[3] At least for this purpose, a class-for-itself should be thought of as a community with a General Will, as opposed to the somewhat fitful will of all its members which is the most that a sectional grouping (or class-in-itself) can hope to muster. Cf., briefly, John H. Goldthorpe (ed.), *Order and Conflict in Contemporary Capitalism*, Clarendon Press, Oxford, 1984, Introduction.

[4] Benjamin Constant, *De le liberté des anciens comparée à celle des modernes*, (Constant, *Cours de politique constitutionelle*, Bechet, Paris & Rouen, 1820, Vol. 4, pt. 8, 238–74). Constant's *Political Writings* are now available in English for the first time, edited by Biancamaria Fontana (Cambridge University Press, 1988).

[5] As is very helpfully brought out in Michael Taylor, *Community, Anarchy and Liberty*, Cambridge University Press, 1982, the anarchist tradition, too, where it hopes to retain any contact with social and political reality has little choice but to adopt the same focus.

the persisting limitations of the conceptions of economic policy that have accompanied it.[6] But it seems likely that there is another and even deeper source of these divagations in the fundamental unclarity involved in its attempt to locate value at the level of a fictive community. (What is to forge the forgers, or educate the educators?) I cannot pretend to have a clear idea of how best to express this unclarity, though I emphatically share the standard Anglo-Saxon suspicions over the contribution to keeping it unclear that has been made and continues to be made by a sound intellectual socialization in the idioms of Hegel.

What I am relatively confident of is the intellectual and practical undesirability, at least in modern political and economic conditions, of thinking of a fictive community as a locus of individual-transcending value.[7] It is not that community, insofar as it happens in fact to be historically present, fails to play a vital and predominantly benign role in giving stability, definition, and potential viability to modern politics. It is certainly not that the historical absence of community is other than a major existential burden for vast numbers of individual lives today in a multiplicity of societies across the world. It is simply that the attempt to forge political community through ideological declamation and massively concerted coercion, whatever its incidental benefits (and burdens) along the line, is in the end self-frustrating. The posttotalitarian or postcultural revolution exhaustion that comes over modern socialist states in early middle age is a deeply revealing feature of their histories. The need to take community *broadly* the way history provides it and not to deceive oneself by obsessional fictions of one's own was, I think, quite well understood by the youthful Marx, whatever his temperamental resistance on occasion to this understanding. It comes out not merely in his sober critique of the Jacobin overestimate of the socially shaping power of politics, but also in his firm insistence in the *German*

---

[6] See Dunn, *Politics of Socialism* and *Rethinking Modern Political Theory,* Chaps. 5 and 6, drawing heavily upon Alec Nove, *The Economics of Feasible Socialism,* George Allen & Unwin, London, 1982, and Michael Ellman, *Socialist Planning,* Cambridge University Press, 1979. Much the same judgment (more decorously expressed) can now also be found in Perry Anderson, *In the Tracks of Historical Materialism,* Verso Editions, London, 1983.

[7] For a purposeful contractarian attempt to pin down a more immanent conception of political community on the basis of an individual-respecting conception of value see Salvatore Veca, *La società giusta,* Il Saggiatore, Milan, 1982.

Ideology[8] on the practical futility of conceptions of community spawned over the millenia by moralizing intellectuals and on the comparative historical and political substance of modes of community which practically involve millions of human beings and are firmly immanent in the directional movement of history. Of course the distinction between historically immanent and externally fictive community is not an easy one to draw clearly even in theory, and in practical politics the judgment of where to draw the line between the two is a difficult feat for anyone. What is essential in modern political theory is to keep clearly in view the fact that in politics there always is such a distinction to be drawn and to sense without undue resentment the political weight of the need to draw it with as little self-deception as possible.

I think the point is definitely better put this way round – as a scepticism about fictive community as a potential locus of rational human value, and not as a dogmatic affirmation of the metaphysical validity of a radically individualist value pluralism (as in the thought of Rawls, Nozick, Dworkin, or perhaps Scheffler).[9] Individualist moral scepticism at present serves as a powerful critique of prevalent public standards of value.[10] It is more lucid and cogent in its presumptive metaphysics than even the most systematic and adventurous of recent attempts to theorize human value.[11] But it would be a very bold political theorist indeed who was, as yet, at all confident which version of modern theorizing about human value can reasonably hope to be in good intellectual order in a few decades time. And it is quite unclear at present if the more sceptical (and metaphysically relaxed) of current value conceptions do in fact yield any real determinacy

[8] See Karl Marx, *On the Jewish Question* (Karl Marx and Frederick Engels, *Collected Works,* Lawrence & Wishart, London, Vol. 3, 1975, 256); Karl Marx, *Critical Marginal Notes on the Article "The King of Prussia and Social Reform"* (*Collected Works,* Vol. 5, 1976, 54).

[9] John Rawls, *A Theory of Justice,* Oxford University Press, Oxford 1971; idem, "Kantian Constructívism in Moral Theory," *Journal of Philosophy,* 77, 1980, 515–72; Robert Nozick, *Anarchy, State and Utopia,* Basil Blackwell, Oxford, 1974; Ronald Dworkin, *Taking Rights Seriously,* Duckworth, London, 1977; Samuel Scheffler, *The Refutation of Consequentialism,* Clarendon Press, Oxford, 1982; but cf., particularly on Rawls, Michael J. Sandel, *Liberalism and the Limits of Justice,* Cambridge University Press, 1982.

[10] Amartya Sen and Bernard Williams (eds.), *Utilitarianism and Beyond,* Cambridge University Press, 1982, Introduction.

[11] Contrast Bernard Williams, *Ethics and the Limits of Philosophy,* Fontana Press, London, 1985, with Derek Parfit, *Reasons and Persons,* Clarendon Press, Oxford, 1984.

even at the individual level. (It is also at least equally unclear whether such determinacy as they do yield is conceptually combinable with a clear recognition of whatever cultural residues of a distinctively moral point of view are still to be found amongst them).

Community as such, then, must be taken as it happens to be available. And the content of individual valuing must also in the first instance be taken as it comes, even if, in situ, it may be adjusted quite sharply through a process of active and even moralistically belligerent shared deliberation. It must be taken essentially as it comes in the first instance because what we first need to sense is the shape of existing political possibilities. It is to aid our grasp of this that we need a political theory at all[12] – and in sensing this shape the full contingency of existing individual valuing is not merely an external moral constraint upon the theory. It is also a relatively robust imaginative aid in constructing it, and the supplanting of the contingencies of individual valuing by the fiction of nonexistent community is not merely a purposeful evasion of external moral constraints, but also a voluntary abandonment of the most effective source of assistance for focusing upon political possibility rather than personal fantasy. It is impossible to exaggerate both the importance and the difficulty of attempting to sustain this focus.[13]

On the whole modern political theorists set great store by their attempts to specify human good at either an individual or a social level. In historical perspective it is not difficult to see why they should elect to do so, but there is in my view considerable reason to doubt the soundness of this feature of their strategic judgment. What principally makes modern political theory unstable and confused is not the political struggles that swirl around it and into which it enters with, for the most part, such naive alacrity. Rather, it is the extreme intellectual difficulty of discerning clear and reassuring relations between the other two components of a modern political theory: the constitutional order of power and the pragmatic determination of economic policy. In the now rather distant days when ideology was presumed (by some)[14] to have ended, it was implicitly – sometimes even explicitly[15] – the relatively high de-

---

[12] Cf. Dunn, *Politics of Socialism*, 1–3 and passim.
[13] Dunn, *Politics of Socialism*.
[14] Cf. Daniel Bell, *The End of Ideology*, Collier Books, New York, 1961.
[15] Andrew Shonfield, *Modern Capitalism*, Oxford University Press, Oxford 1965. Contrast John H. Goldthorpe, *Order and Conflict*, Introduction.

gree of consensus about the successful conduct of economic policy that was taken to have placed the character of the constitutional order beyond rational criticism, or even rational doubt. (Don't look a gift horse in the mouth.) This sequence of thought was always a source of very proper scandal to the moralistic, but in retrospect what is more striking about it is its extreme simplicity of mind. The felicitous determination of economic policy is hardly in itself an appropriate topic for political theorists, or even a wholly appropriate one for political scientists. (It is also one of which I myself have, as will be all to obvious, only the feeblest glimmerings of an understanding. It would be nice in fact to be confident that anyone at present has a very robust comprehension of it.) But although it is hardly for would-be political savants to prescribe what is well considered or ill considered in the way of economic policy, it certainly is a fairly self-evident judgment at present, as John Goldthorpe has recently pointed out,[16] that economic policies, class actions, and political institutions in advanced capitalist societies are to be understood, if at all, only by an attentive study of their mutual interactions.

Here those political analysts who decisively favor either capitalist or socialist economic orders tend to be pronouncedly better at discerning beams in each others' eyes than they are at locating motes in their own. But both ideological tendencies, except in their most extreme fideist versions,[17] tend to accept without undue discomfort an essentially domestic focus of constitutional order, a view of the essence of the political problem as the right disposal of powers of agency within a sovereign territorial unit. This is not, of course, in itself simply incorrect. We all live today in territorial units which are sovereign at least for some purpose, and within these units powers of agency do need to be institutionally disposed in some determinate way. But correct at a relatively basic level though it plainly is, it does nevertheless offer a deeply unhelpful imaginative frame in which to assess modern political problems. Some of these problems, to be sure, transcend the contrast between capitalism and socialism: particularly those concerned with modern weapons systems and the structuring of mutual menace, but also those concerned with the use of natural resources and the custody of the globe as a human habitat. Others,

[16] Goldthorpe, *Order and Conflict.*
[17] See, for example, the writings of Friedrich Hayek, Samir Amin, and Ernest Mandel.

more specifically focused on the basic legal framework of production, distribution, and exchange however, touch directly upon the contrast between capitalism and socialism. As they do so, in the case of each, they still tend in modern political thinking to presume a domestic territorial frame as the domain of problems and their potential solutions and to conceive human social life and its right ordering in terms of the fashioning and sustaining of some determinate form of domestic political community. It is far from clear that this image of an essentially national and sovereign political articulation and expression of human social flourishing any longer makes good sense. If we are to think seriously today about the relations between constitutional orders and either a socialist or a capitalist organization of production, one issue which we must certainly press vigorously is the question of the intellectual defensibility of this continuing domestic focus.

One reason for suspecting its viability goes back as far as modern political ideologies themselves. Anglo-Saxon critics of the political theory of Rousseau and liberal critics of its supposedly totalitarian progeny have attacked both, not always altogether justly, for resting their political trust in the last instance on an essentially fictive General Will or commonality of interest. But it is important to be alert to the extent to which analogous fictions of commonality of interest lie at the heart of *all* modern political ideologies. These differ assuredly – sometimes rather sharply – on the demographic scope of commonality of interest, excluding for example parasitic estates of the privileged or exploitative classes of owners of the means of production. But almost all – certainly all with any great ideological resonance: Who, after all, would be willing to lay down their lives for the political conceptions of Schumpeter or Robert Dahl? – do offer a definite social locus for political membership and good health. Consider, for example the philosophic radical theory as set out by James Mill in the political prelude to the Great Reform Bill.[18] Government is a risk-reducing mechanism for mediating between creatures (human beings) that present the most extreme risks to one another. It is carefully engineered to combine possession of the maximum of power to impede mutual threat with the minimum of power to exert such threats on its own behalf. Tacitly

---

[18] Mill's *Essay on Government* is now conveniently available in Jack Lively and John Rees (eds.), *Utilitarian Logic and Politics*, Clarendon Press, Oxford 1978, 53–95.

premised on a simple and exceedingly confident economic theory, it promises to guarantee to each economic agent the full fruits of her labor[19] (as these are assessed under its own economic theory). And it rests the principal weight of its own ideological viability not upon the careful mechanical balancing or mutual arrest of powers or on the happy intellectual self-evidence of its own economic theory,[20] but upon a class-specified social psychology of political belief in which the middling ranks happily enjoy perfect ideological taste and causal judgement and still more happily exert a sustained hegemony in these terms over the, in themselves, potentially far more erratic taste and judgement of their social and economic inferiors.[21]

Mill is on the whole remarkably specific in his contentions. But so too, in their different ways, in the firm contrasts which they drew between the parasitic few and the vast productive majority and in their highly specific assurance of the absence of any real structural conflicts of interest within this majority, were, for example, Sieyes and Thomas Paine.[22] And their tendency to exhaust a sense of potential structural conflict in identifying an existing and presumptively illegitimate group that needs to be eliminated from the texture of society (and perhaps even – since these animals tend to *méchanceté* and may well seek to impede their own elimination – from the texture of nature also) is handed on all too evidently to the socialist tradition. The struggle to prevent the advent of socialism is a real and present historical threat to this advent, but once it has been met by one last bold effort[23] the historical residue of modern societies is a potentially integral and harmonious social and economic whole. Its integration and harmony, as in the case of the Third Estate or the middling ranks, is not a property identified by direct inspection.

---

[19] Lively and Rees (eds.), *Utilitarian Logic,* 57: "The greatest possible happiness of society is, therefore, attained by assuring to every man the greatest possible quantity of the produce of his labour."

[20] No theory which required Harriet Martineau to expound it at such length could plausibly be said to be self-evident.

[21] Lively and Rees, *Utilitarian Logic,* 93–5.

[22] Thomas Paine, *The Rights of Man,* J. M. Dent & Son, London, 1915; Emmanuel Joseph Sieyes, *What is the Third Estate?,* tr. M. Blondel, Pall Mall Press, London, 1963.

[23] Filippo Michele Buonarroti, *Conspiration pour l'églaité dite de Babeuf,* Editions Sociales, Paris, 1957, Vol. 1, 58n. "Il ne tint, peut-être, qu'à un acte de sévérité de plus, que la cause du genre humain ne remportât en France un triomphe complet et éternel," (On Thermidor, 1794).

Rather it is read off – and largely by rhetorical bravado – the contrast with the miserable chasm that runs through the center of existing historical society: in the case of socialism, the chasm between the subjugated proletarians who only own their own labor and the owners of the means of production who hold the former in subjection through this monopoly over access to the means of livelihood.

It is plainly not just an accident that all modern ideologies of political incorporation attempt to specify an identity of interest at the level of political or social membership. Civil equality – equal participation in a system of civil rights – or political equality – equal participation in an institutionalized scheme of political action – are ideological pretensions rather than social facts. Even the most intrepid specification of political equality – the classical Greek right of *isegoria* within a genuinely sovereign process of political decision making – was a right exerted effectively in practice by only a relatively small group of *habitués* of the political life.[24] And modern attempts to specify what true political (or for that matter true civil) equality might genuinely consist of today either dissolve rapidly into complete incoherence[25] or trail away into edifying but essentially marginal reflections on how it might be possible to synthesize and sustain a somewhat greater sense of personal effectiveness in the teeth of modern work organization[26] or how it might be possible to wheedle a rather larger percentage of the population into interesting themselves more regularly in the workings of local government.[27] It is hard to avoid the suspicion that what we are dealing with here is a certain narcissism of political value itself – or, to be more concrete, of its modern social bearers.[28] It is quite easy to exaggerate the charms of unstinting involvement in the workings of local government which, in this perspective, have a great

[24] Compare M. I. Finley, *Democracy Ancient and Modern*, Rutgers University Press, New Brunswick, N.J., 1973, with idem, *Politics in the Ancient World*, Cambridge University Press, 1983.

[25] Cf. Philip Green, *Retrieving Democracy: In Search of Civic Equality*, Rowman & Allanheld, New York, 1985.

[26] Cf. Carole Pateman, *Participation and Democratic Theory*, Cambridge University Press, 1970; idem, *The Problem of Political Obligation: A Critical Analysis of Liberal Theory*, John Wiley, Chichester, 1979.

[27] Cf. Benjamin Barber, *Strong Democracy: Participatory Politics for a New Age*, University of California Press, Berkeley and Los Angeles, 1984.

[28] Cf. John Dunn, "Social Theory, Social Understanding and Political Action," in Christopher Lloyd (ed.), *Social Theory and Political Practice*, Clarendon Press, Oxford, 1983, 109–35.

deal in common with the existential appeals of incessant participation in university committees.[29]

But however ideologically flimsy or practically consequential the modes of constitutional expression for civil or political equality, it is not at the constitutional level (outside South Africa, Namibia, and a handful of recently conquered territories like the West Bank) that modern political incorporation really is problematic. Neither the excessive claims for the institutional substance of egalitarian political incorporation in modern states, nor the equally excessive lucubrations over the varieties of more concrete political extrusion which these institutions in fact secure, really capture much of what is significantly happening in the modern world. What they offer us is in large measure a world of ideological shadow-boxing in lieu of a world of real political action. To put the point more polemically and starkly, I doubt very much whether it is even with the second component of a modern political theory – the constitutional order of power – that our political comprehension of what is now going on really is profoundly at sea. Rather, it is the third component – the pragmatic determination of economic policy – for which our understanding is at present almost completely incoherent. It is the endless and extreme instabilities of this third component which resonate out into the second, preventing it from assuming for any length of time a clearer and more definite profile.

That this judgment is in fact well founded can be quite readily confirmed by anyone who studies the history of modern constitutional dispute since the American Revolution and who pays close attention to the extreme plasticity of that handful of categories that carries the ideological weight of political incorporation in the face of the presumed consequences of governmental action. It is quite easy

---

[29] For two disabused perspectives see Michael Zuckerman, *Peaceable Kingdoms: New England Towns in the Eighteenth Century,* Alfred A. Knopf, New York, 1970, and Thomas Hobbes, *De Cive: The English Version,* ed. Howard Warrender, Clarendon Press, Oxford, 1983, 136: "To see his opinion whom we scorne, preferr'd before ours; to have our wisedome undervalued before our own faces; by an uncertain tryall of a little vaine glory, to undergo most certaine enmities (for this cannot be avoided, whether we have the better, or the worse); to hate, and to be hated, by reason of the disagreement of opinions; to lay open our secret Counsells, and advises to all, to no purpose, and without any benefit; to neglect the affaires of our own Family: These I say, are grievances. But to be absent from a triall of wits, though those trials are pleasant to the Eloquent, is not therefore a grievance to them, unlesse we will say, that it is a grievance to valiant men to be restrained from fighting, because they delight in it."

to explain both elements in this relation: the apparent continuity of the categories of constitutional order and civic membership and the real plasticity of these same categories in the face of the erratic trajectory of intuitions about the sound conduct of economic policy.[30] The apparent stability of the constitutional categories themselves comes from the continuity of the presumption of the territorial shape as frame of both political membership and political responsibility. The all too blatant instability of the policy intuition comes partly from the sheer complexity and opacity of global exchange as such and from the insistent importunities of perceived interest which intervene permanently in its analysis from an immense variety of angles. It also comes, as suggested earlier, partly from the discontinuity between a national frame of political responsibilities and an international field of causal process.

To revert to the terms of Constant, ancient liberty was a conception for which the ancient state (or at any rate the small self-ruling *polis*) was not merely part of the specification of the value itself but also a wholly apt historical location for it. Ancient states were not just intrinsic to the realization of ancient liberty. They were also perfectly capable out of their own resources (for as long as they could sustain the capacity to defend themselves against other states) of exemplifying it in practice. But modern liberty has an altogether more elusive relation to real modern states.[31] Partly, of course, Constant fully intended it to do so, deploying it with some vehemence in the attempt to cut ideologically down to size first the Jacobian dicatorship, then the empire of Napoleon, and finally the restored Bourbons. But the point which matters is one of conceptual necessity, not one of contingent political intention. Modern liberty is an assemblage of rights of private enjoyment. It does not intrinsically require a particular state for its site at all. Its votaries have severely provisional loyalties to the particular states to which they happen at the time to belong. They are strictly fair-weather citizens. And this is not simply a matter of attitude; it is also a matter of power. In contrast with the role of a right of

---

[30] I am particularly indebted in my view of this aspect of modern political thought to a series of penetrating studies by Pasquale Pasquino and to the powerful work of Istvan Hont on the history of political economy.

[31] I have tried to develop this point of view more systematically in an unpublished paper, "Liberty as a Substantive Political Value" (United Nations University, August 1984).

emigration at adulthood in seventeenth-century jusnaturalist theories of political legitimacy and political obligation, a comfortably theoretical and abstract role, early-nineteenth-century votaries of modern liberty possessed, in Constant's view, not merely a robust sense of their entitlement to private enjoyments but also a form of property which they had little difficulty in carrying off with them wherever they happened to choose to go.[32] (It is apparent that modern liberty is a fairly class-specific endowment.) States that fail to respect the requirement of modern liberty will find themselves in practice deserted with some ease by its indignant votaries. They will lose – and deserve to lose – the rigorously provisional allegiance of their better-off subjects: those who possess what in the days of Henry Ireton used to be referred to as a stake in the country. (A hazy foreshadowing of the clash between political sovereignty and the international mobility of capital comes into focus at this point.) Modern liberty, Constant wished to argue, can and will largely police itself.

Seen through the prism of modern liberty, the state retains the responsibilities incumbent on its ancient predecessor. For most of its citizens, presumably, it retains rather more, remaining not merely a community of provisional residence but a community of historical fate. What it no longer enjoys is an array of powers which match its responsibilities at all neatly or adequately. Modern political theory – the political theory of modern liberty in all its political heterogeneity – is an extended dilation upon this anomaly. Thus far it has also proved a remarkably unsuccessful dilation upon it. There are two clear and definite forms that such a theory might adopt, one highly ambitious, robustly reassuring if credited, but perhaps also impossibly implausible, and the other strikingly modest, decidedly less fulsome in its reassurances but also mercifully easy to credit. The first clear and definite form would align a determinate constitutional order of power with a trustworthy agency of economic policy in such a manner that the former guaranteed the preservation of the latter. The second clear and definite form would seek to do the same with the crucial proviso that it would also openly acknowledge that no constitutional order can guarantee any given practical outcome. The second, that is to say, simply

[32] Constant, *De la liberté des anciens,* 249; 267–69.

specifies a *compatibility* between constitutional order and the benign management of an economy. The first clear and distinct form is plainly in danger of promising too much for its promises to be credible. The second promises so little that its promises may seem barely worth having. What is needed is some intermediate structure that combines some of the realism of the second, without the *guarantees* of the first but at least with something more committing than the second: a constitutional order, for example, that renders the benign conduct of economic policy not merely possible but actually probable – more likely than not. Put in these terms, this does not seem an extreme hope, but there is very little reason to believe that such a theory – for the world in which we now live – has in fact yet been constructed.

If it is to be constructed, then the weight of transposing it from the possible in principle to the probable in practice has to be carried somewhere specific within the theory. (It is perhaps worth underlining the implied judgment that the possibility of constructing such a theory is in fact today a precondition for giving human beings on any extended scale coherent rational grounds for sustained political cooperation.) Faced with this demand it still seems natural to political theorists to seek to bear the weight by juggling with the constitutional order of power. Partly it is natural for them to do so out of simple professional *amour propre*. The limited economic and social viability of modern states is emphatically a political problem, and any political theorists worth their salt are likely to feel needled by the challenge which it represents. At least for political scientists or political theorists, it is natural to assume that political problems must have political solutions. But in addition to this relatively trivial professional self-regard there is a second and intellectually somewhat deeper stimulus for political theorists at least to locate their principal intellectual response in their casting of the constitutional order of power. The history of Western political theory in fact begins with the theorization of ancient liberty or some transcendent surrogate for it, with a deep ideological and intellectual engagement with the vision of a self-subsistent and participatory political community as the locus of some of the finest and least-dispensable elements of a good human life. The conflation between the pressing moral and spiritual exigencies of the Greek *polis* and the practical organizational realities of the modern state is a ready source of intellectual confusion and bad faith.[33] But it remains such an insistent imaginative option precisely because, in the tradition of understanding to which we belong and which defines us to ourselves, the alternative to it still appears to be the effective demoralization of collective social life. There is, however, every reason to doubt the cognitive adequacy of this semblance of two exclusive and exhaustive alternatives: an overmoralized and monopolistic community of political fate or a nihilist and disaggregated collision of individual wills.[34] And even if one abstracts from the dimension of military self-defence (where the overmoralized conception of political community, along with its practical accoutrements, now threatens to bury us all), it is extremely hard to believe that much aid in reconciling conflicting human interests can now be hoped for from a moral heightening of the sense of content of political membership as such.

Other things being equal, there is certainly something to be said for equality as opposed to inequality[35] or for fairness as opposed to unfairness,[36] and the design of a constitutional order of power is plainly one appropriate setting for these values to be exemplified. It no doubt is true that those who are given the regular opportunity to play a consequential part in determining the details of their work life or domestic life or the government of their local communities have in general not merely a greater sense of personal effectiveness in these settings but also a more informed and even perhaps, on average, a more prudent conception of how these are best disposed.[37] The view that impotence is bad for one is quite easy to defend and decidedly more cogent than its complement, the fond hope that power will necessarily prove good for one. But it is not necessary to be as sceptical as Hobbes of the existential rewards of political participation to be pretty confident that the more fundamental problems of modern political organization are un-

---

[33] Dunn, *Western Political Theory,* chap. 1.

[34] For two balanced protests see Marshall Cohen, "Moral Scepticism and International Relations," *Philosophy and Public Affairs,* 13, 4, 1984, 299–346; Michael Walzer, *Spheres of Justice,* Martin Robertson, Oxford, 1983.

[35] Cf. Ronald Dworkin, "What is Equality? Pt. 1: Equality of Welfare," *Philosophy and Public Affairs,* 10, 3, 1981, 185–246; idem, "What is Equality? Pt. 2: Equality of Resources," *Philosophy and Public Affairs,* 10, 4, 1981, 283–345. Bruce A. Ackerman, *Social Justice in the Liberal State,* Yale University Press, New Haven, 1980.

[36] Rawls, *Theory of Justice;* idem, "Kantian Constructivism."

[37] Pateman, *Participation and Democratic Theory.*

likely to yield to participatory solutions as such. On the whole, theorists of socialism have been particularly inclined to rely upon the merits of participatory solutions,[38] seeing these as not merely edifying in themselves – intrinsically desirable – but also as edifying in their prospective impact upon the consciousness of those involved: as an effective specific in the age-old war against the canker of egoism. Theorists of capitalism, even where they have taken a clear stand in favor of some elements of political participation (voting in elections to select a representative legislature, etc.) have seen the principal and indispensable domain of adult social participation as the market in goods and labor. The principal task of politics (and hence the main causal outcome which the constitutional order of power must be contructed in order to guarantee) is thus the protection and sustaining of the market itself. Beyond this point, defenders of both capitalist and socialist economic orders find it difficult to extend their theories in a very commanding manner.

What makes such extension difficult is the absence of any satisfactorily self-equilibrating or self-maintaining organon for the benign conduct of economic policy. This absence is particularly blatant in socialist theory. A socialist economy in one country, following a revolution in that country, may or may nor be a contradiction in terms. But, thanks to the history of the Soviet Union since the late 1920s, it is at least a more determinate conception than a socialist world economy.[39] Because socialists transcend egoism (or transcend corrupt egoism) by definition and because uneven development is a historical product of capitalism, socialists will not merely trade with each other in a more benign mood than their historical predecessors; they will also, in the fullness of time, trade with each other from market positions of less dismaying inequity. What is less clear is what sorts of terms they will in fact trade on thereafter or how exactly they can expect to make their way to this happy condition of international market equity. It is very hard to believe at present that there is any coherent conception whatever of an international political economy appropriate to the socialist organization of domestic production and international trade.

[38] Not, of course, *all* theorists of socialism. This is hardly a charge that could be leveled against Stalin, and it takes a high degree of selective inattention to wish to press it against Lenin or Trotsky.

[39] Cf. Dunn, *Rethinking Modern Political Theory,* Chap. 6.

(Only under autarky could there be a political economy appropriate to the socialist organization of domestic production which was not also appropriate to a socialist organization of international trade.) It is far from clear at present how one could hope to design a constitutional order of power that would for any length of time guarantee the reproduction of a socialist domestic economy on terms beneficial to its citizens at large. (The view that the design of such a constitutional order can safely be left to the winds of history is an insult to the millions of human beings who have suffered under socialism in the last seven decades.) It is not in fact even clear how to design such an order so that it would make the reproduction of a socialist domestic economy on these terms reasonably likely.[40] And as to how such an economy could be expected to interact internationally with other domestic economies (socialist or otherwise) in a mutually beneficial manner, that question has scarcely yet even been addressed by socialists. It is therefore hardly surprising that none of them should have thus far produced anything very cogent in the way of an answer to it. This lacuna is of very great importance, for, short of world socialist government (a facility for the supply of which there might prove to be candidates) it is only the ready rational complementarity of theories of mutual advantage that could hope to secure smooth and uncoerced cooperation between domestic socialist economies. (International capitalist exchange depends upon a subtle balance between the ideological semblance of uncoerced cooperation and the firm availability of eminently coercive guarantees for the basic framework within which exchange will take place. Those who hope to generate international socialist exchange will have to choose – as some have already chosen – between fashioning an at least equally cogent ideological semblance of uncoerced cooperation or providing even more coercive guarantees for the basic framework within which exchange is to take place. Neither project is going to sit very comfortably with the remainder of socialism's ideological pretensions.)

But if the economics of international socialism are, intellectually and politically, a blank check drawn on a future imagined with tactful vagueness, at least they are not evidently contradictory in the first instance. Partly, the absence of evident contradiction is simply a func-

---

[40] Cf. Dunn, *Politics of Socialism;* idem, *Rethinking Modern Political Theory,* Chap. 5.

tion of the extreme vagueness of what is being asserted. But partly also it is a product of the very strong political will, at the center of the socialist impulse, to conceive social membership as profoundly advantageous for any true human being and to envision society as a frame of meaning and experience orderly and enticing enough to render this conception compelling.[41] The dangers of fairly blatant self-deception in this orientation are apparent enough. But so too is one element of rather simple common sense which it also embodies. To present a society as a framework of evident mutual advantage it is manifestly helpful for that society (as described) not to display gross disparities, unrelated to the efforts of living individuals, in the advantages which it furnishes its members. It is not difficult on the whole to persuade human beings that there are benefits in market exchange, and it is particularly easy to persuade human beings whose forebears have been habituated to market exchange for many generations. What is rather more difficult is to persuade a given set of human beings that any particular basis on which to divide up the rather evident benefits of market exchange is a clearly and commandingly fair and appropriate one. (Hence the philosophical fascination – and the political futility – of the theory of social justice.)

The ideological history prompted by this lack of moral transparency is a vivid and complicated one. Two of the more important moments within it are furnished by Hume's careful analysis of justice as an artificial virtue and Hayek's swingeing assault on the deceptions of social justice.[42] A less important but instructive moment is Robert Nozick's attempt to present the discretionary disposal of all one has legitimately acquired as a human right lying at the very center of modern freedom.[43] Common to all three is a recognition of the indis-

---

[41] Socialist thinkers (including Marx) have had great difficulty in finding convincing ways of expressing this view, though it is constantly presumed by all the more important and ambitious socialist thinkers in their criticisms of a capitalist social order. Since it is a fundamentally aesthetic critique of existing social arrangements it is not surprising that it should have been most successfully captured by aesthetic theorists like John Ruskin.

[42] David Hume, *A Treatise of Human Nature*, J. M. Dent & Son, London, 1911, Bk. 3 pt. 2; F. A. Hayek, *Law, Legislation and Liberty*, Vol. 2, *The Mirage of Social Justice*, esp. chaps. 8 & 9, Routledge & Kegan Paul, London 1976. (And see, helpfully, Frederick J. Whelan, *Order and Artifice in Hume's Political Philosophy*, Princeton University Press, Princeton, 1985; John Gray, *Hayek on Liberty*, Basil Blackwell, Oxford, 1984.)

[43] Nozick, *Anarchy, State and Utopia*.

pensability of a determinate system of property rights to the beneficent working of market exchange and of the systematic disharmony
between the workings of any determinate system of property rights
and the natural emotional responses of the population subjected to
this.[44] (It is not that socialists have any particularly commanding response to the latter difficulty. But they are, of course, decidedly less
committed to the former judgment, and they are also committed
instead to fussing doggedly and ingenuously about the question of
what schema of property rights might in fact be self-justifying. They
take the provision of such a schema as their responsibility.) For the
young Hume in a society where the possession and inheritance of
property was not as yet under immediate political challenge, the inter-
fering emotions were seen mainly as those of natural sympathy and
good fellowship. For Friedrich Hayek, a good two centuries later and
in a political environment in which the challenge to capitalist property
relations was sometimes quite urgent, the intruding emotions are
seen more severely as a blend of envy and sentimentality and subjected to corresponding abuse. But Hayek in large measure shares
the judgment of Hume on the necessary artificiality of any system of
property: the need to buffer it against the spontaneous (individual)
responses of its (collective) beneficiaries. Nozick, more bracingly,
seeks to revive as a coherent intellectual option a vision of a system of
property rights as profoundly natural in their origins and strongly
related, at the point at which they come into being, to the efforts and
deserts of those who acquire them. Within a rationalized and instrumental modern culture it is uphill work sustaining the degree of artifice in property relations commended by Hume and Hayek, and the
more invigorating ideological attack of Nozick's work thus promises
to provide some much needed assistance in defending the belea-
guered artifice. But the aid that it does provide, of course, depends in
its turn directly upon the ideological currency of the conception of
legitimate appropriation which it presupposes. And this conception in
turn could only seem plausible in a society in which capitalist property
relations still were (as perhaps in the United States of America) essentially politically unchallenged.

[44] Compare, Istvan Hont and Michael Ignatieff (eds.), *Wealth and Virtue: The Shaping
of Political Economy in the Scottish Enlightenment*, Cambridge University Press,
1983, Chap. 1.

The ancient Greek conservative equation of democracy with the subversion of property rights – the abolition of debts and the redistribution of land – has not proved a felicitous predictor of the experience of capitalist democracy, any more than its early-nineteenth-century *reprise* by Scottish Whigs in the era of the Reform Bill.[45] But postwar explorers of the contradictions of capitalist democracy (like Claus Offe) and students of the travails of corporatism have certainly dissipated any sense of dependable and stable harmony between the constitutional order of representative democracy and the developmental dynamic of a thriving capitalist economy. They have not, to be sure, replaced an expectation of dependable and stable harmony with any single and clear putative guarantee of ultimate structural incompatibility. (One reason why the political theory of capitalist democracy is seldom as flighty as the political theory of "true socialism" is that there is so much more of the real world with which to compare the former and find it obviously at odds.)[46] But what these writers have contrived to make apparent is the decisive weight of a variety of intervening variables between markets (international and domestic) and the formal constitutional orders of capitalist states. The most important of these intervening elements is the political party, both as articulator of the subjective political significance of class membership and as bearer of a relatively definite strategic practice,[47] brought to bear in the initial contest to form governments and, once success in this first venture has been achieved, brought to bear more decisively in the exercise of governmental power.

Political parties in practice have many important properties, but in modern political theory they tend to figure in one or other of two extremely simple guises. Either (in the optimistic perspective of practical reason) they figure as the potential vectors of potentially perfect distributive taste and potentially perfect causal understanding of the workings of an economy or (in the, properly, more chastened perspective of theoretical reason) they figure as vectors of all too predictable

[45] See Biancamaria Fontana, *Rethinking the Politics of Commercial Society: the Edinburgh Review 1802–1832,* Cambridge University Press, 1985, Chap. 5.
[46] Cf. Dunn, *Politics of Socialism.*
[47] Two of the most interesting recent treatments of these themes are Alessandro Pizzorno, "Sulla razionalità della scelta democratica," *Stato e Mercato,* 7, April 1983, 1–46, and Idem, "Interests and Parties in Pluralism," in Suzanne Berger (ed.), *Organizing Interests in Western Europe,* Cambridge University Press, 1981, 247–84.

deformations in either distributive taste or causal understanding. They are part of the apparatus through which we sustain such personal political optimism about the prospects for our own national communities as we can muster and through which we also seek to explain the moderately dismaying circumstances which usually in fact obtain. There is no doubt at all of the services which they can sometimes furnish in this second and explanatory project. In the face of the morning newspapers we do need to have some coherent beliefs about why matters have come out politically just as they have. It would take a very hardened skeptic to doubt that much of the answer to these questions could be helpfully expressed in terms of the vicissitudes of political parties, in and out of office. But in some respects this is not a satisfactory level of judgment, and it is especially unrewarding when we attempt to clear our heads on the issue of what, of a more desirable nature, might conceivably come about in the future. It is difficult in thinking about modern domestic politics not to become in some measure an imaginative prisoner of a particular political party, committed well beyond clear intellectual consent to envisaging the future through the potential fortunes of a specific political *équipe*. In the more fundamental issues of modern political theory, the questions of how individual value, constitutional order, and economic policy can in principle be aligned for the best (or even for the better), it is unclear that political parties as such offer any direct aid in understanding. Rather, the benign action of political parties itself depends upon coherent conceptions of how these elements can be aligned for the better.

What this analytical evanescence of the political party brings out is a distressingly abstract shape. Constitutional order and economic policy can be benignly aligned (in tasteful conformity with the dictates of individual value) if and only if they happen to be benignly aligned. The relation is one of pure contingency. This is not a surprising state of affairs in politicial theory. Even Plato would not have been *surprised* by it. But it certainly is not an especially encouraging one. And it is particularly discouraging once one comes to suspect also that any stability and determinacy that is inserted into it of a potentially benign kind will have to come not from the axiomatically perfect taste of particular social groupings (the proletariet, the middling ranks, the enlightened court) but from the intellectual cogency of the conception of sound economic policy. (It is not necessary to be a structural Marxist or a devotee of Economism to suspect that individual value and political judgment expressed at the level of the constitutional order are both likely today in any open political system to be in large part derivatives of a conception of benign economic process. All that is necessary is the recognition that, where either is not in fact substantially contaminated by such a conception, the economic, social, and political prospects of the society in question are likely to be fairly grim.)

It is plainly of key importance to which precise social groups or interests the conception of economic policy can be cogently presented as sound. The actual politics of capitalist countries (and no doubt more surreptitiously, much of the actual politics of soi-disant socialist countries also) is quite well represented in the first instance in the idiom of game-theoretical conflict over highly individuated advantages, exacerbated by envy and malice. But this picture is too charitable and rationalist to provide a full rendering. In particular it massively understates the causal weight of tedium, irritation, the fitfulness of attention, sheer cognitive incompetence, and the limits of analytical imagination. To get a clear understanding of the politics of anywhere at any time requires a fearsome level of intricacy and specificity, a bewildering depth of knowledge, and delicacy of insight for which any proffered substitute can only be bogus. Between the purely contingent and highly abstract alignment or divergence between constitutional order and sound economic policy and the dense particularity and determinacy of the politics of real societies at particular points in time there just is no neat intermediate level of analysis. I should like in conclusion to list a few simple points which seem to me to offer some preliminary direction on how to conceive of the intervening space.

There are two principal relevant dimensions – a short-term dimension conceived predominantly or exclusively in terms of distribution and a longer-term dimension in which all distribution is recognized more or less self-consciously to depend upon the reproduction of a system of production. The former, with some consistency in an open political system but also more erratically even in closed systems,[48] is a

---

[48] See particularly Domenico Mari Nuti, "The Polish Crisis – Economic Factors and Constraints," in Ralph Miliband and John Saville (eds.), *The Socialist Register 1981*, Merlin Press, London, 1981, 104–43. For an analytical model that sharpens the

domain of what Hume called the 'violent passions': importunate, myopic, often deeply ill advised. The latter, insofar as it registers politically at all, is a domain of the 'calm passions': unhectoring, discerning, impressively prudent in its directives. No student of modern politics would be likely to dispute the prominence of the former within their chosen subject matter. What is a good deal more contentious is where (if anywhere) within this subject matter the latter can be confidently located. One answer, which enjoys a stalwart following amongst professional politicians and bureaucrats in both capitalist and socialist states, is that it can and must be identified in the workings of the state itself (*L'état c'est nous*), seen in Durkheimian terms as the reasoning and calculating instance of modern societies.[49] There is plainly something in this answer. The public bureaucracies of most modern states do secrete an economic policy of a kind, though it would be easy in most instances to exaggerate the degree of rational integration achieved within this policy. As an answer, in addition to its natural clients, this view also has natural enemies: certainly moralizing intellectuals in both capitalist and socialist countries (at least outside government or public bureaucracy), frequently businessmen in capitalist countries, and perhaps almost everywhere much of the grumbling common sense of the demos in any sort of modern society. There is much to be said, on different occasions and in different settings, for both fundamental points of view. It certainly is the case that the productive systems of modern societies always require a powerful rationalizing instance, and it equally certainly is the case that public bureaucracies that offer themselves as such are often wildly cognitively at sea in their conception of what they are doing[50] and not infrequently, from the viewpoint of many of their subjects, far from trustworthy and disinterested even in their basic intentions. (Consider the Philippines.)

There is no doubt at all that in this matter the calm passions ought rationally *on the whole* to dominate the violent passions: that the reproduction of a system of production ought in general to enjoy

explanation of the Polish case contained in this essay see now Domenico Mari Nuti, "Political and Economic Fluctuations in the Socialist System," *European University Institute Working Paper,* 85/156, March, 1985.

[49] Cf. Bertrand Badie and Pierre Birnbaum, *The Sociology of the State,* tr. Arthur Goldhammer, University of Chicago Press, 1983, 13–14.

[50] So too, often, are governments that fulsomely proffer the market in this guise.

priority over immediate distributive purposes. It ought to do so not because there is some point to production other and grander than eventual consumption,[51] and certainly not because delayed gratification is in itself somehow morally superior to immediate gratification, but simply because there cannot be anything to distribute except what has already been produced. In the devising of economic policies, therefore, modern governments have an evident responsibility to exemplify the calm passions and to attempt to cultivate the good judgment which these make possible. But so too, in any moderately democratic understanding,[52] in responding to economic policies, do modern citizens have an equally evident responsibility to do just the same. And at a very slightly less simple level – and beyond the frame of domestic political participation and authority – both governments and citizens also face an evident responsibility to devise for themselves and respond to the formulation by others of policies for mediating the relations between their own productive systems and those of other societies. The genesis of a world economy, as Marx long ago saw and as Adam Smith saw before him, has generated in its turn the practical need for a rigorously cosmopolitan extension of some aspects of civic virtue. It has also generated the corresponding need for the credal foundation for the practice of this virtue to be furnished by a popular political economy that is directed towards international economic exchange as much as towards domestic production. Both domestically and internationally, these popular political economies are at present in very poor order, deeply confused, and even more deeply marked by suspicion of the motives of each other's exponents. This confusion is not simply a product of defective intellectual socialization, of the insufficiently firm impress of valid economic cognition upon popular belief. Rather, it is a function of the very limited coherence and force of the best of professional economic understanding, considered not as a discrete structure of logical reasoning but as an instrument for understanding the world. There simply do not at present exist clear and powerfully generalizing conceptions of mutual economic advantage that apply convincingly to much of the real eco-

---

[51] Spirtually rewarding work and decent working conditions are important human goods, but they are not a surrogate for producing.

[52] Any understanding, that is, that does not take it as a premise that most human beings because of their nature require their more important exercises in prudence done for them by their rulers.

nomic world. The political synthesis of mutual advantage in practice requires more than valid understanding of where such advantage is to be found, but it is scarcely possible, except by intermittent accident, in the latter's absence.

Even within a purely domestic framework it is far from clear that such conceptions really are still at present available.[53] The advantages of more efficiently functioning and extensive markets (to take a current example) cannot readily be demonstrated to those protractedly or even permanently removed from employment in the effort to restore this functioning.[54] (They cannot, of course, readily be demonstrated to anyone if the markets in questions fail to respond as prescribed.) The merits of systematic rational planning of an economy are equally difficult to demonstrate to those who have begun to suspect (also on the basis of disagreeable experience) that the systematic rational planning of an economy may be a natural impossibility – or at least that it will at most prove to amount to a subjective experience on the part of a set of public administrators rather than an illuminating description of political and economic causality at work.[55] Socialism in one country, either in a democratic or an authoritarian vein, is just as dependent for its potential viability on the possession of a coherently conceived political economy, located in the consciousness of the demos or in the party *apparat*. Even the most successful instances of economic policy in recent decades prove on closer inspection to have depended upon extremely simple causal elements, put together in settings which distinctively permit their sustained combination and which cannot readily by replicated in most contemporary societies. The dramatic success of Japan in recent decades in planning the process of industrial innovation, for example, has not depended merely on the devising, through painful trial and error, of a highly culturally idiosyncratic political organization through which to carry

---

[53] Compare Shonfield, *Modern Capitalism;* Goldthorpe, *Order and Conflict,* Introduction; Robert Keohane, *After Hegemony,* Princeton University Press, Princeton, 1984; Charles Lipson, "International Cooperation in Economic and Security Affairs," *World Politics,* 37, 1, 1984, 1–23.

[54] Cf. Goldthorpe, *Order and Conflict, 13.*

[55] Cf. Ellman, *Socialist Planning;* Nove, *Economics of Feasible Socialism;* Dunn, *Politics of Socialism.* This does not, of course, mean that planned economies are in general certain to perform *worse* than (comparatively) open and unplanned economies: Frederic B. Pryor, "Growth and Fluctuations of Production in O.E.C.D. and East European Countries," *World Politics,* 37, 2, 1985, 204–37.

out the planning. It has also depended on a clear recognition of the need to restrict tightly the responsibilities of the state in the practical running of the economy and on the persistence for more than two decades of an elected party government whose continuity of power permitted a corresponding continuity of state policy and whose eventual success could thus in due course vindicate in practice (and benefit from) the rationality of the policies followed.[56] (While the Japanese state in the late 1930s was all too apparently under the control of the violent passions, its successor since the mid-1950s has been more convincingly and consistently under the dominion of the calm passions than even a country like Switzerland.)

There is no obvious a priori reason why coherent, powerfully generalizing, and currently applicable conceptions of mutual economic advantage must always (or ever) be available. But since the eighteenth century there have always been some human beings, thinkers or political actors, who believed that they had succeeded in identifying one.[57] What we may by now be confident of is that it is predominantly the ebb and flow of intellectual and political plausibility in such conceptions on which any coherent modern conception of political action must in the end rest. To hope to impart and retain definite shape in modern political theory by refining conceptions of the nature of individual (or class) value or by recycling past interpretations of just or fair constitutional formulae for the distribution of political power is a necessarily futile pursuit. The historical domain in which we live is the domain of modern liberty (or modern servitude). Within this domain, coherence and definition in political action and in political community has to be constituted, if it is to be constituted at all, fundamentally on the basis of the cognitive force of the theory of political economy. At present this is hardly a very cheering thought.

[56] Chalmers, Johnson, *MITI and the Japanese Miracle: The Growth of Industrial Policy, 1925–1975*, Stanford University Press, 1982. For other perspectives on the prerequisites of this trajectory see, for example, Robert J. Smith, *Japanese Society: Tradition, Self and the Social Order,* Cambridge University Press, 1983; Rob Steven, *Classes in Contemporary Japan,* Cambridge University Press, 1983; Bruce Cumings, "The Origin and Development of the Northeast Asian Political Economy: Industrial Sectors, Product Cycles, and Political Consequences," *International Organization,* 38, 1, 1984, 1–40.

[57] See Hont and Ignatieff, *Wealth and Virtue,* Chaps. 1 and 11; Keith Hart, *The Political Economy of West African Agriculture,* Cambridge University Press, 1982. For the centrality of this premise to socialist internationalism see Dunn, *Rethinking Modern Political Theory,* Chap. 6.

Index

221